KNOWLEDGE AND VIRTUE IN TEACHING AND LEARNING

"This book is a lovely description and analysis of an alternative educational theory that emphasizes the primacy of dispositions embodied in epistemological presence. . . . It stimulated my thinking in ways I neither anticipated nor thought possible."

Richard Osguthorpe, Boise State University

"Hugh Sockett brings to the fore the philosophical admonition that the 'what' and 'how' in educational decision making must be framed within one's purpose—'the why.' Accordingly, he grounds his work in an Aristotelian frame, and then uses that lens to define and operationalize 'dispositions' which are then seen as intellectual virtues, 'the moral centrality of teaching.'"

Erskine S. Dottin, Florida International University

The challenge this book addresses is to demonstrate how, in teaching content knowledge, the development of intellectual and moral dispositions as virtues is deeply embedded in the logic of searching for knowledge and truth. It offers a powerful example of how philosophy of education can be brought to bear on real problems of educational research and practice—pointing the reader to re-envision what it means to educate children (and how we might prepare teachers to take on such a role) by developing the person, instead of simply knowledge and skills. Connected intimately to the practice of teaching and teacher education, the book sets forth an alternative theory of education where the developing person is at the center of education set in a moral space and a political order. The book's pedagogy is invitational, welcoming its readers as companions in inquiry and thought about the moral aspects of what we teach as knowledge.

Hugh Sockett is Professor of Education, Department of Public and International Affairs, College of Arts, Humanities, and Social Sciences, George Mason University.

KNOWLEDGE AND VIRTUE IN TEACHING AND LEARNING

The Primacy of Dispositions

Hugh Sockett

Routledge
Taylor & Francis Group

NEW YORK AND LONDON

First published 2012
by Routledge
711 Third Avenue, New York, NY 10017

Simultaneously published in the UK
by Routledge
2 Park Square, Milton Park, Abingdon, Oxon OX14 4RN

Routledge is an imprint of the Taylor & Francis Group, an informa business

© 2012 Taylor & Francis

Library of Congress Cataloging in Publication Data

Sockett, Hugh.
   Knowledge and virtue in teaching and learning : the primacy of dispositions / Hugh Sockett.
     p. cm.
   Includes bibliographical references and index.
   1. Education—Philosophy.   2. Teaching—Moral and ethical aspects.   3. Virtue.   I. Title.
   LB14.7.S644   2011
   370.1—dc23   2011022856

ISBN: 978-0-415-89997-0 (hbk)
ISBN: 978-0-415-89998-7 (pbk)
ISBN: 978-0-203-15550-9 (ebk)

Typeset in Bembo
by Apex CoVantage, LLC

Printed and bound in the United States of America on acid-free paper by Walsworth Publishing Company, Marceline, MO.

CONTENTS

FOREWORD

In an educational world shaped by targets and performance indicators, and then by the audits of those targets, and where the learners are customers, parents, clients, and teachers—the deliverers of whatever those customers and clients need in order to hit those targets—in such a world it is refreshing and important to read a thoroughly and persuasively argued antidote to the impoverished language taken from performance management.

There are two things wrong with such a language. First, it has nothing to do with education; the "newspeak" of management is applied equally to the production of cornflakes as it is to the production of learners. Second, and arising from that, it has a seductive "logic of action"—a logic that separates the end to be achieved from the means of getting there. The means of achieving the end are selected for their efficiency and cost-effectiveness, as though the ends to be reached are in no way affected by the means adopted in reaching them.

Welcome therefore Professor Sockett's book. It shatters that illusion, restores the language of education to the moral sphere to which it belongs and puts the development of "persons" at the centre of educational endeavor, not the economy or whatever targets those in power instruct the teachers to deliver.

Central to that moral world is the development of virtues—that is, the dispositions which characterize a distinctively human form of life and which influence how we think and act in the particular situations that confront us. The person with well-developed intellectual virtues will be moved by a concern for seeking and telling the truth. The person imbued with moral virtues will act courageously, judging how to act when confronted with danger. The means by which we pursue the ends of education affect the very conception of those ends themselves.

The book draws upon a tradition in moral philosophy, going back to Aristotle, that centers on what it means to be a person and to become one more fully.

Education, in such a moral context, addresses the kind of learning that fosters that personal development. But that in turn broadens the educational landscape, no longer concerned just with the transmission of knowledge or with training in useful skills. The "whole person" lives by more than useful knowledge, but also and primarily by the values that shape his or her life and that are embedded in the dispositions or virtues acquired through informal and formal learning.

Professor Sockett makes an important and distinctive contribution to this tradition. No one else has so systematically shown how, in thinking educationally about the development of persons, that moral language of virtues not only questions the prevailing emphasis on individual autonomy, not only challenges the narrow view of knowledge acquisition, but also transforms our view of teaching and of the relationship between teacher and learner.

Richard Pring,
Professor Emeritus, University of Oxford

The Human
Common Core

PREFACE

I have been trying for some years to articulate the arguments in this book. George Mason University granted me leave for the Fall of 2010 to complete it, a privilege for which I am deeply thankful, not least because it also enabled me to work on it during that summer. This was a time of profound personal sadness, as between the end of May and the beginning of August, three of my longtime friends died, and it is to their memory that this book is dedicated: John Gooders, philosopher and ornithologist; Ken Green, philosopher and first Vice-Chancellor of Manchester Metropolitan University; and my sister-in-law's husband, John Lewis, a radical, a philosopher, and a reluctant but exceptional administrator at the University of Plymouth.

I was fortunate to begin studying education, and particularly philosophy of education, while teaching at a London comprehensive school that turned out to be more a period of learning than teaching. I now have the privilege of sharing its memories with two friends, formerly sixth-form pupils in my class at the school: Conal Condren and Bernard Barker. I am indebted to two immensely gifted scholars—Richard Peters, who supervised my PhD, and Paul Hirst, who came to the Chair of Education at Cambridge when I was there. Along with Richard Pring, David Bridges, Charles Bailey, John Elliott, and Peter Scrimshaw, we formed what we called the Cambridge Group, which was a golden age for all of us, meeting constantly academically and socially, and writing a series of books together.

I moved into academic administration on moving to Ulster, and to directing the Institute of Continuing Education in Derry at a time of considerable civic turmoil. Again, I was fortunate to work with people of exceptional quality, such as Bill Cockcroft and Willie Ewing, but my philosophical agenda (and competence) lagged during those intensive years. At the University of East Anglia, initially as a founding Professor, then as Dean, I continued my administrative work but began to work my way back into philosophy, primarily through my Inaugural Lecture that deals primarily with the nature of educational theory. At UEA I worked closely with Lawrence Stenhouse, whom I had known for some years, but also with Martin Hollis, possibly the best philosopher of his generation. Both Lawrence and Martin died at an early age, tragic losses to intellectual life.

Before coming to the United States in 1987, I took study leave at the University of Chicago in 1986 with Philip W. Jackson in the Benton Center and led a graduate seminar that included such distinguished young students as Kal Alston, Rene Arcilla, Bob Boostrom, and David Hansen. I am sure I learned much more from them than they learned from me. But in moving from England to the States in 1987, the more immediate professional challenge was to work out the practical implications of teaching within a framework of moral professionalism and reflective practice, through the development of a master's degree for serving teachers. I learned a great deal from the many experienced and committed teachers taking the program and from conversations over the years with my colleagues at GMU, notably Diane Wood, Pamela LePage, Betsy DeMulder, Mark Jacobs, and Jim Finkelstein. I owe special thanks to Sandy Gammons, Director of Secondary Instruction and Career and Technical Education in Henry County Public Schools, Virginia, for allowing me to base the character of Janet in chapter 3 on her initial experience of teaching.

Part of the analysis in chapter 3 draws on my "Moral and Epistemic Purposes of Teacher Education" in *The Handbook of Research on Teacher Education: Enduring Issues in Changing Contexts*, published by Routledge in 2009. In chapter 4, the discussion of institutions was first aired in the two lectures I gave as a Distinguished Visiting Professor at the University of Alberta in Edmonton in 1997, titled "Lies, Secrets and Institutions," and I have also drawn in that chapter on my contribution to *The SAGE Handbook of Philosophy of Education* (2010) titled "The Wider Ethical Dimensions of Education and Teaching." Chapter 10 includes material from two recent papers: (1) "Character, Roles and Relations" in the American Association of College of Teacher Education monograph *Teacher Dispositions: Building a Teacher Education Framework of Moral Standards* (2002), which I edited, and (2) "Dispositions as Virtues: The Complexity of the Construct" published in the *Journal of Teacher Education* in May 2009.

I am particularly indebted to Bill Hare for his excellent work on open-mindedness that provided me with a model for framing other virtues and for his careful reading of the manuscript. To my colleague Diane Wood, to Richard Ogusthorpe, and Erskine Dottin, I must also express my thanks for their penetrating and helpful comments. Nor could this have been done without the help and advice of Naomi Silverman and Kevin Henderson at Routledge. Finally, my dear wife, Ann, has tolerated the rigors of having me writing at home, and for that, and much else, I am eternally grateful.

Ashburn, Virginia, 2011

INTRODUCTION

Contemporary education neglects the knower at the expense of knowledge and skills. It rewards right answers and memorization. It discourages open-minded consideration of alternatives, the development of judgment and of understanding who one is. The moral and intellectual virtues constitutive of the democratic citizen seem tangential to its purposes. In this book, the developing person is the center of education set in a moral space, a political order, and a framework of public and personal knowledge, all of which demand the development of personal dispositions or virtues. Public knowledge comprises truth, belief, and evidence; the congruent dispositions are truthfulness, open-mindedness, and impartiality. Personal knowledge comprises experience, commitment, and identity, severally matched with integrity as wholeness, courage and risk-taking, and self-knowledge.

Teaching knowledge in what has become the default school curriculum can be integrated with developing student personal dispositions as stable and continuous qualities that have both personal and social utility: useful personally in developing a meaningful life; useful socially as the adult person's contributions to society. There is little point in business and industry's demanding people with knowledge and skills from the schools, if graduates lack integrity, are closed-minded, lack judgment, are not prepared to take risks intellectually, and have little self-understanding. Required are not people with critical thinking "skills" but people who are critical thinkers. Being a critical thinker demands an epistemological perspective—that is, the acquisition of knowledge and understanding must be underpinned with grasping such matters as what counts as evidence, what makes a statement true or false, or whether I ought to believe what I believe. Understanding such epistemological puzzles through content in which dispositions can develop, not the trivia of memorizing the oft-forgotten right answer, must therefore be education's central target. Education's primary emphasis must be on those moral and intellectual dispositions that characterize the free, autonomous individual in a democratic society, developed through content embedded in official educational standards.

Recently teacher education in the United States has begun to focus on the teacher's dispositions, a development initiated by the National Council for the Accreditation of Teacher Education. While there is debate, even confusion about what the council anticipates, the implication is clear: teaching technique has to be subservient to ethical and moral goals, as teaching is primarily, predominantly, and pervasively a moral activity. This applies to teacher education, but also to the curriculum in the teaching of children and undergraduate students, and indeed to the teaching of adults, even if the content is training in specific skills. Classroom teachers of children should be experts in their subject and have the adaptive expertise to get things across (Darling-Hammond et al., 2005), but at its center the educational enterprise is one in which children and students are developing as persons, not merely memorizing information.

The moral center of the classroom goes well beyond the to and fro of interpersonal relationships. It demands intellectual virtues and dispositions such as accuracy, consistency, and effort as well as such moral virtues as courage and open-mindedness. If you teach math, you teach children the importance of accuracy, a virtue they will retain long after how to solve a quadratic equation has been forgotten. If you teach history, you should be teaching impartiality necessary to their future in making all kinds of judgments. If you teach civics, you should be teaching open-mindedness, an immensely desirable virtue for a citizen, though it sometimes appears more honored in the breach than the observance. If you teach science, you teach respect for evidence. Therefore, a much stronger educational focus on who the individual in education is becoming would be not merely a bonus for the individual learner, but a critical element in the stability of members of a democratic society because it will contribute to coherent intellectual functioning, enabling the individual to flourish as a human being and as a citizen. A democratic society thus needs a full-blooded approach to the development in children of intellectual and moral dispositions seen as intellectual and moral virtues; for this educational task content knowledge is a necessary but inadequate vehicle.

However, if the emphasis in the aims of education were to shift to dispositions rather than to content, contemporary educational theory and educational research would change too. It is still largely construed as an empirical science, on Thorndike's principles, with little attention to moral or other values, except insofar as they are research objects. There is therefore little to distinguish educational research in this genre from sociological or psychological research, with the various methodological systems available in those disciplines, as the objects of research do not determine a discipline's characteristics. As teaching is a moral activity, however, educational research should also be normative theory and be rooted in the development of dispositions, the efficacy of teaching practices in a moral perspective, the moral office of the teacher, and the moral ethos of institutions. The moral will therefore be at the center of how we understand education and the theory we develop from it, instead of being seen as a mere "dimension" of the practice of teaching, a rather troublesome sideshow to the empirical.

Three matters are germane to the book's construction. First, any exercise in philosophy must be one in which the right questions are asked. So it is no accident that the book opens with a quotation from Mary Belenky and her colleague authors of *Women's Ways of Knowing* that articulates a set of questions both moral and epistemological: a herald's trumpet call to the ensuing arguments.

Second, philosophers of education can continue to write for each other, but needed are philosophical books that are accessible to teachers, policy makers, and indeed anyone with a serious interest in education. That is problematic, as few teachers study philosophy of education in their training. Indeed, philosophy of education is at a crossroads. Inside the discipline there have been huge strides in quality, depth, and range in the last century (see Waks, 2008). Yet, apart from the IMPACT strategy in the United Kingdom (see White, J., 2007), it appears to have little influence at all on public policy in the United States. Educational think tanks in the United States (e.g., the American Enterprise Institute, or the Fordham Foundation) don't contain much, if any, serious philosophical reflection. Moreover, philosophy of education, once a major element in the undergraduate curriculum, was merged into "Foundations," which is increasingly being obliterated from teacher-education institutions. With this in mind, as with my 1993 book, I am seeking to write for teachers and administrators, for teachers of philosophy of education, for philosophers of education, for teacher-education institutions struggling with NCATE standards, and for the educational community at large, national and international.

Third, the book is therefore to be seen as "introductory," that nice adjective with which Mill labels the opening of that majestic essay *On Liberty*. First, it embraces a trajectory of difficulty. That is, part I is written with teachers and educators in mind who have little background in moral and epistemological issues in education, and it introduces ideas explored in parts II and III. Second, these two parts are then much more philosophically complex, opening up major problems from moral philosophy (e.g., agency), epistemology (e.g., belief), and philosophy of mind (e.g., memory). The treatment of the many topics within these philosophical areas is not to be regarded as in any sense exhaustive; rather they provide an introduction to each topic mentioned, scaffolding if you like, on which further inquiry can be developed and more in-depth pursuit of the problems can be encountered. But third, the introduction to this range of philosophical problems is not a tour of available arguments but articulates a strong point of view, specifically that classrooms demand an epistemological presence, an atmosphere in which the complexity of knowledge and the knower's experience of it is constantly in play. That classroom is one in which truth is searched for, not just delivered. Yet a philosophical examination of such complex matters needs to be the base for practice. In part IV I articulate the features of the classroom with an epistemological presence that has been a theme throughout the book. But that presence demands teachers with moral and intellectual virtues and dispositions. I suggest these may be grouped under the three categories of character, intellect, and care, and I end the book by describing proposals for a teacher-education assessment program built on the rationale of parts II and III. My hope is that this structure makes the issues raised in part I accessible enough to a serious nonphilosophical reader so that part II and part III become enticing. Each part has its own introduction to the content of its three chapters.

The direction of the book will open up for graduate and doctoral students in philosophy of education a field for research, which would demand the conceptual, the normative, and the empirical. The future challenge is to articulate educational theory as a normative theory. Such a view of educational theory can build on two important intellectual developments: first, that of virtue epistemology in philosophy, and, second, what has come to be called positive psychology, in which empirical psychologists work on a range of personal strengths and virtues rather than on the various psychological weaknesses, which has been the transcendent focus of much psychological work.

PART I

Knowledge, Morality, and Authority in Teaching

Introduction

Chapter 1 begins with a quotation from Mary Belenky and her coauthors (1986) that puts fundamental questions about our knowledge and how we know at the center of our lives and suggests that there lies the core curriculum for children and young adults. Exploring this curriculum can be effectively done in a classroom with an epistemological presence, which means briefly that all the complex questions of knowledge are in play in that environment. The chapter focuses on the broad scope of knowledge—of persons, ourselves, events, and ideas. Its complexity and tenuous character are illustrated through examining four questions for the teacher.

Chapter 2 then provides an overview of what are called public and personal knowledge, within the framework of the individual as seeker after knowledge. Public knowledge is seen within the traditional categories in philosophy: truth, belief, and evidence. Personal knowledge has different categories in this account, namely those of commitment, experience, and identity. In this chapter the character of the epistemological presence emerges in more detail described through (1) *belief questions*: How do I know what I believe? (2) *self-revelation questions*: How do I see myself? and (3) *search for truth questions*: What is truth? What is authority? To whom do I listen? At the end of the school day, the child clambering on the school bus or the undergraduate returning to her dorm should have a mind full of questions about the day's work, not a mind filled with worry about what time she has tonight to memorize for tomorrow's test.

Promoting an epistemological presence in a classroom, however, demands that a teacher pay careful attention to his or her authority. Through examples of three teachers and one child, chapter 3 examines the distinctions among contractual, moral, and epistemological authority. These are set against differing conceptions of the teacher: as scholar, as nurturer, as clinician, and as moral professional. Part I thus exposes the questions tackled in much greater philosophical detail in part II.

1

THE EPISTEMOLOGICAL PRESENCE IN TEACHING AND LEARNING

epistemological virtues

> We do not think of the ordinary person as preoccupied with such difficult and profound questions as: What is truth? What is authority? To whom do I listen? What counts for me as evidence? How do I know what I know? Yet to ask ourselves these questions and to reflect on our answers is more than a truly intellectual exercise, for our basic assumptions about the nature of truth and reality and the origins of knowledge shape the way we see the world and ourselves as participants in it. They affect our definitions of ourselves, the way we interact with others, our public and private personae, our sense of control over life events, our views of teaching and learning, and our conceptions of morality.
>
> *(Belenky et al., 1986, p. 3)*

Answering these challenging questions is a primary task of this book. First, they connect the intellectual and the moral life—knowledge and virtue. Second, they set both in the context of the individual, the "ordinary person," demanding that answers to the questions not just be theoretical statements about the nature of knowledge or virtue, but examine how individual human beings are to be understood and understand themselves. Third, as children, too, are ordinary persons, the questions put formidable tasks before their teachers. Indeed, if its wide-ranging questions are important, how do we help children grow up to develop their perceptions of the world and their place in it? How do we help them come to terms with these complex issues of truth, reality, knowledge, and authority? For that matter, how do we handle these matters in our own personal and professional lives? How do we become who we are? Above all, these are questions that should permeate a child's education alongside or integral to the subject matter being taught. Where these questions rumble around the work in a classroom, that classroom will have an epistemological presence.

Many teachers may not be familiar with problems of knowledge, even though this is central to teacher professionalism. That lack of familiarity has diverse origins, among which are the dominance of the empirical and developmental traditions, the weakness of philosophy of education, and the uncertain quality of teacher education. Americans also tend, in Cornel West's phrase, to evade philosophy

(1989). The terrain of this book may therefore be unfamiliar to teachers and to teacher educators, because it grapples with the problem of the epistemological and the moral, arguing that we need sophisticated understanding not just of "content" or of "method" but of the problems of knowledge that lie at the heart of teaching—specifically, of how knowledge and virtue are profoundly linked in each part of the teaching enterprise. Of course, teachers, like other professionals, "argue that it is impossible to meet heightened societal expectations for their performance in an environment that combines increasing turbulence with increasing regulation of professional activity" (Schön, 1995, p. 7). But they also have not had a thoroughgoing intellectual preparation for teaching.

It is, however, this shift from being technicians to becoming moral professionals that demands understanding the nature and character of knowledge and developing intellectual habits in transactions with children. For, it is inconceivable to think of a "knowledge-less" education, whether we are talking about knowledge of skills, subject disciplines, oneself and other people, or moral agency. Like morality, knowledge is right there, in the classroom, day in day out, in the interchange between teachers and learners. It is crucial, unavoidable, essentially human, and immensely liberating. Gaining knowledge expands the boundaries of one's ignorance and thereby of oneself, as Plato suggested in his *Apology*. Of course, there are other critical matters in the presence of knowledge in the classroom, such as how decisions are made about which knowledge is taught and how knowledge is connected to belief, truth, evidence, experience, and oneself as an individual. The place of knowledge in teaching is therefore central, but complex and tenuous. In classrooms, however, there must be what I will describe and illustrate throughout this book as an epistemological presence. Four questions, extracted from those posed by Belenky and colleagues, lie at the heart of problems of knowledge and truth in teaching, and they constitute significant problems for a professional teacher:

1.   When I teach students the information, am I giving them knowledge?
2.   How do I teach children that what I teach is true? What counts as "true"?
3.   How can I aid the understanding and development of children who lack crucial background knowledge?
4.   How do I cope and how should I handle the issues of my own power in teaching knowledge to children?

Each of these questions is explored in the following four sections.

I. Knowledge and Information: How Do I Know What I Know?

The problems of the predominance of high-stakes testing in one form or another are not often examined through the prism of knowledge—that is, what is *internal* to the material taught. Look at this example of a Grade 3 history test, a model sample item from a Virginia Standards of Learning policy introduced in 1994.

> The Ancient Chinese built the Great Wall mainly to—
>   a. provide water for their crops
>   b. honor their emperors
>   c. protect against invaders
>   d. teach their building methods to other people.

Treated just as information drawn from a prescribed text, the child answering this multiple-choice question will remember that the correct answer is "c." No one knows, of course, how many children get the answer right by guessing—in which case, while testers may say a child has the right answer, we don't know from a test that the child actually *knows* its content.

But information and guessing aside, what if we treat this as a test of knowledge? The child could claim alternative interpretations—for instance, that if "other people" ("d") includes other Chinese, then manifestly teaching was a main purpose, of importance equal to "c." The child might speculate about the accuracy of the phrase "ancient Chinese"—what philosopher Stephen Toulmin would call "a grand political abstraction" (1972). It makes as much sense to say that the Americans built the American interstate highway system: true but empty. Thus a child could reasonably argue that it was Emperor Ch'in Shih Huang Ti, not "the Chinese," who was mainly responsible for building the Great Wall, just as it was President Eisenhower who built the interstate highway system. There is more than one viable answer, but only one is deemed correct: the one the children have been taught. In classrooms with an epistemological presence, children might consider these and other kinds of explanations of why the Wall was built and search for evidence to support their conclusions—even if that evidence was simply supplied by the teacher. Yet, it would be safe to assume that this has not happened: for, as in the construction of many such multiple-choice questions, testers will simply dream up plausible alternatives, not those that actually can be treated as serious alternatives in the intentions of those who built the Wall or that children have examined in studying ancient China.

How significant is this difference between information teaching and knowledge teaching? First, the politician, the tester, and the bureaucrat may happily sacrifice these quibbles for the testing goals they have in mind—namely, to measure teacher and school performance through the facility with which children recall what they have been taught to reproduce. Whether that is intellectually honest or not seems to be another matter. Second, it is the word "mainly" in the Great Wall question that gives the testing game away: it invites judgment. So, in the interests of the child's knowledge, the test might ask the child to rank these possible answers in order of importance and *explain why*. Explanations demand not mere recapitulation but getting inside the subject, explaining motives and context, and making judgments about evidence. Having children make grounded judgments and explaining their rationale does not fit with the priorities of simple testing, but it is essential to classrooms with an epistemological presence.

If content is taught as knowledge rather than information, that immediately invites the question "How do I know what I know?" The dominant mode of testing children means that teachers feel obliged to have them learn (i.e., memorize) material that they are then asked in writing to recall. It is wrong to assume that success on a test provides proof that knowledge has been transmitted. The conceptual difference between information and knowledge is simple. Knowing something can be claimed only where an explanation can be given, a judgment can be made, alternatives can be considered and examined, and some kind of evidence provided. Being informed about something does not require any such backing or understanding. Information is just stuff. It can simply be an item committed to memory, and then maybe forgotten, or perhaps misremembered. Of course, information, in terms of the details of given events, incidents, predictions in science, is not to be ignored in classrooms; rather, it must be set within the quest for knowledge and will be treated as such in a classroom with an epistemological presence.

II. Knowledge and Truth: What Counts as True?

Many teachers are very wary of saying that something is true, especially as the word "truth" sparks off all kinds of debate in American public discourse. Some will speak of there being "absolute truth," usually connected to a religious belief. Others will say that there cannot be any such thing as "truth" (absolute or otherwise) since "truth" is either relative (dependent on one's own culture or society) or subjective (dependent on how individuals experience the world, so truth is a matter of opinion). (For further discussion of these differences, see part II.)

Especially difficult for teachers, for different kinds of political reasons, is the difficulty in coping with the notion of "absolute" truth. If they have profound religious beliefs and are faced with handling moral issues in the secular context of the school, their integrity as persons may appear threatened. If they have no religious beliefs but work with children of profound fundamentalist beliefs of whatever religion, they may find the integrity of the curriculum threatened, whatever their own position on truth. However, if they reject the notion of absolute truth, and believe truth to be relative, then they are reluctant to impress on children what they see as "their" views of truth. This latter pedagogical position gained notoriety in the values-clarification movement, and that legacy lingers.

As teachers work with knowledge, they will need a view of truth as well, since knowledge and truth are intimately and necessarily connected. Part of the problem is that these harsh dichotomies of absolute or relative, objective or subjective can be traps that force us unnecessarily to extremes of epistemological choice. We know that there are things that *are* true, in what we can momentarily call an "ordinary" view of truth, such as Belenky's "ordinary person" would accept.

"Ordinary" here means the kind of truth we all use throughout our lives. For we make statements all the time that are "ordinarily" true (the teacher's late; my friend is sick; the school bus is yellow). Statements of truth can be regarded, for the moment, as assertions that claim knowledge (see chapter 2). Supporting evidence can be very full, uncertain, or unclear; what happened can be in dispute, exemplified most obviously in a criminal trial, where a jury struggles to come to a balanced and fair judgment on batteries of actions and interpretation that have been laid out before them. Teachers need to understand how to handle the concept of truth with children and its closely related concepts, evidence, experience, and meaning.

The controversy about truth often inhibits teachers from using the word, except perhaps when a child blatantly lies. The following two examples indicate that we can teach children things that are true without needing to use terms like "absolute," "relative," "objective," or "subjective," and both are matters that call for the child's judgment. If we accept that there are things that are true (in this "ordinary" way), that will open up the way to building a more detailed account of truth and its relationship with knowledge and simultaneously release us from the tyranny of the harsh dichotomy of relative and absolute that traps teachers into confusion about truth. For the search for truth is the hallmark of a classroom with an epistemological presence: truth cannot just be delivered to children as a package of information. One way to further an examination of knowledge and truth is to look at examples of coincidence and proof.

Knowledge and Coincidence

[handwritten margin note: narrative ethics]

The history of the African American in American history is so central that, from an early age, children need to encounter it. This is often done either through the history of the Civil War or through literature or poetry. But the story told by Alex Haley in *Roots* is accessible to children at an early age, though they may not be ready to read the whole novel. Anyone who has read the story of Kunta Kinte and his family in this "epic drama of one man's search for his origins" must be impressed with the power of the narrative legacy handed down from "the old African" to his family on this side of the Atlantic (Haley, 1976). Slavery was not simply inhuman; it was dehumanizing in the strict sense, stripping countless human beings of their personhood and their identity, not least by prohibiting the use of their own given names when they were first sold. The American story originates in the Gambia, where Kunta Kinte of the Mandinka tribe went out one day to collect wood and disappeared—captured, it was assumed, by slave-traders. Down through the family came this story, the stuff of legend, the one link for this family with their African origins, which Alex heard on his grandma's porch.

To use this story in a classroom opens up several epistemological issues: the verifiability of oral history, at what point fictional or semi-fictional stories constitute history, and whether such stories provide any truth or even certainty. One passage in *Roots* embodies each of these epistemological factors, for Haley's search for his roots culminated in his visit to the village of Juffure in the Gambia:

> When we got within sight of Juffure, the children who were playing out-side gave the alert, and the people came flocking from their huts. It's a village of only about seventy people. Like most back-country villages, it was still very much as it was two hundred years ago, with its circular mud houses and their conical thatched roofs. Among the people as they gathered was a small man wearing an off-white robe, a pill box hat over an aquiline-featured black face, and about him was an aura of "somebodiness" until I knew he was the man we had come to see and hear....
>
> ... After a while, the old man turned, walked briskly through the people, past my three interpreters, and right up to me. His eyes piercing into mine, seeming to feel I should understand his Mandinka, he expressed what they had all decided they felt concerning those unseen millions of us who lived in those places that had been slave ships' destinations—and the translation came: "We have been told by our forefathers that there are many of us from this place who are in exile in that place called America—and in other places."
>
> The old man sat down, facing me, as the people hurriedly gathered be-hind him. Then he began to recite for me the ancestral history of the Kinte clan, as it had been passed down orally across centuries from the forefathers' time. It was not merely conversational, but more as if a scroll were being read: for the still, silent villagers, it was clearly a formal occasion. The griot would speak, bending forwards from the waist, his body rigid, his neck cords standing out, his words seeming almost physical objects. After a sentence or two, seeming to go limp, he would lean back, listening to an interpreter's translation. Spilling from the griot's head came an incredibly complex Kinte clan lineage that reached across many generations: who married whom; who had what children, what children then married whom; then their off-spring. It was all just unbelievable. I was struck not only by the profusion of details, but also by the narrative's biblical style.... To date things the griot linked them to events, such as "in the year of the big water"—a flood—"he slew a water buffalo." To determine the calendar date, you'd have to find out when that particular flood occurred....
>
> The old griot had talked for nearly two hours up to then, and per-haps fifty times the narrative had included some detail about someone he had named. Now after he had just named [these] four sons [Kunta, Lamin, Suwadu, and Madi], again he appended a detail, and the interpreter translated—"About the time the King's soldiers came"—another of the griot's time-fixing references—"the eldest of these four sons, Kunta, went away from his village to chop wood...and he was never seen again." And the griot went on with his narrative.

I sat as if I were carved of stone. My blood seemed to have congealed. This man whose lifetime had been in this back-country African village had no way in the world to know that he had just echoed what I had heard all through my boyhood years on my grandma's front porch in Henning, Tennessee, of an African who had always insisted his name was "kin-tay": who had a guitar called a "ko", and a river within the state of Virginia, "Kamby Bolongo"; and who had been kidnapped into slavery while not far from his village, chopping wood to make himself a drum.

(1976, pp. 676–679)

Is it *true,* then, that Alex Haley's distant ancestor, Kunta Kinte, went out to collect wood and was captured by the king's soldiers? Is the American legend confirmed by the old griot? Manifestly this extraordinary story has all kinds of powerful images and opportunities for connectedness with the African American story. But is it true?

Assuming *Roots* to be part of a school curriculum, we do not of course want children to think that just because the story is there in print, it is true. The story requires an examination of the circumstances and coming to a judgment. Yet persuasive here is the fact of coincidence. That is, the same basic story about a man's life 200 years before seems to have been handed down on both sides of the ocean. There are many possibilities, including the account is fictional or the Kunta the griot referred to was not Haley's ancestor. We don't have all the details, of course, but we could still reach the judgment that it is true that Kunta Kinte went out one day to collect wood and disappeared, was captured by slave-traders, and was brought to America, and this person was Haley's ancestor. We *know* this to be *true.* It will be critical in a classroom with an epistemological presence that this story be taught not just as information, but as an important example of how we understand whether a given story is true and the grounded judgments we need to make in deciding its truth.

Knowledge and Proof

As teachers we frequently make mistakes about what is true when we are teaching. For many years, it was a staple of history that "Columbus discovered America in 1492." At almost any level of interpretation, this is simply false. What is meant by discovery, for example: Do you mean it wasn't there before Columbus? How about Erik the Red, the Viking? One such common belief in Europe is that the first circumnavigation of Africa took place in 1497 when a Portuguese expedition led by Vasco da Gama rounded the Cape of Good Hope on the way to India.

What then, would children make of this passage from Herodotus? In the fifth century BC Herodotus, a young Greek scholar, toured what we now know as Africa and the Middle East. He wandered through the towns and villages of the Nile, commenting on the geography, showing how the Greeks had borrowed so many Egyptian ideas, picking up stories and writing them down, and particularly writing the story of great wars between the Greeks and the Persians. He is constantly referring to his sources "soothsayers in Memphis," and "priests of the temple at Thebes," for example, and he is very careful to qualify stories or explanations with "people say" or "some believe." Herodotus's work has earned him the title "the father of history." The nine books called *The Histories* are without doubt one of the greatest achievements of the ancient world; they are also funny, vulgar, erudite, and highly observant (Herodotus, 2003).

> As for Libya [Africa] we know that it is washed on all sides by the sea except where it joins Asia, as was first demonstrated, so far as our knowledge goes, by the Egyptian king Neco [r. 610–595 BC], who, after calling off the construction of the canal between the Nile and the Arabian Gulf, sent out a fleet manned by a Phoenician crew with orders to sail round and return to Egypt and the Mediterranean by way of the Pillars of Heracles [the Strait of Gibraltar]. The Phoenicians sailed from the Red Sea into the southern ocean, and every autumn, put in where they were on the Libyan coast, sowed a patch of ground, and waited for next year's harvest. Then, having got in their grain, they put to sea again, and after two full years rounded the Pillars of Heracles in the course of the third, and returned to Egypt. These men made a *statement which I do not myself believe,* though others may, to the effect that as they sailed on a westerly course round the southern end of Libya, they had the sun on their right,—to the northward of them.
>
> *(IV:42, pp. 228–229; my italics)*

Notice that Herodotus appears to believe the detail of the men's story, though he doesn't believe that part of their story that proves they did it. For, Neco's Phoenician sailors must have been right not only about sailing around Africa. When they said that the sun was on the "wrong" side at midday and that they were sailing westward, that is itself proof that they had entered the southern hemisphere. Ergo, they must have been beyond the southern tip of Africa. The paradox for Herodotus is that the evidence he disbelieves actually provides additional evidence for the veracity of the navigators. For this reason, we *know* it to be *true* that Africa was circumnavigated over 2,000 years before Vasco da Gama's expedition. Internal to the story is the additional evidence. In a classroom with an epistemological presence, each of the strands in this complex story would be unraveled and understanding will begin to emerge about different criteria for proof of things we can judge to be true. If we are to have children grapple with truth, they must be well-equipped through being encouraged to challenge received wisdom, to pursue alternatives, and to examine evidence, but not thereby to become skeptics.

Ordinary Truth

So whatever people may aver about truth being absolute, relative, objective, or subjective, we know what happened to Kunta Kinte, and we know that Neco's

Phoenician sailors circumnavigated Africa in approximately 600 BC. We know these two statements to be true, and we can justify teaching them to children—but not as mere information. For their *truth depends on the evidence* set out: they are not true just because Alex Haley, Herodotus, or I say so. Rather, to show you they are true, I have presented evidence that explains why I have written this down, why I make these claims to knowledge. Evidence is always in principle disputable, but on this evidence, these things happened, so my statements about those events are true. If they are true, then the notion that there is no such thing as truth (or that it is all relative or subjective) is seriously undermined. Classrooms with an episte-mological presence are environments where there is a search for truth, not where truth is just delivered.

Of course, if we somehow always avoided telling the truth, social life would disintegrate—quickly (see Hart, 1961, especially chapter 9). Try to imagine a world in which telling the truth was *not* the norm of behavior, even though the actual extent of deceit may increasingly contribute to undermining social life and civility. Robert Putnam and colleagues (1994) have described how important networks, norms, and trust are to the coherence and the economic viability of groups within society, based on studies of contrasting regions of Italy. The key is trust and the adherence to norms of conduct, and at the heart of trusting someone else is knowing that they are not deceiving you, or, more positively, that they are telling the truth. With children, rather than avoiding issues about the truth, we must embrace them.

Equipped with this "ordinary" view of truth, and being prepared to use it when we discuss knowledge, is something of a relief, for we can now stop being embarrassed by talk about truth, but relish its complexity, especially in our classrooms, where dialogue about evidence and thereby of truth is intellectually and morally critical. How else are "ordinary children" to begin to encounter the problems Belenky and colleagues lay out for us? Without that dialogue, one might say that teachers keep epistemological *secrets* from children, by not letting them see the complexity of truth—about how evidence connects to truth, to knowledge, and to belief, among much else (see chapter 2). The problem is significant. In an age of relativism and subjectivism (see chapter 6) or even in a culture of absolutism, how can a teacher provide evidence for children who are often skeptical? How can that evidence in the classroom be powerful enough to be convincing, such that the child accepts it as true? Do teachers back off when a child says his dad, priest, or guru says "that's not true"? In science teaching, of course, there can be palpable evidence produced in laboratories, though even here there are conflicts—for example, about climate change. In social studies, history, or literature, that presents a much harder task. We therefore face major problems not about truth, but about producing good evidence, and the unusual character of Kunta Kinte's descendants' history and the history of Neco's sailors are excellent indicators that convincing evidence can be forthcoming, even without primary documents. But, if a teacher is to create an epistemological *presence* in a classroom, one where knowledge and truth are valued, then the story of Kunta Kinte or the circumnavigation of Africa can be examined both for their content *and* as provocative examples of the relation between evidence and truth.

III. Knowledge, Perception, Background, and Perspective

We have so far noted the problematic relationship between knowledge and facts, and the difficulties that the absence of a clear concept of truth and evidence can make for a teacher. We can now turn to focus on Belenky and colleagues' ordinary person, the knower—the person to whom, in teaching, knowledge is being conveyed or transmitted or learned. For a classroom with an epistemological presence will contain a teacher and children, each with their own view of the world. All are knowers.

Two issues illustrate the significance of considering the knower: (1) the individual's capacities of perception and (2) the background he or she has of the world, both of which can include the capacity for memory, reason, intuition, and introspection. First, the acquisition of knowledge requires certain kinds of mental and physical abilities. For example, a patient in an advanced stage of Alzheimer's disease appears from all the evidence to have lost the capacity to acquire new knowledge or to remember anything much—for instance, where Oxford professor John Bayley (1999) wrote so movingly about his wife Iris Murdoch, the philosopher and novelist. Second, each of us brings a social, cultural, or intellectual *background* to the world, our perspective on it, and our views about it. The Nobel Prize winner Amartya Sen, for instance, grew up in what is now Bangladesh and has worked in Britain and the United States: his book *The Idea of Justice* (2010) is a remarkable study drawing from several different cultures. Children in our schools, too, have diverse backgrounds.

First, we will deal with problems of perception as one of many important human capacities. Our knowledge of the world around us comes to us through language, which as children we acquire predominantly by being able to see what spoken words represent (see also chapter 7). The key issue in the movie *The Miracle Worker* was Ann Sullivan's continuous and unflagging attempts to get Helen Keller to connect the tapping out of the letters on her palm (a sign language) with the objects to which they referred. For a sighted child, we pick up the ball and say, "ball," and the child gradually learns the word. Of course, the child learns the huge complexity of language, its nuances, and tones of voice that accompany different emotions. It is not merely a matter of parroting words, too often the upshot of vocabulary tests.

Perception, Seeing, and Seeing As

What might we learn from the case of an adult who has been blind since childhood and suddenly has his vision restored? Oliver Sacks (1993) studied Virgil, a 50-year-old Oklahoman who regained his sight after 45 years. The physical details need not concern us. Briefly, Virgil was operated on in 1991, shortly after he had become engaged to Amy. The family had been largely opposed to the operation; Amy believed it would change Virgil's personality, for the better. He himself was phlegmatic about the possibilities. Amy kept a journal in which the path of Virgil's recovery was documented. He had lived for years negotiating the world as a blind man. The restoration of his sight created a massive problem of learning for him. Sadly, as he was struggling with his new acquisition, he had a severe illness that, "at a single stroke, deprived him of job, health and independence, leaving him a gravely sick man, unable to fend for himself. For Amy, who incited the surgery in the first place, and who was so passionately invested in Virgil's seeing, it was a 'miracle' that misfired, a calamity" (p. 73).

The major threads of the progress of Virgil's recovery, however, were as follows. Initially, he was unable to trust his vision; he was unsure of what seeing was. There was no cry of "I can see!" when the bandages were removed. Not until the surgeon spoke did a look of recognition cross Virgil's face. There was plenty of light and shadow but no way to put the images together with his experience and understanding of the world. "When we open our eyes each morning," as Sacks says, "it is upon a world we have spent a lifetime *learning* to see" (1993, p. 61). When Sacks met Virgil, he felt that his behavior was "certainly not that of a sighted man, but it wasn't that of a blind man either. It was the behavior of one *mentally* blind, agnosic, able to see but not to decipher what he was seeing" (p. 62). Five weeks after surgery, "he often felt more disabled than he had felt when he was blind, and he had lost the confidence, the ease of moving, that he had possessed then" (p. 63).

The specific examples of his difficulties are interesting: he had to "put a tree together," learning it bit by bit (leaves, trunk, etc.). He could not understand how a skyscraper stood up without collapsing. He began to define things in terms of color, which had not been available to him before his operation. Shapes and solid objects presented major difficulties, probably because we come on objects from different angles and so they "look" different. He needed to walk in his house on a particular learned line, or he became disoriented. "As Virgil walked the rooms of his house, investigating, so to speak, the visual construction of the world, I was reminded of an infant moving his hand to and fro before his eyes, waggling his head, turning it this way and that, in his primal construction of the world" (p. 66). He had severe difficulties in distinguishing the dog and the cat. He began to buy toys (buildings, soldiers) and it seemed by having these models, he could begin to put the real world into order in his (visual) mind. With eating, and with other ordinary tasks, he would start off well, but then relapse into his "blind" life, picking food up with his hands. "In the newly sighted, learning to see demands a radical change in neurological functioning and, with it, a radical change in psychological functioning, in self, in *identity*" (p. 70; my italics).

Virgil's experience points up the crucial difference between "seeing" and "seeing as." "We see, by the gauge, that we need gas; see, by the newspapers, that our team has lost again; see by her expression, that she is nervous"—all different forms of perceptual knowledge or what we see things as (Dancy & Sosa, 1992, p. 334). Seeing the gauge is empty or that, by her expression, she is nervous are things we see because we have come to know what "the gauge" and "her expression" signify. Both Amy and Sacks ruminate about whether Virgil's learning process is like that of a young child—though physiologically it cannot be.

Background Knowledge

There are many classrooms in the country to which children come without the basic tools of understanding that have not been developed, as for example with adolescent refugee children from rural Central America who have never seen a pair of scissors. Equally, whether from teenage culture or ethnic differences, understandings of words, symbols, and signs can differ markedly. Much education, therefore, is the process of having children "see as." Children's inability to see things *as* can often be deeply confusing to teachers and is too often equated with a lack of intelligence.

So it is not just forms of deprivation, or the Virgils of this world, that present teachers with problems they don't understand. Moral education, for instance, demands teaching children to *see* other people *as* worthy of their respect. Teaching children to face difficulty implies having them *see* difficulties *as* challenges and not obstacles, just as mothers teach their infants to *see* fire *as* dangerous. Problems children have in geometry are often introduced by such howls as "I don't *see* what I have to do!" So dominant is sight in our understanding of the world that it is the eye that is the organ that seems to dominate our acquisition of knowledge (see Rée, 1999). But objects, colors, and everything else do not just present themselves to us: we have to learn them, to know them, to *see them as*...colors, objects of specific kinds with certain qualities.

What we learn to see as becomes what John Searle (1992) calls "background knowledge." We can do things, think things out, dream dreams, fulfill our intentions, *only* if we have a set of background capacities—that is, a range of knowledge that stands behind the specifics of our intentions, dreams, thinkings, and other mental acts. Searle takes a simple example, like the word "cut." Cutting a cake is different from cutting the grass or a cloth. There is nothing different here in the literal meaning of the word "cut," but our knowledge of the background is what we know about cakes, grass, and cloth and how they are different (pp. 178–179). These differences we are taught, or we learn. The same is true of our perceptions: we see this object as a table, though it could be in a doll's house, a palace dining room, or the table in a morgue. This background understanding facilitates linguistic interpretation and perceptual interpretation.

There is never enough that teachers can put into a child's background, and many contemporary advocates of a common-culture curriculum are talking about this background. Our individual perceptions act as enablers for everything else, and they need constant and continuous development. It is this lack of perceptual knowledge and understanding that so incapacitates Virgil. The absence of background knowledge, seeing as, is a major obstacle to the development of knowledge, indeed to the development of mind. That is a serious problem for many deprived, less able, or simply inexperienced students and their inexperienced teachers. Why? Because background here does not mean just curriculum "stuff": it incorporates everything we know from our first days of consciousness and how we have built understanding and our vocabulary and then more built more understanding and more vocabulary (see chapter 5). The problem for most teachers is that children's background, in this sense, is heterogeneous, and therefore the importance of John or Jane as individual children (as opposed to "third-graders") becomes critical.

Background and Perspective

Yet it is not merely background, but perspective. How Jane or John perceive things, how what all may see is seen as, influences our ability to communicate with them and therefore to communicate knowledge to them. In Charles Dickens's *Hard Times,* young Sissy cannot get hold of the idea of "national prosperity" in what she is being taught because she can understand it only in terms of the people and the life she lives, not as an abstraction. What has been selected as the known is incomprehensible to the knower. That lack of comprehension arises not because Sissy doesn't speak the language, or because she is stupid, or because she lacks the perception, or because she lacks the background. Simply put, she cannot comprehend how the matters of which the teacher speaks can be so treated, how things of great moment (wealth, starvation) can be reduced to statistical fact. *This is a matter of perspective, not background.* At the root of this is Sissy's background and upbringing, with her belief in the fierceness of her father's love for her. She cannot become a vessel to be filled up with facts or information: she is not that kind of vessel. Unsurprisingly, many children come to school with perspectives on life that differ from each other and from their teachers, but this is not, repeat not, a handicap for the child but an opportunity for the teacher. Perspective reveals a different sort of background, not a lack of it.

How does this seem to the contemporary teacher? Who are the children we teach whose perspectives are so foreign to us? As a teacher of educational philosophy, teachers who study with me present me with considerable challenges. They sometimes have worldviews I cannot comprehend, and I am sure that much of what I say to them, and how I say it, is as meaningless to them as was Sissy's problem with national prosperity. Because we are knowers with certain kinds of knowledge, we cannot simply treat students, whether children or adults, as under some kind of compulsion to imbibe the knowledge we teach in the curriculum. Nor will finding a motivational hook or some kind of connection be sufficient to get the knowledge to *this* knower. It is perhaps unnecessary to point out that here lies the challenge of multicultural classrooms with children from diverse backgrounds and how different school contexts will afford different opportunities and challenges in developing an epistemological presence. That classroom must be a place in which any child's perspective can be articulated.

IV. Knowledge, Power, and Authority

Because of the difficulties of handling truth and evidence, especially with children who lack an assumed background, teachers may resort to non-rational means to transmit some piece of knowledge (e.g., "it's right because I said so," or "the text-book can't be wrong," or "it's on the test"). The teacher resorts, in other words, to an open or disguised form of power. "Because I say so" can take many forms.

The tyranny and power in a state can have people come to believe things that are false through brutal treatment and conditioning, as Orwell's novel *Nineteen Eighty-Four* illustrates. One of Orwell's biographers suggested that his early school experiences are thinly disguised in the novel's politics. Certainly English private schools of Orwell's time (known as preparatory [elementary/middle] and public [secondary] schools) could manifest many of the features of the civic situation in which Winston Smith (the hero of the novel) is placed. These schools were often tyrannical systems forcing children to think "their way." Those school establishments manifested a puritanical and hypocritical attitude to sex. Unfair and degrading punishments, sometimes outside the school rules, were common-place. A fascination with inter-school competitions (or in-school competitions) became a meaningless, noisy rhetoric of "warfare." There was often a despised group outside the culture unable to get any place or rights, and there was often a school language, a series of slang terms and phrases that have to be learned to remain part of the culture, as in William Golding's *Lord of the Flies.* Finally, be-cause these were boarding schools that children attended 36 or more weeks of the year, the institutions almost became total (see Goffman, 1961). Once initiated, they created dependencies among their students, so that many students came to love being there, to admire the people running the organization, indeed to "love Big Brother." Schools can have immense power over children, usually mediated by teachers.

Yet many modern teachers often look askance at the notion that they can tell children what they ought to think or believe, especially in terms of values of any kind. Even so, some educational institutions do still manifest vestigial institutional characteristics of Orwell's tyrannical state, through a puritanical and hypocritical attitude to sex (pedophilia), unfair and degrading punishments (hazing) sometimes outside the school rules, and a ritualistic fascination with inter-school competi-tions as in high school football. There is sometimes a despised group in the school defining itself outside its culture (tragically illustrated at Columbine High School in 1999), and there is frequently a school language, a series of slang terms and phrases that have to be learned to remain part of the official and unofficial culture. Some of these phrases are specific to an institution, others to adolescents across society. Crucially, in all these aspects, the teachers and the student culture (Grant, 1990; Hersch, 1999) drastically influence the knowledge that a student acquires, along with a perspective on values, beliefs, and views *of what is true*.

So teachers exercise power through the knowledge they teach. To begin with, their basic competence as professionals inevitably influences how well children master the material on which they will be tested and which will open up (or not) life opportunities to them. Teachers also can exercise personal power by their own predilections as teachers, the material they choose to present, though testing systems may reduce that possibility. Personal influence can also be connected to knowledge, especially of oneself: think of teachers who have been rude, uncivil, or downright nasty to you as a child or to a child in your presence, and remember the impact that had. People begin to think of themselves as unable to progress because of the treatment they get from teachers; in other words, their knowledge of themselves is formed inaccurately. This is especially true where old habits of racial or ethnic superiority linger (Delpit, 2006). This sense of power can also inhibit teachers from saying what they believe to be the truth and/or leave them free to manipulate the truth to their personal predilections. Such power is rarely physical, nor is it just emotional: it is centrally connected to the *knowledge* the teacher conveys, especially on the content material that excites, fascinates, intrigues, or bores young learners. Knowledge is at the core of the power relationship, however attractive or repulsive a particular teacher's personality may be.

Knowledge as power is not merely the province of a teacher-student relationship. As Orwell demonstrates, there are power structures in any society that can seek to determine what counts as knowledge. The cultures of disciplines (such as medicine, history, and chemistry) themselves can be powerful and epistemically privileged, demanding a specific understanding of what counts as knowledge and acting as gatekeepers to the truth. Part of the resistance to a national curriculum, or even to national testing in the United States, is a residual suspicion of the good intentions of those who propagate such ideas. The fear of state or federal control is exemplified in the heterogeneity of school boards—some 15,000 across the nation. Yet the states and the testing agencies seem to be doing the nation's work for it, as the press for high academic standards becomes the rhetoric of education. Popular culture, of course, is also a powerful source for the transmission of knowledge and values, shaping our culture, our values, and our knowledge.

The word "power" has been used in this section because it is common currency, but it ignores the more sophisticated term of "authority": authority implies rights under a contract, an issue that will be examined in chapter 3. Nevertheless, the teacher's power often intervenes in a classroom, and not always productively in the search for truth. It is the teacher's responsibility to remove the element of power and live within a relationship of authority with children. The teacher creating a classroom with an epistemological presence will need a firm understanding of the complexity of his or her authority.

Conclusion

This chapter has portrayed some major challenges for teachers beginning to consider the epistemological framework of their teaching:

1. When I teach students the information, am I giving them knowledge?
2. How do I teach children that what I teach is true? What counts as true?
3. How can I aid the understanding and development of children who lack crucial background knowledge?
4. How do I cope and how should I handle the issues of my own power in teaching knowledge to children?

This light introduction to the agenda provides a framework that will constantly be revisited and substantially expanded throughout this book. Its purpose has been to begin to locate the problems of knowledge for teachers. If teachers pay attention to these matters as they teach, they will see it as their duty to create in their classrooms an epistemological atmosphere, an epistemological presence. This presence, to repeat, is to assert that matters of knowledge, truth, belief, commitment, experience, and identity are always in play in a classroom (see part II especially).

However, teachers have professional expertise. In writing about teaching in classrooms, no prescriptions are laid out in this book for teaching methods. The challenge is to provoke teachers' interest in daunting questions that will be productive for them, which they may not have thought of, but which they must face, and from which they may choose to modify their professional work. Why are epistemological considerations so important? Because human beings are at once moral beings and epistemological beings: they are persons, and they are knowers. This is the crux of Belenky and colleagues' remarks, which now bear repetition:

> We do not think of the ordinary person as preoccupied with such difficult and profound questions as: What is truth? What is authority? To whom do I listen? What counts for me as evidence? How do I know what I know? Yet to ask ourselves these questions and to reflect on our answers is more than a truly intellectual exercise, for our basic assumptions about the nature of truth and reality and the origins of knowledge shape the way we see the world and ourselves as participants in it. They affect our definitions of ourselves, the way we interact with others, our public and private personae, our sense of control over life events, our views of teaching and learning, and our conceptions of morality.
>
> *(Belenky et al., 1986, p. 3)*

Not only is it important for teachers to understand that, they need to be prepared to induct children into the human problems these features of our humanity create for us, but that presupposes having a good grip on the issues involved.

2

THE INDIVIDUAL AS SEEKER
AFTER KNOWLEDGE

The child, in other words, is seen as an epistemologist as well as a learner.

(Bruner, 1996, p. 57)

An initial knowledge agenda for teachers comprises matters of truth, background, the contrast with information, and the question of authority when seeking to introduce children to knowledge in classrooms. However, acquiring knowledge is not easy. Rather when we are trying to learn anything, our minds constantly shift focus in and around the subject matter; we sometimes lose our concentration, sometimes without being aware of it, and start thinking of other things. The psychological experience, the mental states, and the character of our consciousness as we acquire knowledge do not match any logical or analytic division between types of knowledge and/or between types of knowledge as constructed for learning. Our experience as learners or seekers after knowledge runs across traditional epistemological categories, sometimes haphazardly, sometimes directly, and often with some confusion. If in acquiring knowledge we are trying to discern the truth—in that ordinary sense—we are on a search, so that it makes sense to see ourselves not as knowers but as seekers, as Bruner describes. The seeker (after knowledge) experiences learning in two ways: the experience of the subject matter *and* of him or herself and how he or she stands in relation to that subject matter. We might mark this complexity by saying that, in learning, the material we are learning and ourselves as individuals are in some way interdependent. This is precisely where the questions by Belenky and colleagues (1986) pick up the complexity of the knowledge–individual relationship. In a classroom with an epistemological presence, the intricacy of the relation between public and private knowledge will be pervasive. We need to understand the distinction in order to help the child grasp it too.

In section 1 of this chapter, the distinction between public and personal knowledge is described. Searches for true beliefs backed by some kind of justification, such as evidence, are conducted within the *public* domain of knowledge with its three central concepts of truth, belief, and evidence—the last term being at this stage a placeholder for differing kinds of justification. They are also conducted within what may be called the *personal* domain of knowledge, with its three central concepts of commitment, experience, and identity specific to the individual seeker.

In section 2, the three conditions of public knowledge are outlined as preliminary to their full treatment in part II. Discussion of personal knowledge follows in section 3, where three aspects of our personhood—the historical individual, the belief-holding individual, and the self-conscious individual—are outlined as ways of understanding experience, commitment, and identity. These will form the basis of part III.

In section 4, the description of the individual passes to a teacher's reflexive awareness in the context of the development of an epistemological presence in his or her classroom. Knowledge in an environment of investigation is shared as much as it is transmitted, and conversation and space for dialogue are as important as instruction, so that the individual seeker is an active participant, not a passive receiver of information. This implies that problems, uncertainties, and ambiguities taxing the seeker's judgment will regularly occur, demanding investigation of epistemological secrets—that is, topics in the theory of knowledge that are not often discussed in front of the children. The opening up of these secrets in classrooms expands the individual seeker's developing self-consciousness as a learner, providing the epistemological ground for the student's reflexive self-awareness characteristic of Belenky's "ordinary person." This is the basis on which an epistemological presence in the classroom is constructed.

I. Public Knowledge and Personal Knowledge: Introduction

Possessing knowledge is a characteristic of sentient beings. Horses, dogs, cats, elephants, and kangaroos seem to have it. Hummingbirds, snakes, ants, and mosquitoes perhaps have it. Human beings have it, but stones, rivers, plants, buildings, and mountains, computers, smart houses, smart cars, and Deep Blue (the programmed machine IBM people used in a chess match with Kasparov) do *not* have it. Inanimate objects can't *know* anything, although the growth in computerized technology has given rise to some charming and some bizarre metaphors about intelligent machinery. As we learn about animals, we begin to see the extent of what appears to us as knowledge: for instance, chimpanzees know *how* to use long sticks of grass to thrust into rocks to harvest ants. Cats know *when* it's time for dinner and *whom* to sit pleadingly in front of. Horses know *that* this person is the master, or the food-giver, or the apple of their eye. Our dogs *know us,* and they can apparently make distinctions between different members of a family. Even sea-bed octopuses carry coconut shells to hide inside. Most animals usually *know the place* where they live, sleep, and eat. Cows have routines about their milking order and where to stand in line.

In many different ways, therefore, many animal species seem to *know* "how," "when," "who," "what," "where," and "that." We will disagree on animals knowing "whether" (since that implies reasoned choice, as in "whether to choose this or that banana"). Yet animals also *recognize* and get to know other animals, specifically their threat potential and mating possibilities; where their bed is; and, remarkably, in the case of homing pigeons and many other returning birds, where to come home to. Many animals seem *to know their way around* homes, streets, parks, and woods. Human beings are animals too. These prepositions ("how," "when," "who," "what," and "that") are, grammatically speaking, the "objects" of knowledge. They are the sorts of things animals and humans can sensibly be said to know.

Public Knowledge

To try to get a grip on the complexity and variety of knowledge (what human beings say they know), philosophers have worked from hugely varying perspectives. Without attempting to survey these differences, the common currency in philosophical work is of the objects of knowledge as falling into three groups: (1) skills, (2) persons and places, and (3) propositions. This is a useful basis on which to begin.

First, we have knowledge of *skills* of many kinds—the how's and the how-to's of everyday life, from using a knife and fork to flying a 747.

Second, like many animals, we can know *persons and places:* our family, the other kids in the class, our friends, ourselves, people at work, but also towns or cities, mountains or lakes we visit, or the schools and colleges in which we work.

Third, there are the "knowing when, knowing who, knowing whether, and knowing what" to be accounted for, all of which can be contained under one category, "knowing *that.*" (Without explaining the argument here, the "when, who, whether, and what" cases can logically be subsumed under the category "that": public propositional knowledge. See Ryle, 1949, especially chapter 2.) The object of our knowledge in this category is a public proposition, not a skill, or a person or a place. For example, if you know that you left your textbook at home under your bed, the proposition you know is "I left my textbook under the bed"; equally with every proposition/belief you hold. This type of knowledge is difficult to interpret with animals because we have no common language with them, but it is the major constituent of human knowledge. (See Further Reading.)

For the purposes of analysis, then, the *objects* of knowledge can be captured within these three types. The distinctions are useful and they arise from our experience of the world caught by the grammar of language: verb (know) plus three types of objects—*skills, persons and places, propositions.* The formal analytic boundaries between these three are immensely permeable in practice. Each type does not just stand on its own in a neat logical or psychological box. A professional tennis player, for instance, needs to know something about her opponent's character on the court; she has to exercise a huge amount of skill; and she also has to know a good many propositions—for instance, about the effect of the climate on the clay among other things.

The use of the adjective "public" as describing knowledge is not casual. By qualifying the notion of the propositional by the term "public," I am emphasizing that, while the discussion of an item of knowledge may in this instant be private between you and me, it is in a public language and *in principle* accessible to everyone. The evidence or warrant for the belief is also in principle open to all. Hereinafter, I will use the term "public knowledge" to refer to propositional knowledge.

Personal Knowledge

Personal knowledge is focused not on the formal characteristics of knowledge but on the *individual* seeker after knowledge and three elements in that personal knowledge: experience, commitment, and identity.

First, what the individual experiences comprises insights, memories, intuitions, judgments, understandings, and my reasons and motives for actions. These are more or less complex characteristics of seekers after knowledge. Some of these intuitions, insights, and understandings may become assertions to public knowledge, although the evidence may not be palpable. I may be more or less committed to my intuitions but am definitely committed when I regard them as true. The child who has been regularly bullied, say, because he is fat, has knowledge through experience that those of us fortunate enough not to have been subjected to that kind of torture do not have. Sometimes, intuitions and insights prove to be untenable, though not necessarily false, for that would assume they can always be tested for truth. If I have an intuition about an individual and you ask me why, I may be able to say no more than "He just makes me uneasy." Children sometimes, hopefully not often, begin to feel that way about a teacher.

Second, commitment is seen as commitment at varying degrees to the beliefs we have. That can of course include prejudices, political, social, and religious. There are important distinctions here to be made in terms of categories of belief: we may not be committed to some trivial belief or other, really not caring whether it is true or not, though we can be intensely committed to theories about the world, scientific, religious, or ideological. Our judgment issues in commitments and decisions and enters into both our assessment of individuals and our experience of events, though it is obviously a feature of our public assertions too. As Polanyi (1962/1974) puts it, "an element of personal judgment is involved in applying the fundamentals of mechanics to the facts of experience" (p. 19).

Finally, personal knowledge includes knowledge of one's own social and individual identity—for example, as a teacher, father, and as being Bill Smith. But we also have an understanding of self that is necessarily private. We know who we are: we can get clearer about our identity through self-knowledge. Yet, a comment "that's not like him" reveals that an individual is understood as, say, wise and generous by others, and this appraisal indicates he is acting out of character.

Personal knowledge in each of these three areas is educationally critical—for example, in identity where teachers seek to correct stereotypical views of themselves that children have that inhibit their growth and development. But we now need to examine each aspect of knowledge, public and personal, in turn, and see in a preliminary way how each will feature in the classroom with an epistemological presence.

II. Public Knowledge: Truth, Belief, and Evidence

The fundamentals of public propositional knowledge are truth, belief, and evidence. This is the historically long-lasting and well-known formal account of knowledge as justified true belief, not defeated by the idea that knowledge is constructed. Philosophers have sought to articulate these three characteristics as conditions of knowledge—that is, both necessary and sufficient for any assertion to be a case of knowledge. As one might expect, each characteristic has had extensive scrutiny and detailed argument, none more so than the evidence condition. In recent decades the idea that "evidence" is a critical condition has come under severe scrutiny, so, for the moment, I am using this word as a placeholder for all possible forms of justification or warrant—that is, how we justify what we know. So no claim is being made here for these three as the precise conditions of knowledge, but they provide a good working start, and we will see the alternatives, qualifications, and complexities later (see part II).

To summarize this view of public knowledge briefly: First, to know something is to assert that something is true, however clear or obscure the *criteria* for a statement's being true are. The point of drawing attention to the connection between knowing something and making some assertion that it is true is to distinguish it from such mental acts as imagination, intention, speculation, or daydreaming. If I tell my wife I am now imagining the first house we lived in, I am not making any sort of assertion. If the kid in the third row is looking out of the classroom window daydreaming, he is not asserting anything. So knowledge is unique: it is not a mental state or an activity, such as reporting, imagining, intending, speculating, or daydreaming. We don't spend time knowing something, as we do when speculating. To say one knows p (where p is any proposition) is to assert that p. And, as it has been frequently argued, not only must something be true for your assertion to be correct (i.e., that you know something), but you must believe it and have evidence for it. We will deal with each condition in turn.

Truth. In chapter 1, Belenky and colleagues (1986) used the notion of the ordinary person that was extended to the notion of ordinary truths. Truth is a property of statements. That is, if I believe something and it is true, the truth of the matter lies in the statement about that something. For example, I make a true statement in a witness box that the driver who hit my car was traveling 60 miles an hour as he turned the corner. That event is the source for my true assertion in court some days later, but the event itself cannot be described as true or false, only my assertion about the event. Yet statements are of very different kinds. "God exists" is different from "The Chinese built the Great Wall as a tourist attraction." "The Second World War was won in the Pacific" is different from "My grandmother used to paint beautiful pictures of flowers." The statement "2 + 2 = 4" is different from "the earth moves around the sun." In what lies the difference? The differences between statements are matters of not just their content but how we can decide whether any given statement is true. Different statements will have different criteria of truth marking the core differences between disciplines.

The search for truth is the hallmark of the epistemological presence in a classroom. This is a moral classroom arranged to promote challenges to received truths, seek for reinterpretations, steadfastly examine sober or outrageous assertions, wrestle with such problems. We use inquiry in the light of truth as a constant defense against irrationality, indeed, as Williams (2002) put it, as the medium through which liberty is tested and in the end guaranteed. Notice this is not here an insistence on honesty as a virtue (though that is important; see chapter 4). Attention to the truth inhibits self-deception, the tendency as described by Shulman (1999) of undergraduates holding beliefs about themselves that are manifestly false. Yet the capability to examine statements for their truth in any area does not just spring up in the child like his or her fingernails. It can grow for an individual only in a climate that respects it and insists on it, hence its critical place in the epistemological presence in a classroom. Notice, if it is not already clear, that nothing is claimed here for truths being absolute or relative, objective or subjective, half or whole truths as discussed in chapter 1. Truth here is a formal concept that governs our conversations and patterns of instruction and ensures that we root those discussions in the use of reason to figure out what is true; which, of course, in many instances, we may not be able to do.

Belief is integrally connected to truth and evidence. When we know things, we are making or have made assertions as to their truth, but we are not just making an assertion but saying something about ourselves, namely that *we believe* p to be true. So it is not imagination or intention or speculation or daydreaming that are the mental acts associated with knowledge, but belief. So all-encompassing are the beliefs we have for our lives and our futures that a person may be said to be composed of his or her beliefs, or, at least, that they are a vital constituent of who a person is (see chapter 5). Your beliefs constitute, in large part, what and who you are, ranging across the whole sphere of human experience: from superstitions (like not walking under ladders) to premonitions ("I will die young"), intuitions ("My boss doesn't really like me"), insights ("I'll bet she'll marry him"), and much else. Beliefs are of course different, like statements of truth, and can also be religious, aesthetic, historical, philosophical, or scientific; where they are true, they will count as knowledge. But beliefs guide human beings, along with emotions, and so not all beliefs need be framed as assertions to knowledge. Fortunately we don't have to keep all our beliefs, true or false, at the forefront of our minds all the time; we would go crazy. But if beliefs do have this central place in who we are, the importance of the teacher's understanding the task of helping the child to form beliefs, as well as to examine those the child already has, is integral to the epistemological presence.

Three additional interesting things need to be said about belief. We can believe in things; we can't believe impossible things, and not all our beliefs are our individual achievements.

First, we can believe *in* things or deities. The list is endless—health foods, the Dallas Cowboys, or, of course, Allah, God, and other beings to be worshipped. Such a "belief in" carries special devotion to its object, but it also contains propositions that, in principle, can be candidates for truth.

Second, you can't believe *impossible* things (i.e., things that are empirically impossible or which seem impossible to you), *pace* the White Queen in Alice (*Alice Through the Looking Glass,* chapter 5). A belief must have coherence for the believer, and that coherence is the coherence of truth as seen by the believer. People do believe extraordinary things, but they do not see these extraordinary things as impossible. There is an internal connection between what we believe and what is true (see chapter 5)—namely, that we can believe only things that seem to us true, putting on one side questions of evidence or the experience. People who read astrology columns can make the most banal statements about their prospects cohere with their perceptions and expectations. Why exactly is this important for teaching and learning? One classic danger with having children memorizing information is that it need not have coherence for the child. The child can easily avoid confronting the truth and, for the sake of the test, just believe impossible things, without a concern for their truth.

Third, our beliefs are not necessarily our achievements in ways that our knowledge often is. We garner beliefs from all kinds of places. We believe what we are (often) brought up to believe—in the superiority of our race or class, in kindness to animals, or in odd religious rituals (see, for example, Carolyn Jessop's 2008 book *Escape,* about growing up in a fundamentalist Mormon sect). Progress toward becoming rational will often mean evaluating and changing those beliefs. But many of our knowledge-warranted beliefs are recognizable achievements of ours, when we have studied to acquire them, or when we have changed our views and shaken off the prejudices of our youth.

Evidence. Evidence can be changeable, inaccessible, and of radically different types. This condition of a statement's being a correct knowledge assertion is the most perplexing and difficult. Recall the case of Alex Haley, Kunta Kinte, and the old griot. We did not have any direct evidence as such that Kunta Kinte was captured as he went to gather wood: no photographs, no vessel inventory, no written accounts by sailors. It was the coincidental circumstance of two legends or oral records, separated by the ocean, that gave us—how shall we say it?—enough to have us assert it as true. So evidence is always tricky; not least because the evidence for a proposition is itself a proposition, which demands evidence that is also a proposition and so ad infinitum. But life demands judgments (see chapter 6), as any juror will tell you.

However, when we acknowledge the validity of a knowledge assertion made by a person, we assume they believe it. So we are entitled to ask them, "How do you know?" That is, publicly, we want the evidence, the support, the reasons, the warrant, the justification to support the assertion made. "Show me why," we are apt to say, of course, because we are interested in believing what is asserted and we want some justification for it. (Evidence, once again, is used here as a short-hand to cover all manner of justifications we might make in justifying our knowledge. The details of the differences will be examined thoroughly in chapter 6.)

Four things are important about evidence of this general kind. First, it can turn out to be false and it may not be publicly accessible. Evidence can become false as new material comes to light. Earlier assertions to knowledge turn out to be untrue. When the British liner and hospital ship, the *Lusitania,* was sunk off Ireland in 1915 by German U-boats, it horrified the American public and led, in part, to the country's entry into World War I. The truth about the ship, namely that it was carrying military supplies in its cargo and was not solely a hospital or passenger ship, was not revealed until after the Second World War (see Preston, 2002). Because new evidence arises, however, we should not resort to being skeptical about everything we know; we should accept that we get to learn more and so our beliefs change. Knowledge, we say, is provisional, but it usually demands individual judgment in the assessment of its veracity, and it will be of very different types, depending on the knowledge assertions being made.

Second, some evidence may be publicly inaccessible. So as we have seen with what I am calling personal knowledge, an assertion to knowledge could arise from a person's private experience, and so it is a matter of judgment on our part as to whether the evidence for the assertion can provide sufficient justification. The problem with private experience is that it may be used to justify malicious actions or pernicious attitudes derived from individual experiences of, say, upbringing. One's autobiography is different from the truth of the beliefs it contains.

Third, acknowledging that some kinds of personal experience are publicly inaccessible to us, the public kinds of evidence are either analytic statements like "I know that $2 + 2 = 4$," empirical assertions like "that was a nuclear explosion," or normative assertions like "you ought to keep your promises." Here we can learn from young children who, like the skeptic, test our patience with interminable questioning. Every explanation is met with a further query "Why?" For it is a crucial fact in human understanding that no evidence can be produced for any empirical or normative statement which *on its own* is strong enough without individual judgment. In every case, there must always be judgment: "That evidence convinces me. It's enough."

Finally, as we have seen with true statements and beliefs, assertions are of different kinds. Assertions about the past are not the same as assertions about what one ought to do. An assertion about the beauty of an object is unlike a religious assertion. A mathematical assertion contrasts with a philosophical assertion. There will be distinctive types of evidence appropriate to different types of assertion, an important topic that will be investigated further in chapter 5.

If we are to construct an epistemological presence in a classroom, an environment in which knowledge is at the center, we can usefully work with public (propositional) knowledge as justified true belief. An assertion to knowledge can be justified (by evidence) true (according to judgment based on evidence) and the belief is held by those who assert it to be true. However neat that formal account might sound, two things are worth notice. First, this very formality runs counter to our day-to-day lived experience where issues of knowledge and truth are very disorderly and untidy: knowledge is not some kind of instrument of reason quite apart from human life with its dialogue, context, and vibrancy. Second, we have had to indicate the significance of the individual in the matter of belief, and how the individual is connected to truth, and the importance of judgment in the acceptance of evidence. Key issues about public knowledge arise as we try to connect these fundamentals to people's experiences.

III. Personal Knowledge: Experience, Commitment, and Identity

Much of what we teach children contributes to the development of knowledge of other people. Opportunities, planned moral education apart, are continuously presented to develop children's understanding of other people through subject matter and classroom interactions. Knowledge of others is a major topic in the formal and informal curriculum and in professional life. However, knowledge of others is by no means always benevolent, as we realize when children and adults figure out the other's weaknesses and vulnerabilities. To know other people is by no means necessarily to be good to them or take their interests to heart. (Schrag, 2010, warns that too pious an approach to moral education may leave children defenseless when confronted by villains.)

Our knowledge of others is at once highly idiosyncratic *and* generalizable. Family relationships differ. Children know their parents differently from the way they know their friends know them. We view each other from different perspectives generated by different relationships. We contribute to these differences by showing specific sides of ourselves to distinct people, so each of our relationships is not simply unique by description, but by texture, as Jane Austen's novels brilliantly portray. Yet from the variety of our early experiences with others, we begin to react to other human beings, generalizing from our relationships with our parents or siblings. The indiscriminate smiles an infant girl bestows on any adult in a supermarket aisle need to become highly discriminating when she becomes an adolescent, something she learns from advice and experience.

Equally, our knowledge of others can be at hugely different levels of intimacy. Intimate knowledge can also be as wonderful in its best examples as it can be appalling in its worst. The family life of the Brontës (Barker, 1994) was a splendid kind of intimacy, with continuous conversation and with any sister being able to continue the story another was writing. The Wittgenstein family, of which the philosopher Ludwig was a part, seemed to have a succession of violent rows among very highly strung and opinionated members (Waugh, 2010, p. 114). Knowledge of others doesn't demand intimacy, but the intimacy of relationships deepens knowledge of each other and oneself. This can be both problematic and rewarding in the relationships between children and teachers.

Moreover, we do naturally talk about *other people* believing this or experiencing the pain of that. I can't see your belief, because I cannot look inside your head: I see how you act and infer your beliefs. I see what you do on the basis of your beliefs. But we don't make these statements on the basis of what we see with our eyes, for I can't see your pain; what I see is your broken leg. When we talk in an "ordinary" way about other people, we assume that they have pains and beliefs just like us, on the basis of our experience. But what evidence and justification do we have for generalizing from our own experience (which is all we have to go on) to the assumption that others *are* just like us? All we have is our own experience, and in general terms that is a flimsy basis of evidence from which to generalize. Indeed, we often make huge mistakes, indicating the fragility of such knowledge. We get very angry precisely because other people make assumptions about how we feel that are quite unjustified. "How do you know what I believe?" and "You don't know what pain is!" are common enough phrases in our experience to make us very uncertain about precisely how we do know other people, specifically in respect of their beliefs and their pains. The key to grasping our personal understandings and knowledge lies, for the most part, in how we understand people like us.

In this book, personal knowledge thus incorporates these three distinct elements: experience, commitment, and identity. Why these three?

Experience locates the *historical individual,* especially memories, but also the cultural, social, and familial location of the individual and how that individual understands his or her experience.

Commitment describes the *belief-holding individual:* it picks out how an individual stands in relation to what he or she knows and/or believes, essential as an element in personal knowledge if our beliefs in large part comprise who we are.

Identity describes *the self-conscious individual:* who we are, how we make ourselves (or not) out of what we believe and what we experience, for which knowledge of self is critical.

Experience, commitment, and identity are, therefore, significant concepts for a classroom with an epistemological presence.

Experience and the Historical Individual

What is experience?

First, people have experiences. Those who watch a total eclipse of the sun have *an* experience. However, it makes a huge difference whether those enjoying the experience are astronomers or those fictional chiefs in Rider Haggard's *King Solomon's Mines* who, having captured a band of marauding colonialists, were conned into saving their lives because these heroes predicted an eclipse. To the chiefs and the tribe, this appeared to be some kind of miracle controlled by man, not a rare, spectacular, but eminently predictable natural event.

Second, experiencing something is not just in objects getting into touch with our senses as if the sudden warmth of the sun on our skin on a spring day was the paradigm of experience. Philosophers have worried that such an understanding of experience ignores that we can be mistaken about what we see or feel, touch or taste. In any encounter with our world of objects, there must be something of our own understanding that we bring, just as we must bring our commitment to theories, and a theory to our observations. As in the case of Virgil, a child blinded in childhood has limited resources when vision is restored in adulthood (see chapter 1, section 3). His world is reshaped by the sighted experiences he is having. This is not a rearrangement of objects, but, to emphasize the central point, what Virgil now comes to *see them as.* We have to bring a framework of perception and language, a framework of public knowledge, to mere objects. The local chiefs did *not* see the same thing *as* the colonialists. Indeed we understand the episode in the story only because from our vantage point, we can understand (1) *seeing the eclipse as* a natural event of rare but explicable character and (2) *seeing the eclipse as* something to be terrified of.

Curriculum in school is often based on the erroneous assumption that the experience will be the same for everyone, giving rise to such phrases as children going through a program "in lock-step," which is a misunderstanding of the nature of experience. We can share experiences with others, yet in the curriculum, *each brings to that experience their own perspective and the baggage of their individual historical and cultural resources.* Similarly with classrooms or being brought up in a family. Ryan summarizes Dewey's position acutely: "nobody has ... *an* experience without bringing to bear on the raw materials of an encounter with the world the cultural resources that allow him to turn it into *an* experience" (Ryan, 1997, pp. 337–338). The perceptions that individuals have of shared experiences (e.g., of a lesson in a classroom) and the differentia of what they each bring (by virtue of their former life experience) complicate any teaching task.

Whereas evidence is public and our assertions can be verified, it might seem as if our experiences are private, unverifiable, and therefore privileged. Not necessarily so. For if we are in conversation, in a dialogic space, and we are committed as responsible people to facing up to Belenky and colleagues' (1986) questions, we can examine another person's experiences with them (and vice versa); but there has to be that space, a characteristic of the epistemological presence in a classroom. Within that space, we can test the validity of the individual's experience as a check all of us expect where we use our own experience as public evidence in our assertions. Here a child puzzles out his or her understandings of, say, slavery or heat through dialogue and reflection. The prerequisites for classroom dialogue are very clearly articulated by philosopher Tazos Kazepides in *Education as Dialogue* (2010).

Experience therefore is intimately connected to what we, as individuals, see the world *as*. That will in turn depend on the historical and cultural identity with which we have been brought up, which will also influence how we see the public knowledge we encounter in classrooms. We thus have to bring not only our commitment and judgments to ideas and theories we are presented with but we must also bring our experience, however limited or extensive that may be. In no other way can our knowledge of ourselves and our knowledge of subject matter become interdependent. The classic danger in teaching is to ignore the child's real-world experiences as a historical individual and provide for them ersatz experiences that they know quite well are unreal. However, knowledge of all kinds has to be shared if it is to be effectively communicated and if it is to become a part of the individual's identity.

Commitment and the Belief-Holding Individual

If we accept that knowing other people is a crucial human area of our knowledge, how does this relate to how people in general comprehend public knowledge? In the context of a discussion of the epistemology of science, Polanyi (1962/1974) argues that knowledge of theories (i.e., an integrated bunch of propositions) in practice cannot be cut off from the individuals who are the seekers. There is no such thing as objectivity in science, says he, and the ideal of strict objectivism is absurd (see also chapter 6). In his view, we have no objective theories, only *theories to which we are committed* (see also chapter 8). In the process of argument (both one-on-one and across the centuries), our theories (yours or mine), he asserts, are challenged by rival theories to which other people are committed, often with great passion. The ideal of objectivism (i.e., that scientific facts are value free) cannot deal with the necessary human element of judgment that we make about such theories to which we become committed. If we are to be responsible people concerned about the truth, we must understand the significance of our knowledge of ourselves and the appraisals and the judgments we make, for they are interdependent with our public-knowledge assertions. We cannot easily disentangle our personal judgment from our understanding of theories (and thereby also of any proposition) and from our commitment to them as we make an assertion. Polanyi (1962/1974) describes a relationship between the individual and the way he or she sees the world: through the theories to which he or she is committed. "When we accept a set of presuppositions and use them as our interpretative framework," he writes, "we may be said to dwell in them as we do in our own body" (p. 60). That includes the interpretative framework and theories we have about other people specifically or generally.

Polanyi's notion of a commitment can be seen as a *development* of the notion of an *assertion that something is true* (see chapter 8). That is, when a person makes this kind of assertion, he is "standing by" his or her judgment—that is, being committed to it. Second, it embodies the sense of the interdependence of the public and the personal domains in knowledge. In so far as a person uses a theory (large or small) consciously or unconsciously he or she is operating on the belief that the theory is true and would assert it as such. In general terms, if we are challenged on most of what we believe, we will seek to defend it—hence assertions like "I am convinced" and "I passionately believe." Not surprisingly, arguments usually embody disagreement in belief. Indeed, in our day-to-day conversations, it is a commonplace for us, if we encounter people saying things we do not think are correct, to judiciously enter the conversation by starting our counter-assertion (a belief to which we are committed). This applies to everything from asking directions to theories of evolution. And, of course, it applies to children.

To a large degree, teaching to the test brooks no passion. This is what you must memorize. Yet that denies children the opportunity to work out and defend positions about all manner of curriculum topics to which they can become committed. They will of course develop commitments on many other things, such as which football team they support or which pop star they admire. To be educated demands the development of the ability to argue, to develop a position and defend it; lessons too often left to a forensics teacher and small minority of students and treated as a skill. That is also a matter of developing in children the ability to detect flaws in arguments deployed against them without breaking off discussion, losing their temper, or turning to ad hominem comments. The level of public debate indicates the need for all children to be taught argument and rhetoric: that's possible only in a classroom context where ideas are in play.

In sum, we cannot simply deal in public knowledge without engaging with these ideas and theories, getting inside them and using our judgment about their application, and becoming committed to them, as knowledge deepens. As we will see later, this development of a commitment to one's beliefs becomes a central part of education, especially if what one believes can itself be an ethical question (see chapter 5).

Identity and the Self-Conscious Individual

In the exploration of knowledge of ourselves, however, we need to go one step further than the judgments necessary in our commitment to such public knowledge as is contained in theories or indeed the passion with which we might believe such theories. Recognizing the place of experience too in the formation of those commitments, we must develop our own identity. Identity is quite different from personality. Our personality is the way in which our identity is expressed (see Sulloway, 1997). Within our identities we make the specific choices that contribute to our personality, although personality will include matters of our temperament and style. The notion of identity picks out both who we are and what we have in common with others who share what we value and with whom, of course, we identify. We can speak of personalities (for example, extrovert or introvert) as abstracted, so to speak, from any individual. Identity conjures up not types of identity but belief systems or value systems that we draw on. The question of my identity is my answer to the question "Who am I?"

For Charles Taylor (1989) identity is something more than just having a set of historical or cultural belief systems or value systems and locating oneself within them. Rather, one's identity is orienting one's self in moral space, "a space in which questions arise about what is good or bad, what is worth doing and what not, what has meaning and importance for you and what is trivial or secondary" (p. 28). Providing that moral space for children can be done if the moral classroom has an epistemological presence, where questions arise about what is good or bad, what is worth doing or not, and so on.

One's identity thus comprises at least the set of beliefs and commitments one holds. One particular identity for an individual may be dominant, say in a person of devout religious faith, and this is just recognition of the salience of this aspect of life for that person. It is not a defining feature of a person's identity, however, that there is one such salient feature. Not only is one's identity historical, as Taylor (1989) puts it, it is contemporary and individual. If the various frameworks he has hinted at above contain fundamental human questions, to have an identity is to be an agent capable of answering for oneself out of certain belief or value systems. In other words, with an identity a person can enter a dialogue, particularly about fundamental human issues, from a particular perspective, even though that perspective may change. But we cannot as individuals just make up a perspective for ourselves. What we desire qualitatively, we adopt from the various traditions or frames we encounter, maybe mainly through family and often through education. We will fashion our specific identity from that maturing individual perspective particularly because the frameworks don't come laden with answers to new questions. One's identity thus "belongs to human agency (existing) in a space of questions about strongly valued goods, prior to all choice or adventitious cultural change" (Taylor, 1989, p. 31).

Clearly we both do and do not create our identity (but see chapter 9). Opportunities are thrust on us in classrooms that influence us, but we can determine them for ourselves. An answer to the question "Who am I?" has thus to be tackled within the language of those frames that make sense to me and that I have either grown up within or embraced as an adult. Richard Rodriguez, for example, explores his "identity crisis" by examining how he grapples with his Mexican parents and his acquired status as an intellectual journalist, and how he moves between the languages and the cultures (Rodriguez, 2004).

IV. From Epistemological Secrets to Reflexive Awareness

Classrooms with an epistemological presence should contain these up-front and persistent problems of truth, evidence, and belief, as well as the learner's (and the teacher's) commitment, identity, and experience as individual seekers after knowledge. Pervasive in that epistemological presence are not the trivial certainties of textbooks but engagement with the confusion, the uncertainty, the wrestling with difficulty, the questioning, and the messy condition of our knowledge and our puzzles about the world. This is not to say that children should as a matter of policy be brought up in a world of complete uncertainty; at what developmental stage the development of doubt and uncertainty is appropriate is, no doubt, an empirical matter, though as Matthews (1996) vigorously pointed out in *The Philosophy of Childhood,* any strict adherence to developmentalist models can seriously underestimate children's capacity for reason and for empathy. Rather, this stance to knowledge in classrooms has moral import, brilliantly clarified in the set of questions from *Women's Ways of Knowing* with which chapter 1 opened. There is no obvious reason that such questions and their implications should be kept secret from children; indeed, it is urgent to introduce them to these exciting characteristics of life as soon as possible.

More positively, this is an immensely profound and instructive passage for educators. It sets out simply the character of the epistemological challenge facing the teacher and its intimate link to the moral in a classroom. If you think of the "ordinary person" as a child, you have a brilliant description of a curriculum and the questing spirit with which it has to be approached. Realize, too, how often these immense and profound questions about human life are left unexamined by many children in the day-to-day life of their public schools. A moral classroom, in this view, is not just one where children are, in a phrase, well brought up, or where the teacher is caring and competent, or where the practice is moral. To repeat, it is a place where the major epistemological questions have to be constantly in play, and where Belenky's questions are not kept hidden from children. Yet many are forbidden entry to the epistemological presence either on purpose or by neglect. We are likely to share such epistemological *secrets* only with selected (gifted?) children (Van Manen & Levering, 1996). Unless all children start to crack open such secrets, they will not get the sophistication of which Belenky and colleagues (1986) speak—namely, definitions of themselves, how they interact with other people, how they understand themselves publicly and privately, how they control their lives*, how they learn, and how they act morally.* Epistemology is therefore not just "theoretical": it is intensely practical. It enables us to understand who we are. And that is a moral matter.

Without such openness, of course, children can come to see their teachers as knowing everything as they are the classroom judges of what is correct or incorrect, irrespective of its truth. Children may come to think themselves stupid, because the teacher's view of the world must be correct, even if it is at odds with their own experience. The child's difficulty in such cases is epistemological: they try, often in vain, to connect the truth or the coherence of what is being taught to themselves and their experience. To protect their authority, teachers may distort truths in the real world and, in so doing, keep epistemological matters *secret.* That is too often true in contemporary education. We keep the messiness of knowledge an epistemological secret, even though we observe in young children a boundless curiosity, a quest to unlock the secrets of the universe. Much of what we say we know is commonplace and incontestable, but our history, our cultural assumptions and mores, and our social, political, economic, medical, legal, and other practices are horrendously complex and controversial. Think of the disagreements about health and diet, about the environment and its pollution, the nature of science, and the complexity of ideological, political, and economic matters—let alone the arts and literature—that burn through public discussion in a democratic society.

Growing up in an epistemological presence enables children to be moral agents and democratic citizens, and so they must get on the inside of this complexity. Postman (1994) suggests that childhood is, in part, a state where the young do not share adult secrets, which may be desirable on some matters, but keeping the fundamental messiness of knowledge a secret inhibits and discourages questioning of evidence, grounds for belief, and an understanding of the truth. Yet what are the secrets from which children get shielded? Belenky and colleagues (1986) list "What is truth? What is authority? To whom do I listen? What counts for me as evidence? How do I know what I know?" These seem very grand philosophical questions, but it is not difficult to imagine how fascinating children would find them, were they not kept secret.

Yet, precisely because Belenky's questions are so difficult and important, the classroom cannot just have an instructional frame, but is dependent on the quality of interpersonal relationships. Knowledge in a classroom cannot be cogently transmitted from a teacher to a student unless it is shared. Where public knowledge is at stake, students must come to view the evidence as public—not true because the teacher said so or just because the teacher guided them to this evidence, or because it's in the book. The fact that it is knowledge at stake, if shared between teacher and learner, creates, influences, and steers the relationship. It is as if teacher and learner should try to look at the world together as seekers, not just to see it from their own position, not from some false kind of objective position, but from a common position, seeking to explore its facts and its mysteries, its problems and its treasures, each as a learner, differently positioned, a view expressed in standpoint theory (Harding, 2003). Profound epistemological questions then are not just for philosophers in ivory towers. They are important to us all, but to growing children they have immense moral importance.

First, the task of the school or the teacher in introducing these communities of language is grossly undermined if it rules out those questions that help a child understand or achieve his or her identity, and those are perspicuously ones that are going to have an epistemological core. Our beliefs are at the core of individual identity. It makes no sense, therefore, for a teacher to assume that the relation between subject matter and identity is just some kind of one-way street. A curriculum that ignores the way in which our identities are formed out of both our specific historical and cultural identities, and how we grapple with them in our contemporary life, is a destructive force in the creation of personal identity.

Second, the curriculum cannot therefore be "out there" if it is to educate persons. Children must make the curriculum and its intricacies their own. This is the complaint of those who talk of the curriculum as irrelevant. It fails to see the child as a human being facing the curriculum as content from one or more perspectives and stances, all of which are serving to make up his or her identity. Rather, curriculum must be interdependent with the individual, seamless as between public and personal knowledge, providing the dialogic space, the understanding of these perspectives and stances, and the attention to issues of the good, if it is to be attentive to the self. If it does not do this, of course, it may be a banal form of training, but it could not be a form of education in a democracy where the upbringing of the individual person is of paramount moral importance.

Third, these six elements of an epistemological presence (truth, belief, evidence, experience, commitment, and identity) should not just float around the classroom as a kind of ethereal presence. The glue binding them together is common to them all, namely the way in which each places demands on the reflexive awareness of the individual, teacher and learner alike. Those who become reflexively aware struggle with the puzzles of public knowledge, think them through, and explore their authenticity and connections to their individual lives. Knowledge of the real world (including of others and ourselves) passes through our reflexive awareness. While our knowledge of other people is categorically different from our knowledge and understanding of ourselves and our individual identity, knowledge of others is contributory to individual identity. Knowledge of other persons is knowledge of other human beings and of the kinds of wants, desires, purposes, ambitions, needs, actions, and intentions they have. In learning about ourselves, we learn about others, and vice versa. However, human ambitions, actions, and aspirations are expressed through and embedded in our understanding of the empirical and normative world, in our social, scientific, historical, aesthetic, religious, and literary understanding, our ethical and moral life.

To be educated, however, such interdependence of knowledge must continuously be understood by individuals thinking about themselves—how ideas, truths, and beliefs influence them as epistemological beings. They become reflexively aware and aware of their ability to reflect. Saint Augustine's maxim about reflexive awareness—subject matter passing through us—demands that we constantly consider our experience, commitment, and identity.

Ms. Jean Brodie

3

THE MORAL AND EPISTEMOLOGICAL AUTHORITY OF THE TEACHER

Unthinking respect for authority is the greatest enemy of truth.

—*Albert Einstein*

"What is authority? To whom do I listen?" are questions necessary to the classroom or the seminar room with an epistemological presence, where problems of public and personal knowledge are always open and shared such that children or students develop reflexive awareness. This chapter introduces an account of the authority of the teacher as a platform from which teaching quality can be described. Section 1 distinguishes between the formal and the personal in teaching. In section 2, four examples are examined that stretch the context of understanding the teacher's authority: three teachers (Mrs. Payton, Terrence's teacher, and Janet) and one child (John). Janet in particular is important in describing the moral and the epistemological aspects of her authority as a young teacher. In section 3, a formal account of authority, drawn from philosopher R. S. Peters, is rehearsed first, leading to a distinction between expertise (Darling-Hammond et al., 2005, see chapter 2) and authority that alone can provide the richness needed to understand the quality of teaching. The first part of the book is then concluded with a provisional account of the contractual, moral, and epistemological authority of the teacher.

for Spencer Seminar

I. Authority in Formal Relationships

In all public institutions, relationships are formal, created for the execution of an established social purpose—for example, education, policing, doctoring, banking, business, the law, medicine, and all public enterprises. We learn the conventions of what is expected in all such formal relationships, relying on both authority and expertise. Different to most such relationships in a complex society is teaching children because it has to incorporate the personal. Like it or not, the teacher has a responsibility for the kind of person the child is and is becoming, through having authority over how the child behaves in school. It is a misunderstanding to demand that teachers stick to transmitting knowledge, because the social matrix demands rules unconnected to knowledge transmission that have to be followed if the enterprise is to succeed. The child has to be taught civil, intellectual, and moral habits: failing to be polite, bullying others, producing slipshod work, doing nothing, or cheating are matters which the teacher cannot ignore or be neutral about. Whatever is being taught to children, or what the child is learning from a teacher has the potential to shape the child's life, indeed to shape who the child is. Moreover, this authority is shared: parents or guardians are also, legally and morally speaking, responsible for children's growth and development. Relationships between schools or teachers and parents become a salient factor in a child's upbringing.

The Formal and the Personal in Teaching

Personal/professional relationships are therefore a teacher's business, because we also cannot separate out the growth of the child's identity from the knowledge he or she is acquiring through these encounters with teachers. So a teacher is not acting outside his or her role in discussing anything with children that affects the school's purposes, especially their personal behavior. A child is being taught how to interact with people with civility. If children are injuring their health, teachers must be concerned. If children break the law in school, there is an educative, not merely a punitive, obligation on the teacher. Finally, children's domestic circumstances directly influence school performance. Quite apart from the curriculum, therefore, teachers cannot avoid a personalized professional relationship with children (see Hirst & Peters, 1979, chapter 6). In every case, teachers have to use their judgment about the ways in which individuals or groups can be influenced, taught, or protected, and different norms will be active at different levels of schooling.

This can be restated and reemphasized in two ways. First, children are learning how to conduct formal relationships and how to distinguish personal informal relationships (with which they have been brought up) from formal relationships (which on the path to adulthood they are beginning to establish). This is not just a matter for teachers acting independently in classrooms; the quality of relationships must pervade the whole institution (see White, P., 1996, p. 5). This mixture of professional and personal in the school environment protects children, so formality has to be treated lightly by the teacher, especially when children are young.

Second, children are in the process of becoming persons, and they are learning how to behave and act as moral agents. They are becoming people as they interact with the curriculum subject matter and others in the school environment. They are, to invoke Norton (1995), on a path of self-discovery about which they need to be self-conscious. So teachers and students will often shift from the informal-personal to the professional and back again. Each teacher will determine what the balance is between the two, from which emerges a repertoire within which this complementariness can be handled with finesse and skill, but the teacher has to see him or herself as part of the institution of the school, not as a lone wolf.

II. Teachers and Children

Mrs. Payton and Her Authority

Hansen quotes one of his subjects, Mrs. Payton, whose emphasis leans heavily to the professional and away from the personal:

> School should be a place where you can leave your problems behind, where you can find good, regular activity, a structured place. . . . I would like them to really become interested in their grade, in their work, what they can do. . . . They shouldn't have to dwell on their problems all the time. I like to give them a place where they can *work*. Kids need rules and structure or else they jump all over me and each other.
>
> *(Hansen, 1995, p. 22)*

Clearly Mrs. Payton is right that children shouldn't dwell on their problems all the time and that children need regular structured activity and classroom discipline. However, we may wonder whether that is not a somewhat narrow view of a classroom, especially one having an epistemological presence, although, of course, Mrs. Payton may well have good contextual reasons for her focus on disciplinary structure. Nevertheless, seeing the interlocking conversations important to the development of individual identity must surely not be reduced to "dealing with children's problems." If a structured environment diminishes dialogic space, it may provide a good socializing program, even a limited education, but it doesn't open the doors for knowledge widely enough. If Mrs. Payton doesn't open up the epistemological secrets that may protect her situation in the classroom ("no jumping all over me"), then she is putting to one side the incessant demands of truth, belief, evidence, and experience.

Yet, Hansen's rich account does contain this nugget suggesting Mrs. Payton is partially aware of epistemological significance and her responsibility in that regard. She is describing a situation where other teachers ask her students how come they knew this process or why they reasoned it out like that. The students say that Mrs. Payton taught them. "And that," Hansen records her as saying, "makes me feel good because it says *they didn't just take a body of knowledge that they may forget. They took a process and I think a process is more deep-rooted than the facts*" (Hansen, 1995, p. 40; my italics). It appears that her students therefore have developed an intellectual habit, what she calls a process. That does not go far enough. Reasoning is not a process, except perhaps in strict deductive logic, for it has to be framed as a task of judgment of what is relevant, what the context is, how the problem should be framed that reason is addressing. Mrs. Payton needs to have her students understand the epistemological complexity of the "process," not merely have it as a habit.

But, whether the children's workplaces are benign or not, Mrs. Payton draws our attention to her situation as one of power—a central feature of the teacher-student relationship. Not quite power. Teachers are certainly bosses: they are authorized (note the verb) to create or impose rules and structures; they order children to work, oblige them to follow prescribed patterns of behavior, threaten them with punishments, choose how their time is spent, and hector them if they are lazy. Mrs. Payton, Hansen writes, has "unqualified belief in her own authority in the classroom. She wants her students to understand unambiguously how to conduct themselves so that they can concentrate on their academic work. In practice, that aim implies that she must herself act, when in the presence of her students, in a clear, consistent and confident manner" (1995, p. 28). Indeed, the teacher determines the topics, the style of study, what is correct and incorrect, what is to be learned, and whether learning has been achieved and how it will be assessed. They implement rules and codes—for example, what it is permissible to wear. The teacher also interprets material (new to the student), which gives the teacher huge latitude to determine what is right and wrong, correct or incorrect, true or false. But the authority they exercise is one governed by a contract, by rules and norms of behavior: the teacher cannot do whatever he or she wants, just because she has the power. Teachers have authority.

Terrence's Teacher and Her Expectations

That authority can be misused and go beyond knowledge itself to the control of the child's future. In the introduction to Lisa Delpit's outstanding book is the following sad account:

> One evening I receive a telephone call from Terrence's mother, who is near tears. A single parent, she has struggled to put her academically talented fourteen-year-old African-American son in a predominantly white private school. As an involved parent, she has spoken to each of his teachers several times during the first few months of school, all of whom assured her that Terrence was doing "just fine." When the first quarter's report cards were issued, she observed with dismay a report filled with Cs and Ds. She immediately went to talk to his teachers. When asked how they could have said he was doing fine when his grades were so low, each of them gave her some version of the same answer: "Why are you so upset? For him, Cs are great. You shouldn't try to push him so much."
>
> *(Delpit, 2006, p. xxiii)*

Here the teacher's authority is being misused. It is restricting opportunities for learning. But how exactly do we understand this? First, there would seem to be a grossly misplaced empathy with the child—of the "don't push him" variety. To be generous to them, the teachers assume that black kids need "love," not hard work; they are mistaken and reveal gross misunderstandings at different levels— for example, of what is implied by equality of educational opportunity, or what social justice implies. Second, it is morally crass not to set high expectations for all children, for how can children acquire knowledge if they are not constantly challenged to produce their best work? If we are not so generous, of course, we must regard this use of authority as simply malicious. Third, the world Terrence experiences is completely shut out from the teacher's understanding, because she is clearly seeing the child as an example of a stereotype, not a person in his own right, to whom the teacher has powerful obligations. We need to get beyond simply categorizing this teacher as incompetent or prejudiced and understand the failures of her moral and epistemological stance toward Terrence and probably, though in other ways, to other children in her class. The irony is that too often (and once is enough) teachers use their authority perniciously but think they are being benevolent.

John and In-School Suspension

Mrs. Payton and Terrence's teacher seem to dominate their classrooms, as seen through these examples, and it is certainly correct that, as employees, they have the contractual authority to do so. But in practice, those over whom the authority is exercised may try to negotiate that exercise of authority. Children frequently struggle to get power in a classroom and sometimes succeed. John is the central character described in a study of the ideology and friction of an in-school suspension system.

> John proved to be a very reflective and intelligent young boy. When asked, "Is there another way (beside the Alternative Learning Environment) that might help you control your anger a little better and help you follow the rules?" John responded, "I truly do not know the answer to that question. . . . I really don't know." It is here that John shows reflection and is truly puzzled by his own behavior. It was deeply saddening to realize that the school was not helping John to understand what causes his behavior. John mentions the control a teacher had over him when she grabbed his hand and squeezed it tight. He didn't try to struggle until he realized she didn't trust him. It wasn't until then he stated: "that he began to add to the problem." It could be surmised here that John's behavior depends to a large extent on the concept he has of himself and that those around him have, but the intuitiveness of children can easily be overlooked. John is far too skilled in the character analysis of his teachers to be misled about the reasoning for his punishment. What are the unintended consequences for the actions we take against these children? Obviously, one consequence for John was that he began to manipulate and control his teachers.
>
> (Dalton, DiGiovanni, & Warner, 1996, p. 28)

John is a student in the second grade. He is eight years old and clearly able to be reflexively aware of his teachers. He provides proof, if it were necessary, that children are not stupid. We find, as the interview and analysis of John unwinds, that this eight-year-old boy knows that his rambunctious behavior is only one source of the problem. He also knows that his teachers do not trust him and have little expectations of him, and so he manipulates himself into the alternative learning environment (ALE) out of his classroom any time he wants too, simply by creating a stir. John shows us, among other things, that the social matrix of a classroom and the authority of the teacher can be negotiable. Clearly the teachers concerned and the school seem to exercise little authority over John. The teacher(s) seemed to regard his stance as simply one of social control, perhaps the most common explanation of such "deviance," but the rationales he provides of why he acts as he does show a total absence of trust in his teachers' authority, whom he sees as not being on his side. The problem is different for adolescents and their teachers, and this extended discussion of Janet's case explains why.

Janet and Authority as Social Control

Janet lives in a country area of the eastern United States. She attended a local university, and it never occurred to her to teach anywhere but the region where she was born. Her field experience was undertaken in the high school to which she was then appointed as a full-time teacher. When she began teaching, she was only four or five years older than many of her students and could easily have passed for one of them. Although her own school days were not all sweetness and light, she had never seen herself as anything but a teacher. Once in college, she saw her field experience as wonderful, but, as with most student-teacher situations, she did not realize that the student-teacher role is quite distinct from that of the classroom teacher. She therefore did not experience the range and dimensions of the real responsibilities of the teacher. These came thick and fast on her first appointment— teaching government and economics, being tennis coach, cheerleading coach, and a senior class advisor all in her first year. The result was that the friendly, though firmly distant, relations with the students established in her field experience were quickly transformed to a level of intimacy engendered by long shared periods of curricular and extracurricular activity as a regular teacher and, of course, living in the school's neighborhood community. Wanting to be a "nice teacher," Janet became the tireless friend, helper, and confidante. When a student approached her with a problem, whatever the problem, she wanted to help.

Adolescents are learning about the boundaries in relationships, specifically authority relationships, however much they may respect or exploit them. To students in schools these boundaries are infinitely explorable and exploitable, especially for many children to whom school is a necessary nuisance and where a teacher allows, so to speak, the boundaries to be negotiable. Some kids would press Janet into writing false notes excusing their tardiness or skipping. She kept quiet about her knowledge of their drug use. Keeping the friendship with them became more important to her than being honest in her role even though she knew she was not setting a good moral example. The moral quandary for her was exacerbated by the fact that she felt allied with them as they faced a harsh school administration.

But she consistently wanted to push the students to learn. They complained about the difficulty of the material and their test results were terrible. So she weakened the tests out of friendship. Sometimes she postponed tests, sometimes she allowed students not to take notes. The teaching structure of her work began to disintegrate. The denouement in her first year was the visit of a guest speaker in her economics class. She sent a student to the office for being rude in this session. He, the student, was annoyed by what he saw as her betrayal of the norms she had set. Yet in the ensuing conference it was she, not the student, who was made by the administrators to feel guilty about the incident. The failure to have the student punished or even reprimanded undermined her completely. She visibly had no support. She still struggled to be a "nice teacher," but now the students' defined her clearly as one of "them," as lax, undemanding, and obviously unreliable as a "friend." She continued to be a soft touch, without support from central administration or from her head of department (a disciplinarian who would ask occasionally how many of "them" she had "knocked out" that day!).

Since that first year, Janet has reestablished herself on an even keel, in part, she feels, because of major changes in the administration. Gradually, over five years, she built for herself a role that respects her students and retains her compassion, while pursuing intellectual integrity. This is not an unusual story of a first-year teacher in a high school. It is the tale of a young person full of ideals. Manifestly her teacher education was a failure in helping her understand how to translate personal ideals and her dispositions into practical teaching, and her first-appointment school torpedoed her by a crude sink-or-swim policy. Fortunately her ideals were not sullied but reinterpreted. She has gritted her teeth and pressed on.

How do we understand this biography? Pragmatically, many teachers would understand this story solely as an issue of social control, which was obviously the way Janet's principal saw it. An alternative mode of understanding would be a moral and an epistemological one.

Janet and the Moral Aspect of Her Authority

For here there are very important moral problems, especially in the specific cases Janet cites, but also more generally in matters of the creation of personal relationships with students and the moral obligations of her role and hence of her authority. (See chapter 9 for a discussion of the teacher's role.) That line of exploration would involve an examination of the notion of friendship and its compatibility with authority. Friends are open to secrets and intimate discourse. Except in highly special circumstances, the very formality of the teacher's role preempts such authentic friendships. Friendship with every child is impractical, as to befriend one child is ipso facto to exclude another, raising matters of equal treatment and fairness. For these two reasons, at least, trying to be a student's friend is a moral mistake because the teacher role rules out that kind of intimacy, as Janet discovered. (Being friendly is, of course, a different matter.) That much is a matter of moral discrimination and understanding. But this matter of authority and personal relationships is also an epistemological one.

Janet and the Epistemological Aspect of Authority

The epistemological issues are different, for in a parent-child or a teacher-class context, the adult person in authority and the child have a difference of *perspective on experience*. First, the child's wish for experience can override parental or teacher strictures. Teachers and parents are continually surprised by how little attention students or children pay to advice based on experience. The parent *sees Johnny as* obeying or disobeying an order. Johnny *sees the context as* wanting to try something out for himself, to get inside the experience so that he can understand it. So he is prepared to risk the dangers the parent is warning him of. The challenge for an adult is to establish ways of proceeding that reconcile encouraging children to experience the world, for good or ill, and insisting on their following adult instruction—for their benefit. Properly speaking, no experience can be secondhand.

Second, the adolescent frequently rejects a commonality of perspective such that adult experience is not valued. There are shared human wants and desires (forbidden or permitted) through which shared reflection on experience or desire might be promoted. Given advice adolescents will frequently tell adults that the world has changed since they were young. "You just don't understand" is a motto spanning any generation gap. For the adolescent it establishes the nontransferability of experience and the irrelevance of the adult perspective. From the perspective of the adult teacher or parent, valuable advice is thus cast off without reflection. Such adults, especially if they are in authority over children, see their treasured experiences scorned or ignored, and they feel disrespected and devalued. The adult's problem is not one where obeying the adult is pitted against the child's wish for experience, but one in which the adolescent's perspective is discounted. We thus have a context in which neither adolescent nor adult places any value on the other's experience. They do not see it as a source of knowledge or understanding. Teachers, like parents, have to put to one side their own experience as necessarily valuable and not seek to transmit that experience as an object lesson. Rather, they need to find ways in which different experiences from adult and children can be shared as material for reflection.

Third, shared transmission or sharing of experience can be stymied where children, especially adolescents, are repeating the (forbidden) experiences of their teachers or parents—for example, in premarital sex, experimenting with drugs, cheating, and a host of others. In class discussions with teachers I often find much righteous indignation about cheating, especially in high schools, with all the best moral reasons being put forward. But, as that explosive wrath simmers down, I ask whether anyone in the room has never cheated, and I have yet to find a single teacher claiming that purity; nor, I should add, do I. That question shifts the axis of the discussion from one of "What do we do about cheating?" to one in which we have a shared problem with children. With cheating and many other issues, if knowledge is to be shared, the sharing of experience must be authentic, not hypocritical, lest it smash the notion of respect for truth. It is educationally important that the (epistemological) perspectives on the experience are shared. That creates fertile ground for the exploration of mutual interests and concerns. Where there is the possibility of shared experience, there can be productive reflection and learning.

In each case of these three adult-child contrasts in perspective, the critical issue is to grasp what each person *sees the context as.* That describes the difference of perspective, of how we see the world, and thus is a matter of knowledge. Janet's case is especially poignant in this epistemological respect, and the question is now how to understand that part of her authority.

First, a major gap in too many teacher-education programs is one of moral education, specifically here in a neglect of the individual *teacher*'s identity. Rarely is any attempt made to have students probe their personal autobiography (not their reflections on their teaching experiences), sense of direction, and moral compass (see part IV). For a concept of teacher education driven by technical performance, this is irrelevant, but its absence abandons student teachers to a nonreflective fate. Students in Janet's class thus have one huge advantage over her: they are practicing a well-defined role; she is struggling to figure out what hers is and experimenting with it naively. Janet's picture of herself as wanting to be a nice teacher, equipped with interesting ideas and methods for teaching government or economics, is a false picture. In this, she is not deceiving us; it betrays a tremendous inadequacy in her *professional* identity. As she lacks a clear understanding of her own role identity, how could she possibly deal with such matters with children or even come close to defining her situation except in the exiguous terms of "loss of control"?

Second, with these misconceptions, Janet can never establish epistemological authority in her relationships with these students. Her concept of that authority and the knowledge she was transmitting was fundamentally incongruent with the personal presence she sought to achieve. If your view about knowledge is that "kids have to learn this," then the limits on being a "nice teacher" are highly circumscribed because that view of knowledge hampers the negotiation that the fragile interplay of teacher and student in "being nice" demands. Janet was not constructing an epistemological presence with any degree of self-consciousness. Her view of knowledge was completely out of step with her view of her authority. Moreover, she did not give up that view of knowledge faced with the students' antagonism to hard work. She simply softened all its edges. It is difficult to see how that perspective on knowledge can be shared in the light of truth, evidence, belief, and meaning. They just must "learn" it, whatever learning means. She therefore failed to establish an epistemological presence, one in which problems of truth, evidence, belief, and experience are the constant themes shared between teacher and learner in a classroom. Indeed, her attempts to be nice undermined the possibility of such a presence.

Finally, she surrendered to the students' definitions of themselves as failed learners, or cheats, rather than setting as the agenda the issues of their identity in relation to their knowledge. Students therefore got control, even commandeered the dialogic space. With that surrender, she mortgaged any possibility of assisting them to change and develop their identity, except as players in the interminable jousts of schooling. Conversations about their "real lives" were left unconnected to issues of their historical or contemporary identity. Her contributions to such topics were being continually marginalized.

This needs further explanation. If we just accept students' definitions of themselves, implicitly or explicitly, we provide no space within which alternatives might be explored. The epistemological cycle is a familiar one in which children often develop mistaken self-knowledge—for example, "I hate social studies"; "I am no good at math." The exploration of curriculum matters of great social and cultural importance to the child is intimately intertwined with a student's emerging identity. Public and personal knowledge are intimately connected. Notwithstanding that the students' self-perceptions are built up over a long (or short) period of schooling, the teaching challenge is to uproot those identities inimical to confrontation with truth, belief, and evidence. Janet demonstrates to us that we need to understand the central features of an epistemological presence if we are to create with and for students a sense of the teacher's epistemological authority.

III. Power, Authority, and Educational Purpose

We need now to solidify the distinction of authority from power made earlier and to note the place of expertise in an individual's authority. We talk of power in almost any kind of human or animal relationship where one party is dominant and the other's behavior is restricted by that dominance. Power, in this view, is a catch-all word insufficiently discriminatory for an educational context. Authority is a narrower notion. For authority implies legitimacy. People exercise authority because, in some form, the authority is given to them and because those "under" that authority recognize its appropriateness. No such notion of legitimacy clings to that of power. Power need not be backed by convention or by law. Authority must be. This distinction is reflected in the way we talk about states that have legitimate or illegitimate governments: we talk of the present U.S. *administration* and the military *regime* in Myanmar, formerly Burma. Of course there can be those who claim authority and legitimacy and are recognized as having it by those over whom the authority is exercised; yet if the source of the authority is in some way illegitimate or immoral, then it dissolves into simply a relationship of power, such as the "authority" of the leader of a fundamentalist sect or cult. (See Further Reading.)

R. S. Peters's Account of Authority

R. S. Peters has written the most sophisticated philosophical account of authority in education (1966, pp. 237–266; see also Peters, R. S., 1959). He builds up
this notion of authority as legitimate to include all kinds of normative contexts
where order is sustained—football games, the military, religious organizations, the
legal system, indeed all the formal organizations of a democratic state. Its origins,
he suggests, lie in children's acceptance of parents or caregivers as "special people
who have knowledge" (1959, p. 238). The kinds of people who are in authority in
such contexts range across football umpires, police officers, military officers, and
anyone who has executive authority. But, Peters points out, we also use the notion
of authority in the sphere of knowledge—for example, Julia Child on cooking.
"Such a person is assumed to have a right to pronounce on such matters because
of his special competence, training or insight" (p. 239). These two types of authority can be distinguished by the way we talk about a person being "in" authority
(like a police officer at a traffic accident) and a person being "an" authority (like
Julia Child). People would have looked to her for her wisdom about cooking and
asked her advice without being bound to do what she said, as her advice was not
a set of orders.

There is often a difference, however, between what is laid down in the rules and
what happens. Peters captures this difference in his distinction between "formal"
authority and "actual" authority. From one perspective, we can see the difference between a teacher who formally has the right to tell children to do things
but, as a matter of fact, is so incompetent that no one does what she says, let
alone listens to her. Janet almost became such a person. From another perspective,
we can see people who are not formally in authority but who nevertheless move
into a situation authoritatively and are treated as such by others—for example, a
bystander directing traffic at the scene of an accident. In matters of social control,
the difference between a person's formal and actual authority therefore seems to
rest on his or her personal qualities of leadership—whether they can, say, actually
be firm, fair, friendly, enthusiastic, and caring.

What does this account imply for teaching?

First, as the teacher-student relationship is governed by rules, we should talk
about it as an authority relationship, as this avoids the arbitrary character of a
"power" relationship. It puts the teacher's authority within a contractual relationship with employers. This entails the teacher having the right, under the rules, to
have students do what he or she decides shall be done. Criminal priests or teachers use power, not authority, in molesting children. Nor should such egregious
behavior be seen as a mistaken use of authority.

Second, how a teacher exercises authority will depend intricately and ultimately on the personal qualities he or she brings to the enterprise, especially on
the moral dispositions he or she has, together with a reflective capacity for personal
knowledge and understanding.

Third, the contractual authority must, in principle, be congruent with the demands of that moral and epistemological authority, which springs from the child's developing as a person and gaining in knowledge and understanding.

Yet the most significant problem for the teacher is how his or her authority is seen by those who are responsive to it. We saw with John the development of distrust and enmity with a teacher who was clearly misusing her authority: "John mentions the control a teacher had over him when she grabbed his hand and squeezed it tight. He didn't try to struggle until he realized she didn't trust him. It wasn't until then he stated 'that he began to add to the problem.'" In schools as institutions, principals and teachers can badly misuse their authority and, of course, they can also act in legal terms ultra vires—that is, beyond the powers entrusted to them in the authority they have. Where someone misuses their authority, they are using it badly in moral terms, for example where principals bully a teacher or gives them increased workloads because they don't like them. But acting ultra vires is to resort to power, typically in cases of sexual harassment or molestation, but all sorts of other aberrant behaviors driven by gain, greed, or excitement. Critical for the teacher, especially in a classroom with an epistemological presence is not the question "Do the kids like me?" but "How do the kids see my authority?" (I am grateful to Diane Wood for her comments on this argument.)

Darling-Hammond and colleagues (2005) have emphasized the notion of the teacher as having "adaptive expertise," akin to that of the medical clinician's diagnosing, surgical skills, and therapeutic advice (see especially chapter 2). The notion of the expert, however, is a very limited term that fails to capture the range and depth of issues coming under the teacher's moral and epistemological authority. For we think of the expert as a person superbly competent in the application of knowledge, like a cardiac surgeon, but we are rightly reluctant to use the notion of expertise in connection with the moral life. Expertise is an element in the teacher's authority, displayed in his or her practical wisdom, but governed by both moral and epistemological considerations and, of course, judgment.

This difficulty arises partly from the fascination in educational research and politics with the medical analogy, especially in teacher education where field experience is described as clinical practice. Of course, the medic's job is therapeutic, not educational. His or her job is to cure you; that's all. Hopefully he or she will be *an* authority on your complaint, say, Lyme disease, but a doctor cannot oblige you to follow instructions. You choose to do so. The diagnosis is rooted in his or her expertise as *an* authority. While teachers may be "authorities" in this sense, children, unlike patients in their classrooms are under an obligation to accept the teacher's authority, to do what the teacher says, not to choose whether to do it. The educational complex is far more intricate in matters of morality and epistemology than the doctor's office or the operating theater, where expertise is dominant, not broad-based authority. In many cases, the teacher has to win the respect of the children, to gain the de facto as well as the de jure authority. Not so the doctor.

IV. Authority and Models of the Teacher

In chapter 1 we noted the significance of knowledge for the teacher, stemming from the challenging questions raised by Belenky and colleagues. In chapter 2, two domains of knowledge were described, one public (with truth, belief, and evidence as its significant concepts), the other personal (with experience, commitment, and identity as its significant concepts). From those discussions so far have emerged characteristics of a classroom with an epistemological presence. In this chapter, examples of teacher authority and what the epistemological presence might mean for the authority of the teacher have been explored. In the final part of this chapter, how that authority is linked to the moral and the epistemological is articulated through four different models of that authority.

Different versions of authority—moral and epistemological—can be discerned with different views of the teacher (see Sockett, 2008) as primarily:

a. a scholar-professional,
b. a nurturer-professional,
c. a clinician-professional, or
d. a moral agent–professional.

A model here is seen as an ideal type, with the label acting as a rough and ready descriptor of emphasis, not carrying exclusivity—that is, (d) does not mean that (a), (b), or (c), individually or severally, lack a moral perspective. How in general might such models be articulated? One could pick out, say, the central tenets of Dewey's moral and epistemological stances to education, including other scholars in this tradition, and describe there from a Deweyan model of teacher education (see, e.g., Dottin, 2010), with different interpretations in different institutions. Alternatively, one could look at practice and seek to build a model from different elements of practice—for example, how children learn, the teacher's authority and responsibility, and managing a classroom. So, as will be seen in the clinician-professional model below, practices may vary in their moral and epistemological frameworks, but their coherence as a model rests on a consensus about specific moral and epistemological positions set within the idea of professionalism. Once again, there will be differences of application.

However, a model of teacher education presupposes a picture of a good teacher. What counts as "good" is culturally and morally heterogeneous. Socrates, Aristotle, Jesus of Nazareth, Mohammed, Saint Thomas Aquinas, Confucius, Jean-Jacques Rousseau, and Julia Child each provide us with glimpses into different aspects of teaching quality, not forgetting such literary heroes as Mr. Chips, or those men and women celebrated across the nation with different forms of good teaching awards and by success, for example, in the standards elaborated by the National Board. Models reveal differences in the conception of the "good teacher." These four models described are therefore not exclusive, but they are articulations of distinctive moral and epistemological positions on teaching and teacher educa-tion: they are therefore both models *of* practice and also models *for* practice. Each implies a different concept of teacher authority.

The scholar-professional. This first model regards knowledge as the pur-pose of education, so that the teacher is dedicated to imparting wisdom and fostering the life of the mind (Oakeshott, 1991, 1962/2010; Hirst, 1972/2010; Barzun, 1959). Moral purpose here is a matter of traditional, even conventional virtue. Epistemic purposes for teacher educators and teachers will not simply be focused on what is regarded as the unique character of disciplines (e.g., history) or inter-disciplines (e.g., classics) being studied but will also focus on epistemologi-cal battles within disciplines and on the nature of knowledge, perhaps with some attention to what has come to be called pedagogical content knowledge. (For a recent account of this, see Grossman & Schoenfeld, 2005.) The model of authority here is the traditional teacher in a traditional classroom.

The nurturer-professional. The second model is primarily focused on the development of the individual. It describes a teacher whose primary focus is on relationships with children: as Noddings (2002) puts it, the child is infinitely more important than the subject. It interprets the parent of in loco parentis as the mother. It can encompass such perspectives as Van Manen's (1990), with his emphasis on intuition and the "personal embodiment of a pedagogical thought-fulness" (p. 9). In other iterations (see Belenky et al., 1986), as teacher educators work with novice or serving teachers, both moral and epistemic purposes are connected to individual development. Throughout, the emphasis is on individual nurture: care or tact demands self-understanding by any teacher, and the cogni-tive is subsumed within the affective. The model of authority here is dominantly interpersonal—as in the aphorism, We teach children, not content.

The clinician-professional. The third model starts from an account of the work of the professional public school teacher in a democratic society and emphasizes the teacher's adaptive expertise, with moral emphases geared to so-cial purposes, such as social justice, with socialization as the educational aim (see Darling-Hammond et al., 2005). Its epistemic character is a strong if guarded belief in the integrity of educational research as a social science with explicit as-sumptions about knowledge, truth, and belief and the significance of the scientific method (see, e.g., Phillips & Burbules, 2000). The model of the teacher's authority here is difficult to articulate, but, without stretching the matter, it could be that of an executive manager.

The moral agent–professional. The fourth model accepts the legitimacy of the conflicting educational purposes and regards none as having priority since its focus is on teaching as primarily, predominantly, and pervasively a moral activ-ity (see, e.g., Tom, 1984; Hansen, 1995; Campbell, 2003). Although Aristotle and his followers provide the ethics of virtue from which this book grows, the model would have different interpretations dependent on the ethic depicted—for exam-ple, that of Dewey. Social and moral in education are a fortiori epistemic purposes, in the Aristotelian tradition, uniting moral and intellectual virtues (Norton, 1995; Sockett, 1993; Williams, 2005). The model describes the individual teacher with a primarily moral purpose focused on the child's comprehensive development and growth, and its epistemic purposes, for teachers as well as children, are to integrate academic content with intellectual and moral virtues, such as accuracy, consistency, courage, and open-mindedness.

This *moral agent–professional model* is celebrated in this book. Teachers in all these four models, however, will have a contract. The contract that gives a teacher authority in a classroom is (a) open-ended with regard to moral and epistemo-logical authority but (b) frequently circumscribed by local conventions and the cultural mores of the community from which the children are drawn. The contract is with public or private employers and gives teachers the authority to have children learn according to their instructions in the formal setting of the school. It will contain all kinds of details about employment, salary, benefits, and perhaps evaluation systems among other things. That apart, such a contract will also usu-ally entail the content of a curriculum often not determined by the teacher, such as where state authorities may lay out standards or guidelines, detailing topics for particular grades. In some countries, there will be public examinations or tests for which children must be prepared, even though comprehensive examinations given to students at age 16 may allow teachers choices of texts or topics to be studied. Practices differ, but only a relatively few teachers in public institutions have ever had carte blanche over curriculum, not least because even in those most prestigious private schools tradition exercised its own authority over the teacher. Within varying elastic parameters, teachers are put in authority, but they are not contracted as "authorities" in the sense that a Julia Child would be, though they need the appropriate expertise. The basis of any contractual authority therefore takes us only so far in any discussion of the teacher's authority and the quality of the teacher required to fulfill it.

Contractual authority cannot tell us much about a teacher's authority, although it is the legal basis for the exercise of that authority. While the formal curriculum to be taught may be implicit in the contract, neither the precise ways in which the knowledge is transmitted nor the conduct of the classroom is usually speci-fied under such contract. The epistemological and the moral responsibilities ger-mane to the teacher's authority are not specified. In that sense, employment details notwithstanding, the teacher must look beyond the contractual authority with which he or she is invested to enrich that authority. However, local conventions or cultures may impose some additional limits to the contract. Topics may be ruled out: sex education invariably contains controversies of one kind or another, for example, should children discuss premarital sex, homosexuality, reasons for divorce, or pedophilia? What is taught about sex and who by is vastly different in New York City and Peoria, Illinois. Similar constraints may be in place over politics and religion. Extramural conventions also apply: in one county in Virginia, no teacher dare ever drink alcohol in public.

How then, finally, do we understand the teacher's moral and epistemological authority, at any rate, within the moral agent–professional model?

The teacher's moral and epistemological authority is definitive of teaching and so, as Einstein's remark indicates, it should be in the service of truth. Moreover, unlike contractual authority, it is *created* by the teacher and is visible in the practical conduct of the classroom. The content and the form of the relationship with children, while subject to due process in terms of contract, are developed and enhanced by the individual according to the personal qualities and virtues the teacher manifests. That creation is an outcome of individual character. The teacher determines what we might call the rules of learning engagement in terms of (a) interpersonal relations, (b) individual conduct, and (c) the character and style of his or her interventions.

Interpersonal relations across a classroom are determined not by what a teacher will allow, as if rules were made to be broken, but by what general or specific rules he or she believes children should be taught in terms of the norms and rules of interpersonal engagement. The teacher's moral authority thus calls for very subtle exercise with all children. Younger children are learning the social ropes of the classroom, whereas adolescents are exploring friendships and relations with the male or female peers that occur in both the classroom and the extramural context. Individual conduct rules relate not merely to these interpersonal relationships but to handling the dispositions the child comes to the classroom with—arrogance, shyness, aggressiveness, politeness, and so on—and trying to have the child establish for him or herself a persona that the child comes to value. Into this complex range of exercises of moral authority comes the style of the teacher interventions, which reveal the moral cast of the teacher behind the speech-acts, gestures, and remonstrances. The practical wisdom a teacher shows in the classroom may be in some cases simply expertise—for example, how to handle a tornado threat, a fire drill, a child having an epileptic seizure, or, of course, teaching complicated long division sums.

Yet, across the range of the exercise of a teacher's moral authority will be revealed the individual's character as embodied in a teaching persona (not a role), sincere, caring, generous, courageous, trustworthy, friendly, even-tempered, and careful. Out of the individual character is built a teaching persona and a content-filled conscience about the appropriate form and content of his or her authority. This may, of course, be helped by thinking in terms of some moral vision of "who I am to become"; more likely, in my view, the teacher's stable dispositions and virtues are shaped and reshaped as reflection on new experiences as they are encountered. In the process, however, the teacher is the creator: he or she has the initiative, whatever a contract may say. In part IV of this book, how the persona created manifests in the individual teacher's classroom authority will be located within categories of virtue in terms of character, intellect, and care.

On the specifically epistemological side, seekers after knowledge are not agnostics or cynics. Rather, they are prepared consistently to put their knowledge

to the test of truth and alter their beliefs accordingly. The form of the epistemological authority is how teachers hold their knowledge, what their attitudes are to
what they know. Once again, therefore, the teacher's epistemological authority is
manifest in his or her conduct—that is, how individual intellectual dispositions are
displayed. That will include truthfulness, accuracy, consistency, fairness and impartiality, clarity, thoughtfulness, and open-mindedness, among others.

There are therefore three main areas in which epistemological authority will
be exercised: (a) the truth of what is being taught and the character of truthfulness displayed in the teacher's authority, (b) the open-mindedness of the teacher
and thus the extent to which challenges to his or her epistemological authority
are received and handled, and (c) the impartiality and fairness that the teacher
both manifests and insists on in the handling of beliefs held by individuals in the
classroom.

In chapter 4, we will examine the interrelations of truth and truthfulness. Suf-
fice it to say here that being a truthful person creates trust. That does not imply
that the authority of the teacher always demands truth-telling, as judgments about
other principles are involved in different contexts. Yet being truthful in general
terms implies that the teacher's authority can be relied on. From the child's viewpoint in matters of knowledge, it is not that the teacher should self-consciously act
as a model, but that emphasis should be on the creation of trust through that aspect of personal integrity called truthfulness. We see here how an intellectual disposition, truthfulness, necessarily spills over into moral issues and moral authority.

Peters pointed out that for children to grow to rational autonomy, to be able to
think for themselves, will usually imply their coming to make intellectual assaults
on the teacher's beliefs. In this way, the only coherent educational justification for
the use of epistemological authority is to free children to live their own life of the
mind. Characteristically, therefore, the teacher's epistemological authority cannot
be exercised cogently with a closed mind. Part of the difficulty with this claim is
that state-constructed syllabi are obstacles to its realization. To take an example in
Virginia: children at many different grade levels encounter the life and work of
Thomas Jefferson, both as a Virginian and as an American. The implication is that
Jefferson should be regarded as a hero. A teacher may or may not be acquainted
with some of Jefferson's personal and political weaknesses, as for example in his
political conflict with John Adams where Jefferson's truthfulness, to say, the least,
was not perspicuous. An open-minded teacher cannot shut these significant matters off from children. Judgment will differ, but a fifth-grader could perfectly well
understand the fact, too, that Jefferson, after his wife's death, had children by Sally
Hemmings, and they will also come to understand his slave-owning. There is no
valid reason, especially in days where the nuclear family is no longer the norm and
children experience different forms of family life, for this fact to be kept a secret
from children. Open-mindedness demands not merely being receptive to beliefs
contrary to one's own, but being prepared to share all kinds of beliefs with children for them to learn how to be open-minded and to handle contrary beliefs to

their own. These connections between belief and open-mindedness are explored in chapter 5.

More complex still vis-à-vis the teacher's authority is the handling of children's beliefs, especially those that are outside the norms. The challenge is one of fairness and impartiality combined with a tough-minded stance toward the provision of evidence. Yet, complexity arises from children's experience—that is, what they bring to the classroom from their own backgrounds. Partly, this fairness is exemplified in treating children's contributions with care and respect, and frequently showing that what they believe is invalid or simply not true. For example, children frequently bring racial prejudices imbued from their parents into classrooms. They may have irrational fears, beliefs in Santa Claus, and a host of other beliefs. The challenge for the teacher is both epistemological and moral. More difficult will be the injection of specific religious beliefs that may or may not be shared by other children, for example on evolution and creation. But, we need to treat impartiality as an intellectual virtue, specific to the ways in which we examine that controversial notion of evidence, how we justify our assertions that this or that is the truth (see chapter 6).

The character of the teacher's authority, therefore, is manifest in the way a teacher develops or has developed a classroom persona in respect of the moral and intellectual dispositions he or she has, which, for the purposes of analysis, can be understood as moral and epistemological. Dispositions have primacy over knowledge and skills in conceptualizing teaching because the deployment of both carries with it the teacher's view of his or her authority within which created persona these dispositions rest. In part IV, this account of the primacy of dispositions will be developed, following the examination of dispositions and virtues connected to public knowledge in part II, and dispositions and virtues connected to personal knowledge in part III. In the exercise of a teacher's moral and epistemological authority, moral and intellectual dispositions are the core of teaching and are the main criteria of teaching quality.

narratives as necessary
to cultivate
the ground for open-mindedness
in ethics

PART II

Virtue and Public Knowledge

Introduction

An epistemological presence in the classroom is interwoven with the moral character of the teaching and learning enterprise. Such a classroom celebrates learning encounters with both knowledge and virtue, and in part I, we have seen various ways in which it would accommodate such encounters. In the next two parts of this book, the task is to provide a substantial rationale for this argument through connecting each of the six elements of public and personal knowledge described in chapter 2 to their congruent intellectual virtues. As the general pursuit of truth is a moral enterprise itself, intellectual virtues are ipso facto moral virtues, although the reverse need not be the case.

Part II addresses the connections between the elements of *public* knowledge and specific virtues: truth and truthfulness, belief and open-mindedness, evidence or justification, and impartiality. In chapter 4, following Bernard Williams, I suggest that truthfulness can be understood through the virtues of accuracy and sincerity. But in classrooms, in disciplines and institutions, the demands of truthfulness are prominent, for example in matters of plagiarism, cheating in general, lies, secrets, and gossip. Truthfulness is therefore intimately connected to trust, a defining quality of a classroom with an epistemological presence. The ethos of an institution like a school or a university permeates conduct: children need to develop understanding of the temptations of institutional life.

In chapter 5, a detailed account of the complexity and connectedness of beliefs is illustrated through an examination of examples from the Commonwealth of Virginia Standards of Learning. We build up children's beliefs when we teach, however limited our view of education. But changing one's beliefs or getting new beliefs requires open-mindedness, the congruent virtue to belief. The acquisition of beliefs is the central task for the student, but, with adulthood, many such beliefs will challenge the individual's disposition to open-mindedness. Yet open-mindedness signals one further matter of immense importance, which may be called the conscience of belief. We usually associate our conscience, or what we feel obliged to do, with *actions,* but ought we to *believe* what we believe? That question nags away at what teachers and children are examining in a classroom with an epistemological presence, for this is not a private matter. Erroneous beliefs impact other people. So an account is given of open-mindedness in two modes— the discovery (where one is acquiring new beliefs) and the critical mode (where beliefs are being evaluated). Both require the development of specific habits and the development of judgment, further discussed in chapter 6.

If truth has these significant connections to truthfulness; and belief, as the second primary epistemological concept defining knowledge, is embedded in open-mindedness; the third condition, namely evidence, is connected to impartiality. In chapter 6, a brief account of the philosophical problems of evidence and justification is explored, particularly in terms of those who are called virtue epistemologists. To justify what you know, in their view, is not a matter of there being knock-down incontrovertible evidence, such as a scientist might produce, but in the moral diligence that you are bringing to your assertion that you know something. From a discussion of these different positions, the claim is advanced that a knower will make grounded or justified assertions with different forms of justification depending on the context. The justification for what one believes should, once again, be part of the structure of the classroom with an epistemological presence. By the time children are in high school, if not before, they should have acquired a clear understanding of the epistemology of the subjects in terms of the complex distinctions of objective and subjective. Part II ends with an account of what is required in making judgments from a base of impartiality, inside or outside disciplines. Evidence, warrant, justification, whichever term may be used to describe this condition of knowledge demands impartial judgment in which the crucial key is the consistent examination of alternatives.

A classroom with an epistemological presence, therefore, will demand truthfulness, open-mindedness, and impartiality in the quest for truth and for knowledge. Yet clarity on how we are to understand truth, belief, and the complex problems of justifying what we know are the arena within which these virtues are exercised.

4

TRUTH AND TRUTHFULNESS

> The truth is rarely pure and never simple.
> —*Oscar Wilde,* The Importance of Being Earnest *(1895)*

Truth is a property of statements.

Truthfulness is a property of persons.

Persons make statements in which they can express what is true or what is false. They can be truthful, but what they say can be false. They can say what is true without any intention to be truthful—for example, by accident or guesswork. Statements are addressed most frequently to other people. Truthful people create trusting relationships, but the absence of truthfulness promotes a dysfunctional society, whether that be a family, golf club, country, or classroom.

In educating children, we want them to come to believe what is true and to make true statements, assertions, and claims about what they believe and congruently be able to detect where beliefs are false. Without detailed justification here, we want them to become truthful people, especially in being truthful to themselves and not being victims of self-deceit. While they will need to understand connections between what they believe and evidence for those beliefs, in order to judge whether something is true or not, we are also concerned with them as people with characteristics, dispositions, and a panoply of human attributes. Truth and truthfulness are therefore complementary in our educational understanding, and together they create trust between individuals, between individuals inside institutions, and between individuals outside those institutions, for example, customers and those institutions. Truthfulness is the linchpin of trust.

In section 1 of this chapter, the general connection of truth and truthfulness outlined in chapter 2 is expanded, suggesting that truthfulness is a virtue or a disposition with two constituent virtues: accuracy and sincerity. Both virtues are assessed in terms of their function in the establishment of an epistemological presence in the classroom. The account leans heavily on that given by philosopher Bernard Williams (2002) in his book *Truth and Truthfulness.* In section 4, the discussion shifts to institutions, specifically in terms of lies, secrets, and gossip, which points up not merely the significance of truthfulness as an individual or institutional property but its intimate connection with trust and epistemological matters of truth. This offers the opportunity to discuss both plagiarism and cheating in educational institutions and to suggest how truthfulness among students might be promulgated. It is important throughout to have in mind that teachers at all levels work in institutions that certainly influence and in some ways determine their behavior.

I. Connecting Truth, Truthfulness, and Trust

Recall the old griot in *Roots* (see chapter 1) who was retelling a lineage, a familiar activity for those who have read the Old Testament or, for that matter, those who grapple with putting their family trees on contemporary software in a rather different idiom. That old African was making a series of statements about the past; his demeanor, his style, and his obvious sincerity convinced Alex Haley not only that what he was saying was true, but that he was being truthful. Consider too a criminal trial, the most obvious formal occasion for telling the truth. People swear to "tell the truth, the whole truth, and nothing but the truth." Yet cross-examination follows: here the major purpose is to test two interconnected elements: (a) the truth or falsity of what the witness has said and (b) the veracity of the witness—whether he or she is being truthful. That these two elements are needed in a cross-examination is perhaps obvious. A witness might state the truth on one or two precise matters, but actually be totally unreliable, because too much of what he or she claims is false. This is to emphasize that truthfulness is a property of persons and can be described as a disposition, a habit, or a virtue.

You can tell the truth by accident, but you can't be truthful by accident. Teachers often ask children questions and, sometimes, perhaps often, children don't know the answers. So the teacher invites individuals, with pedagogical automaticity, to guess. If a right answer emerges, no doubt the teacher will then explain why that is indeed the right answer. But the child who gets the answer right has been lucky, not truthful, even though what he or she said was true. Being truthful must always be a matter of the speaker's intentions, hopefully drawn from his or her moral and intellectual dispositions. Yet one can be truthful without what one says *actually being true,* as in "I honestly thought that was the case." For I may say something that I believe to be true, and I am indeed a truthful person, but perhaps unknown to me the evidence has shifted, as with the *Lusitania,* and what I thought was true is no longer so.

Truthfulness as a human characteristic does not come upon us by accident, either. It is a desirable disposition—that is, a stable characteristic of the ways a person acts. Stability implies consistency: if a person tells the truth only when it suits him, then we will not describe him as truthful. Since we value the disposition to be truthful, and we see that value as moral, we can satisfactorily call it a virtue. Distinctions are made between intellectual virtues and moral virtues, and truthfulness may easily be thought of as being in both categories. But the conceptual root of truthfulness lies in its character as a moral virtue that is then present, so to speak, in all matters of intellect. Scientist X is a truthful person, and that extends to his work. It would certainly be odd to think of his truthfulness as stemming only from his work, as if his non-work life were a pack of lies. This is not, of course, to say that people cannot lead double lives, as spies throughout the ages indicate.

We can see how truth and truthfulness are not just complementary but inextricably linked, especially in teaching. Telling the truth, as Bernard Williams (2002) points out, is an example of doing something well—that is, reliably communicating information (in a very general sense) to someone else, usually in the form of an assertion. Doing it well is a necessary qualifier because, as human beings, we may well desire to conceal the information in some way. Of course, making correct statements is not just something we do for its own sake; when we say things that are plainly true "they remind us that we share the same world and find the same things salient, and help us to discover where we do and do not agree" (Williams, 2002, p. 72). Needed among human beings, he suggests, are two types of dispositions: (a) those that connect to *acquiring* a correct belief and (b) those containing the *motivation* to say what one actually believes. Williams calls these two dispositions accuracy and sincerity, respectively, and regards them as the basic virtues of truth.

Both virtues, at first blush, would be characteristic dispositions of the moral teacher. Teachers can reasonably be expected, contractually and morally, to be accurate in what they teach to children, but also in their assessments and reports of children's behavior and character. Accuracy can, of course, be undermined by prejudice, favoritism, or simple dislike. Such obstacles to accuracy must form a constant threat to a teacher's truthfulness. Similarly with sincerity, though an interesting pedagogical problem—often used as a teaching technique—is that of the devil's advocate, where a teacher deliberately chooses to defend a position that he or she does not in fact believe. Equally, to seek to be sincere—that is, to have the motivation to say what one actually believes—contains a strong obligation to make sure that what one believes is in fact true. We might reasonably expect both of these virtues, accuracy and sincerity, to be taught to children. As such, they would become part and parcel to the way we conceive the curriculum and, of course, be virtues indicative of an epistemological presence in the classroom.

To put the matter another way, assertions convey information to people who are going to rely on what is said, as in teaching, and "someone who is conscientiously acting in circumstances of trust will not only say what he believes [sincerity], but will take trouble to do the best he can to make sure that what he believes is true [accuracy]" (Williams, 2002, p. 80). Out of these notions of accuracy and sincerity, but especially the latter, questions of trust between individuals naturally arise. The virtue of truthfulness, with its constituent dispositions of accuracy and sincerity, has therefore to be set in the context of trust: this complements the formal analysis of truth as justified true belief, as understood through truthfulness and trust from the realm of the personal and interpersonal virtues, moral and intellectual. Both dispositions of accuracy and sincerity are rooted in trusting relationships.

Indeed trust, in Williams's account, is a "necessary condition of cooperative activity, where this involves the willingness of one party to rely on another to act in certain ways" (2002, p. 88). Teaching is formally a paradigm case of a cooperative activity, simply because a learner has to be willing to learn. Trustworthiness, as a disposition, is always part of a trust-filled context—that is, where people are used to each other, have ends in common, or, for example, are in a professional-personal relationship such as that between teacher and student. Such a context gives rise to the idea that the educational relationship itself is one of trust and the individuals within it are trustworthy; but they value the trust, whatever they think about the intrinsic value of the enterprise. One can trust the math teacher without caring much for math. But an individual, Williams suggests, who wants to be trustworthy must want to relate that virtue to other things he or she holds valuable, and it must connect to his or her ethical emotions (2002, p. 92). So the trustworthy person thinks things through, reflects on how he or she is being seen, and seeks to have a kind of stability in relationships that are always under reflection.

This argument binds closely together the moral and the epistemic. The scientist (or indeed any serious intellectual student) is part of a community for whom seeking to establish the truth or falsify what is believed *is* the point of the exercise. The scientist is truthful, which in the case of science means such things as accurate reporting and scrupulous following of the methodology in pursuit of the truth. It is the virtuous pursuit of truth that makes the enterprise tick. The moral and the epistemic are integrally linked.

How do children become truthful people? How do novice and practitioner teachers either become truthful people (if they are not already) or develop more sophisticated understandings of what it means for them as teachers? How is the relationship between such teachers and the children they teach to be handled and developed? We have noticed that children can get the right answer by luck, so teachers will want to ensure that there is understanding. We have noticed too that we can be truthful when it suits us, and many children may be somewhat devious, but also keen to be the informer. We have questioned briefly so far the problem of the devil's advocate as a method. We have noted too the need to create trust through cooperative, not hostile, relationships. These are a mixture of moral and epistemological matters that will always be on the agenda of a classroom with an epistemological presence. For teachers there are other matters: how to distinguish fact from value and understand their interrelations; how politics can pollute research and how teachers can be critics of research and of scholarly knowledge. Above all, are teachers sufficiently truthful (i.e., committed to accuracy) to examine complex beliefs? We now need to examine in more depth both sincerity and accuracy in turn.

II. Sincerity and Candor

Sincerity does not mean just that one does not lie, but that the way one expresses one's beliefs are in relation to an ethical and emotional commitment. "Hearers gather more from a speaker's making a particular assertion than the content of the assertion" (Williams, 2002, p. 100). In other words, the question of how someone asserts something is deeply and profoundly connected to his or her sincerity and, thereby, his or her trustworthiness. Parents and teachers may feel themselves trapped by children's questions about Santa Claus, God, sex, or many other topics that for different reasons they are disinclined to answer truthfully. It is beside the point to utter such nostrums as "one should never lie to children," for this is to take an unnecessarily blinkered view of trustworthiness. For parents and teachers, the crucial issue is the continuation of a relationship of trust with children that does not demand just stating the truth: "People in friendly and trustful circumstances widely lie to others or mislead them or give them false impressions, in order not to wound them or to expose themselves, and in general to sustain systems of mutual esteem" (Williams, 2002, p. 113). Overwhelmingly the parent or teacher must make judgments about what children should know at this or that stage of their lives. That may involve dissembling, even lying, to sustain the relationship of trust, among other moral justifications. The moral judgment remains: that the sustenance of a relationship of trust, and being trustworthy, is a commitment "which is a central expression of the ethical disposition of Sincerity" (Williams, 2002, p. 111). A teacher thus may be equipped with sincerity as a disposition, but there may be very good reasons, in particular circumstances, for him or her not to tell the truth. This requires judgment, which will be discussed in the context of impartiality in chapter 6.

But is there a way to describe the relationship of trust between teacher and student? It must be a relationship in which a teacher's being sincere is both part of who he or she is and part of the content children learn. But the general practice of teaching in the world at large can characterize differing sorts of relationships: compare a professor teaching 350 students Government 101 with the first-grade teacher and her class of 20 and/or to the teacher of an online course in continuing education for lawyers.

The distinctive teacher-student relationships among these three need not be different with regard to truth or to trustworthiness: students in each context can reasonably anticipate sincerity (and accuracy). Critical is the extent to which the teacher has a responsibility for the student's growth in respect of the sort of person he or she is becoming, which influences the scope, range, and difficulty of judgments about trust. The government professor may properly be concerned about the students' becoming good citizens but be able to exert little influence. The lawyer students may want to become better lawyers but want only information from their teacher. The first-grade teacher has an overarching concern for the child as a person, whatever the formal curriculum. The teacher's relationship with children, qua children, invests the relationship with moral characteristics that cannot be left to one side, as is indeed possible in other contexts without there being any form of moral dereliction. Seen from the student's viewpoint, too, the relationships are also characteristically different. A young child anticipates, though may not literally ask for, guidance on most matters of personal, social, and academic activity, from wiping his nose, to sitting quietly and paying attention, to dotting Is and crossing Ts. Government 101 students would be surprised if the professor told them to wipe their noses, or even asked them not to go to sleep, though they do anticipate exchanges on intellectual matters. The exchanges are varied and sometimes dependent on the students' ages and maturity: freshmen in their thirties have different expectations of the relationship than the 19-year-olds straight out of high school. Lawyers would anticipate full social and professional equality, even though they are learning material they don't know. Such different types of teaching serve to remind us that individual children and classes of the same age in schools may equally require different professional judgments. Williams may be said in the following passage to be speaking of such problems, and it can apply to teachers and students:

> We want people to have a disposition of Sincerity which is centered on sustaining and developing relations with others that involve different kinds and degrees of trust. Reflecting on that disposition, they will think about the kinds of trust that are implicit in different relations, and how abusing them may resemble other, perhaps more dramatic forms of manipulation and domination, inasmuch as it imposes the agent's will in place of reality, the reality which all the parties equally have to live within. The disposition itself enables the agent to think clearly and without self-deceit about the occasions when deceit is required, and to keep a sense of those among them when something is lost by it. Much of one's thought, if one is such an agent, looks outward, to the other people involved and to the relations they have to one, but at the same time, and without any paradox, it involves a sense of oneself and of the respect one might have or lose from people one can oneself respect.
>
> *(2002, p. 121)*

This is a critical passage for teachers: consider candor as an element in one of Williams's "kinds of trust" different in degree and kind from, say, authority (see chapter 6). Not only do students expect fairness in terms of being treated on a par with other students, but they deserve frankness and candor, in a supportive context, on the character of their work, though they may not think they need it. While this applies to children at school, it is often most marked with college students, for whom it can be very painful to come up against the college's academic standards as shown by professors and as represented in the grades they receive. One reaction is shock: "I have never had a C before." Another is "You have graded my opinions" or "You don't like me." A third is "'Professor so-and-so doesn't grade as harshly as you do." A fourth is "My assignment was as good as X's and Y's." Shulman (1999), as mentioned earlier, has pointed out how undergraduate students seem to lack a sense of balance and reality about the quality of their work. The difficulty such students have was also well expressed by Lawrence Stenhouse in his remark that, from the perspective of knowledge, students have to see their teachers as supportive critics, not examiners (see also chapter 9). A seeker after knowledge needs criticism; how else can one learn?

The only requirement of trust with a teacher-examiner is that, through the institutional system (as in SATs) or in the individual relationship (as with a college professor), trust is based on fairness. Yet the requirements of trust for the teacher-critic are much more extensive, involving trust in academic judgments. Candor from a professor does not necessarily lead to confidence without the detail of explanation that would promote acceptance of judgment. When the two roles or functions are combined in a teacher, they present tensions that can challenge the individual's commitment to sincerity and undermine trust, as it were, in both directions. But, even if being able to be candid with students is both the role of the examiner and the critic, the limits of candor and the degrees of it will vary from individual to individual, from class to class.

Candor as a feature of a kind of trust is the product and the process—that is, a teacher may well begin with great care, uncertain of the student and his or her ability to take candid judgment of work. Candor, as philosopher Pat White (1996) puts it, is not "to be equated with brutal frankness, telling people 'home truths' nor with simple loquaciousness" (p. 71). It is a process in the sense that the extent to which a professor can be candid is an ongoing part of the fineness of the moral judgments to be made and the education of the student in being self-critical and open-minded. Procedures undertaken in a classroom will be extremely intricate. Trust in a professor's candor and judgment is not enhanced by a professor's lack of respect, in principle, for student work—for example, grading an essay B and simply writing "shows promise" as a final comment; if a teacher does not care enough to read work carefully, take it seriously, and comment on it, warts and all, how can a student come to accept a candid judgment? Equally, constantly using multiple-choice questions in a course removes the possibility of the subtlety of the "degrees of trust" of which Williams writes: there, evaluation of work is simply mechanical, however much it may be judged appropriate for other instrumental reasons. Yet again, candor is a hopeless quest without setting standards of quality, both in terms of the products and the commitment to hard work and effort the student makes.

Nothing is more difficult in creating the element of teacher-student trust where candid judgment is needed. For complex reasons, too many students approach learning with a sense of entitlement to excellence or with a very vague idea that making the effort is everything, even if judgment of what counts as effort is limited. But they cannot grow in knowledge, both of content and of themselves, without the candid judgments of their teachers, suitably judged for each individual student. Sincerity, as Williams puts it, embodies the motivation to say what one believes. There will inevitably be cases where a teacher at least dissembles, as we have noted, if not lies outright. But these occasions have to be part of that reflection essential to teaching that Williams points to, "the kinds of trust that are implicit in different relations, and how abusing them may resemble other, perhaps more dramatic forms of manipulation and domination, inasmuch as it imposes the agent's will in place of reality, the reality which all the parties equally have to live within" (2002, p. 121).

III. Accuracy and Its Obstacles

Accuracy is another matter: its central motivation is to acquire a correct belief and, in the case of the teacher, to teach it as such. Yet the discovery of truth, Williams suggests, is subject to both external and inner obstacles, and "even the external obstacles have an inner representation and imply inner attitudes toward dealing with them" (2002, p. 124). Accuracy can also be treated as a virtue, not some kind of weak disposition to pick up reliable information. Both sincerity and accuracy operate in "a space that is structured by motivations to conceal or dissimulate" (p. 124). Where we struggle with such inner obstacles and motivations, we are seeking to be virtuous. We want to believe something that we like is true or we like the person informing us of something, irrespective of what they are claiming to be true, and, we can be sloppy in attempting to find things out. Of course, as we saw with the students in college, self-deception is also a form of being inaccurate, of not telling the truth about oneself. Indeed to insist "on getting it right can be a matter of conscience, honor or self-respect" (p. 126).

Accuracy, then, "is directly related to the aims of beliefs: it implies care, reliability, and so on, in discovering and coming to believe the truth" (Williams, 2002, p. 127). That involves two things: (a) the "investigator's will, his attitudes, desire and wishes, the spirit of his attempts, the care he takes" (to get it right) and (b) "the methods the investigator uses" (p. 127). If we are to praise a person for his or her accuracy, then we are also appraising his or her methods of getting at the truth. These virtues can be individual or collective, and indeed they are closely interrelated; they may also be needed, individually or collectively, in the context of political attempts to deny their importance or suppress them.

Accuracy relies on efficient and effective investigation, such that some ways of going about finding out things are better than others—in Williams's phrase, "truth-acquiring" (2002, p. 130). In other words, we have to figure out what are good and not-so-good methods of inquiry. If a method is a good method of finding out whether something is true, it must depend on the character of the something. Figuring out how President Lincoln was shot requires a different method than does figuring out why my stomach aches. All such inquiries demand not just qualities of endeavor, taking care, paying attention, and being persistent (see Sockett, 1988) but having good, as opposed to the right, methods. Methods are not just surefire. "When I don't know how to answer a question, I do not know fully determinately what is stopping me doing so" (Williams, 2002, p. 134). Well, it may be the method won't work, but that raises all kinds of other questions about which avenues should be explored, so that, as he continues, "the external obstacles to finding out the truth turn out, often, to be in alliance with internal obstacles—at the most obvious level, laziness, but, more interestingly, the desires and wishes that are prone to subvert the acquisition of true belief" (p. 134; see also chapter 5).

One major obstacle is self-deception: I may want something to be true because of some other factor—for example, I have published a paper on it, already told my grandmother, or whatever. A second obstacle is that I want it to be true, that is, I want the state of affairs described to be as I want it. I am hugely motivated to believe it, but, of course, I cannot believe something at will, as the White Queen seemed to think. "Self-deception, which is one thing that the accurate agent must avoid, is a homage that fantasy pays to the sense of reality" (Williams, 2002, p. 135). But also, in the realm of wishing something to be true, it is the commitment to accuracy that will subvert it (p. 140). This matters especially in the context of a collective endeavor like science: the only point of science is to get it right. We are confronted in science not by the wills of others, however much sociologists of knowledge may think, but by the world and the sense of freedom that offers. "A central form of freedom, then, is not to be subject to another's will in working toward something that you find valuable" (p. 144). How does this influence education?

> We have to mention the truth in making sense of the virtue of Accuracy, and the same applies to education. . . . The only alternative to incorporating notions of truth and falsehood into an account of education will involve, as it seems to me, the assumption that legitimate, educational, forms of persuasion can be distinguished from others simply by their methods: for instance, they are supposed to be specially rational, or to be uniquely directed to the interests of those being persuaded, *where neither rationality nor the pupils' interests are understood in terms of a concern for the truth* [my italics]. Some education practices may have tried to base themselves on such ideas, but we do not need much reflection to see that appealing to methods simply in this sense gives no results, or unacceptable results; if they draw the required lines in the right places, they do so because they in fact rely on ideas of truth and falsehood.
>
> *(Williams, 2002, pp. 147–148)*

This discussion of accuracy and sincerity has connected questions of truth and knowledge to truthfulness and the qualities and the position of the knower. We cannot teach students or children to respect the truth outside teaching them to be truthful—that is, to be, in this sense, virtuous. That is a heady prospect if we consider the range of moral and intellectual virtues germane to teaching. Finally, on both sincerity and accuracy, it needs to be firmly emphasized that this discussion is primarily about how children and teachers can acquire or develop these virtues, how critical the relationship between truthfulness and trust is, and how trust is created within an environment, a seminar room, a classroom, indeed any educational institution.

IV. Truthfulness and Trust in Institutions

It has been argued that moral and intellectual virtues are the canons through which the methods of a discipline are applied by its practitioners and theorists. Both sincerity and accuracy as virtues of truthfulness have been shown to have wide ramifications in teaching and learning contexts. But those contexts are also institutional. The classroom is part of this school: the seminar room is part of this college. These virtues, we may assume, would be institutional norms, not simply personal dispositions. They are embodied in the ethos of the institution, which is instantiated more or less in every nook and cranny of the institutions. Trust, as an institutional norm and a personal virtue, is undermined by deceit, specifically lies, but also by secrets, especially in a small institution like a family or a classroom, but also in a large business or government entity, even an academic discipline like history. Cheating is also a form of deceit, a specific breach of truthfulness, and it usually includes the written rather than the spoken word. Sisella Bok's books (1978, 1982) on both topics form the groundwork for examination of the problems in educational institutions.

The Protestant notion of "my word is my bond" indicates that, although deceit can be achieved without speech or be embodied in statements, what most often matters is what we say. Unlike lying, which seems always to be prima facie wrong and undermines trust, secrets as such are morally neutral, and there are political and moral justifications for keeping some matters secret, but gossip and rumor are parasitic on the passing around of secrets and form an important institutional aspect of secrecy that can be institutionally corrosive. "Politics without trust," as law professor Stephen Carter remarks, "is simply war" (1997, p. 32). However, institutions confront deceit and lies in three specific areas: institutional publicity, grade inflation, and cheating. First, to lies.

Lies and Institutions

There are two perspectives on lying: that of the deceived and that of the liar. The presumption against lying is illustrated by the fact that lying needs justification; telling the truth does not. The core of deceit, rendering it morally unacceptable, is that a person is placed in the power of another. These remarks are, it seems, true of all cooperative contexts, from classrooms to marriages. In her authoritative book *Lying,* philosopher Sisella Bok (1978, chapter 1) suggests that once deceived and aware of it, the deceived is likely to find it more difficult to trust other people and their word. Consider, for example, the effect of a discovery of infidelity on the person betrayed: the deceived is rendered significantly powerless in a relationship. For the liar, however, successful deceit requires protection, lest he or she be unmasked. Successful lying, as Bok argues, may also open the way to other attempts, and the need to protect oneself will multiply, as well as become easier. Discovered lies influence social cooperation. They make everyone concerned less trusting, and moral corrosion sets in. In institutions large and small, telling the truth and not deceiving others are together the foundation of social relationships and the basis for partnership. Of course, there are levels of deceit. Direct lies are thought to be more immoral than evasions. So are lies in contexts where trust was an explicit part of the contract, as in teaching. Perhaps we don't care if someone lies to us about something we are not interested in. Remember, of course, that liars usually think their lies are justified, even if the rationale is selfish.

In educational institutions, the problem of deceit—that is, a flouting of truthfulness—takes many forms, of which three can be especially corrosive: institutional public relations, grade inflation, and cheating and plagiarism. There are many others.

If Jackall's (2009) complaint about the separation of language from meaning, and truth from reality, is pervasive in an institution, then there will be no concern for what is true. Institutional statistics, measurements, and public presentations, for example, can become so oriented to public relations that they positively mislead. This can run from mere overstatement to downright falsehood. Institutionally the danger is that everyone in the institution is complicit in the overstatement, in the contemporary jargon "spin," and either may have to support it or, worse still for the person, disown the official institutional statements. Universities now employ public-relations teams not merely to "sell the product" outside the campus but also to generate enthusiasm for the university within the student body. Institutional assessment generally is awash in student attitudes and does not much constitute a serious examination of the core of the enterprise.

A second example is grade inflation (see Carter, 1997, pp. 79–82). Carter believes that grading has collapsed as a serious enterprise (p. 80). That this is so is directly connected to the unwillingness of too many academics to be candid (see earlier section). Many academics and teachers feel obliged to be dishonest about the quality of student work both to students and to colleagues. Deceit becomes a habit. It corrodes what we do. We lose a concern for the truth. But why? Carter suggests grade inflation "stems from the desire of professors to avoid the guilty feeling that honest grading might generate, as well as a fear of being disliked by students, or perhaps simply a fear or arguing with them" (p. 80). We use the term "grade inflation" to disguise the fact that when we do this as teachers, we are being straightforwardly untruthful (and, of course, personal references fall into the same trap). Carter indicates a number of results from the practice. First, employers or other recruiters cannot rely on a student transcript. Second, working harder in the classroom, particularly important for minority students, results in grades that are unreliable, so that in employment competitions "the informal contacts become even more important and the old-boy network is back in business" (p. 80). This often drives students into taking courses where the professor is not a harsh grader, irrespective of whether the course is desirable for the student.

Cheating, specifically plagiarism, is also a significant matter of deceit in an educational institution. Recalling discussions with teachers about cheating (see chapter 3) forces us to realize that most people, however virtuous, are tempted to cheat, and we should examine our institutional practices to obliterate the opportunity. However, Judge Richard Posner (2007) writes that "an estimated one-third of all high-school and college students have committed plagiarism or a closely related form of academic fraud, such as purchasing a term paper from a 'paper mill'" (p. 8). Most intellectuals know that you are very fortunate in your work if you ever say or do something original, because what you say has probably been said before. Maybe, but we should also notice that some student plagiarism is not malicious or negligent in intent: some students, especially those not raised in the American tradition, may regard the replication of arguments word-for-word from some distinguished author partly as a tribute to the author's eminence, partly because they don't know how to say it better, and partly because writing it out is a way of fixing it in their minds. Such students may not therefore be intending to deceive, which is of course the core of plagiarism, where one presents the work of other people as one's own. (It is also quite different from copyright infringement. I may own the copyright of the Beatles songs, but if I present them as if I had written them, I would be plagiarizing, but not infringing the copyright.)

David Callahan (2004) reveals that plagiarism is not unknown among academics, but students are more likely to suffer more harshly if caught, a double standard that all but demonstrates the lack of academic integrity. "Plagiarism," writes Posner (2007), "is a species of intellectual fraud. It consists of unauthorized copying that the copier claims (whether explicitly or implicitly, and whether deliberately or carelessly) is original with him and the claim causes the copier's audience to behave otherwise than it would if it knew the truth" (p. 106). In the case of a student, "the fraud is directed at the teacher (assuming the student bought rather than stole the paper that he copied). But its principal victims are the plagiarist's student competitors, who are analogous to authors who compete with a plagiarist" (p. 106).

To answer a question on a paper or a test is to assert that this is what I know, and it is my own work. Where an individual has done neither by plagiarizing there is deceit, and, as Carter and Posner point out, others are harmed. At another level, cheating in learning is self-deceit. That is, if an individual writes a paper and implicitly says, "I know this," and he or she doesn't, it is the student's loss. Institutions frequently try to create a moral barrier against cheating through the solemnity of honor codes and making the responsibility fall on the student, but if Posner's figures are right, they are of singularly little help, indicating the ineffectiveness of such codes and their use as instruments of moral teaching, whatever their rhetorical value.

The moral problem of cheating in an institution is thus often defined as a moral weakness of individual students, but there is at least a case that the institution and its teachers are complicit. First, it is clear that those who cheat have not been brought up to face the question "Is a cheat the sort of person I want to be?" within a morally reflective stance, and that indicates that their teachers have done nothing to assist in that process of students' developing a self-identity. Second, cheating arises primarily from the social effects of competitiveness, rather than cooperation in learning, whereby a student need care about only his or her own progress. In other words, much more attention to students' producing work in groups would go some way to obviating the problem—though, of course, group teaching is much more demanding than lecturing to 350 students and getting multiple-choice questions or quizzes conducted by a teaching assistant, topped off with a term paper. (Sometimes, too, it appears as though administrators are more concerned with issues of test validity than they are about the moral aspects of cheating: witness the Education Testing Service officials and Jaime Escalante's students [Mathews, 1989].) Finally, more pragmatically, why is it not possible to remove this moral scourge in educational institutions by framing work in such a way that cheating is simply not an option because of the way the work is designed? It is surely possible to design assignments to which paper mills cannot produce answers, so that in the one or two instances where students copy the work of others, it is perspicuous, and students can be consistently taught how to describe, say, Mill's analysis of liberty in their own words. This is not rocket science and helps students realize both the gravity of plagiarism while simultaneously supporting the educational task. So cheating is something not to be stamped out by administrators, but for all teachers to regard as an educational challenge, either by being creative enough to design forms of assessment in which cheating cannot occur, or to teach young people to examine themselves and their identity as individuals. Preferably both.

Finally, a frequent arena in academic institutions for a lack of concern for the truth arises between those from different intellectual identities, say between an experimental psychologist and a qualitative researcher. Epistemological differences turn into personal animosities and vendettas, which are then fought out around tables where resources are distributed or where promotion and tenure are discussed. These characteristic academic struggles usually end up, as they have often begun, in simple untruths (sometimes about individuals) but more often about what they are purported to believe. It is interesting in this respect to recall how much detective fiction provides such a fertile context of the academy for jealousy, deceit, envy, and, of course, murder. This is related as much to the need to protect one's career, one's academic capital, as to any smoldering resentment or lack of appreciation for an alternative intellectual perspective. But intellectual animus turns academic units into warring tribes, and honesty is often the first casualty. A person who is unable to examine his or her biases is often an architect of self-deceit. This is especially true for teachers and will be a constant drain on their institutional integrity and individual moral personhood, such that they will not be able to instantiate the significance of the dimensions of truthfulness in their teaching.

Secrets and Gossip

Truthfulness is also often put to one side in gossip. First, a lack of concern for what is true appears at its most dangerous in intra-institutional gossip. Gossip is the sharing of secrets (Bok, 1982). It includes statements made about individuals where the teller and listener's purposes are not primarily to discern the truth, but to share what has been said by others, often told as a confidence. The actual items of gossip may have more or less moral significance; for example, "Did you hear that the dean's husband is going to wear a top hat to the White House reception?" is rather different from "Did you hear that Professor A is salting away money from his research grants?" or "Did you know that teacher X is a pedophile?"

The initial moral difficulty about such gossip is that it usually begins as a secret—that is, an item of information held in some degree of confidentiality. Then, as a way of institutional life, it feeds on itself, creating perspectives that are either inaccurate or not known to be accurate. This leads to (a) a sense by individuals that they are the subjects for gossip, and therefore threatened, and (b) the idea that gossip, true or false, is somehow rewarded. Take, for example, the kind of damage that gossip can do to a person applying for tenure in a university or, where it is possible, in a school. Applying for tenure is a context of enormous threat for the applicant, who can easily begin to feel like a victim, notwithstanding the rhetoric and the rules that usually dictate a clean separation between professional achievement and personal demeanor. Our interest in what the gossip may say frequently overrides our best judgment: most of us like to have knowledge, even if it is gossip.

Roberts and Wood (2007) are particularly trenchant in their critique: "What makes it gossip is that it is nosey. It is invasive, voyeuristic, and often has an invidious edge of put-down about it: and even if it expresses no bad will, it is often to the unjust hurt of another's reputation or to the violation of his privacy. The gossiper exhibits a defect of circumspection, of seriousness about the question: Is this something I, in my circumstances, am permitted to learn, or to pass on to this other in his circumstances?" (p. 175). Casting an ethical eye on gossip suggests that it can, for these reasons, be particularly damaging to institutions. It is not necessarily that gossips don't tell the truth, but invariably they qualify what they say with disclaimers, so the damage percolates unverified through an institution.

Of course, it is assumed that institutional leadership sets norms of behavior, and this implies understanding the character of governance. This is a huge topic, but it deserves our immediate notice. Universities in general pride themselves on being more like republics than corporations. Unlike corporations, which cheerfully embrace bureaucracy as an institutional form, universities profess to despise it (while enjoying some of its advantages), although in recent years, university administrators have begun to behave like corporate leaders. In particular, many presidents at all types of university institutions set exceptionally bad examples, for instance by being directors of corporations for which they are more or less lavishly remunerated (Goldschmidt & Finkelstein, 2001). Examine any set of faculty bylaws, and the committees elected are usually designed for representation of faculty rather than organizational efficiency. The primary problem with governance, however, is the paradox of leadership in a republic, a problem at least as old as Pericles and Cicero. Goodlad (1994, chapter 4) has a nice distinction between leaders who are power brokers, accepting the status quo and managing the relationships between the feudal baronies (or warring tribes) of a university, or transformative leaders who stake out a moral ground, hopefully with faculty support, and go for it. Nowadays, the growing model is that of the corporate executive, which presidents seem to follow, governing bodies seem to admire, the phalanx of administrators emulate, and faculty detest but are powerless to uproot.

Few leaders will welcome open governance, where transparency counts, even though O'Neill (2002) believes this to be an overrated virtue. For the power broker, secrecy is necessary to the deals he or she will make. The task will be to settle the differences (resource allocations, paid sabbaticals, additional posts) behind closed doors, before they are publicized. For the transformative leader, the trick will be to construct the debates on the institution's horizons so that opponents are finessed for lack of information. For the corporate executive, the task is to inhabit the position, not make it a job. The difficulty for the institution is that those matters on which secrecy, as far as possible, is important and justifiable—for example, to protect the personal life of an individual—can become a norm of institutional operation, denying any influence to those outside a given circle.

The impact of this brief analysis is that the quality of an institution is the responsibility of all its members. Truthful people need to take care of their institutions. These examples have to be seen as warnings, rather than judgments about institutional specifics or generalizations from empirical evidence. If we delude our "customers," are dishonest with our students about their abilities, fail to see how cheating undermines us, allow gossips, and cannot achieve a maximum of openness in our governance, then our institutions will be corroded. Trust is the primary quality that suffers. Truthfulness is the virtue demeaned. Institutions are, of course, purveyors of beliefs. They demand loyalty—of different kinds, and educational institutions from kindergarten upward seek to fashion those loyalties, in their own self-interest, but also in terms of members' understanding the obligations and demands of membership of a group. This can lead to vicious closed-mindedness, where students and alumni are blind to institutional weaknesses, refusing to confront them.

All of these issues apply to schools. "Institutions are like fortresses. They must be well designed and manned" (Popper, 1962, p. 126). At the core of a well-staffed institution is the trust that is based on individuals' truthfulness and the student body's being educated to value that virtue and cultivate that disposition. The ethos of a school, the pervasive moral attitudes that are invested in it, can be profoundly educative for children. However, the search for truth, the pursuit of knowledge, is also centrally a matter of belief, not merely truth. The second condition of knowledge, namely that A believes p, and its connection with open-mindedness, is the subject of the following chapter.

5

BELIEF AND OPEN-MINDEDNESS

> By and large, all of us are capable of being reasonable through being open-minded about welcoming information and through reflecting on arguments coming from different quarters, along with undertaking interactive deliberations and debates on how the underlying issues should be seen.
>
> *(Sen, 2010, p. 45)*

Coming to know people is, in large measure, coming to learn what they believe, because our beliefs are central to our lives. Indeed, the distinctive agglomeration of our beliefs makes us the individuals we are, because the beliefs we have are continuously implicit in how we think and act. It will be argued that such a grandiose claim ignores temperament, personality, and character. Yet if we consider an elderly Alzheimer's patient, it is apparent that the person, gripped by neurological damage, is losing a hold on reality, however rich and complex his or her past. A patient's temperament or desires may change in the course of the disease, but what is gradually lost is the conscious mind, full of all manner of beliefs that have enabled that person to sustain a hold on reality. At the other end of the life span, the neonate may have some temperamental attributes but is without beliefs, because he or she has yet to have a language within which a belief can be framed. While language may be the distinctive characteristic of the human being qua human being, it is the beliefs generated in thought through language that are a necessary constituent in a distinctive human individual. Our conscious mind, and therefore what we believe, has the major place in defining who we are. As Roberts and Wood (2007) put it, "we believe it to be a non-negotiable fact of human nature that human beings live by believing" (p. 193).

In section 1 of this chapter, the task will be first to give a more thorough account of what a belief is; then, in section 2, to locate the concept of belief in the classroom, through considering examples from Virginia's Standards of Learning, the interconnectedness and complexity of beliefs, and how they are differentiated, specifically in how we teach and how students learn. In section 3, the task is to answer the question of conscience: "Ought I to believe what I believe?" This question reaches far beyond those people we think are bigoted, prejudiced, or simply unable to face up to the facts of a case; it will have a major influence on both curriculum and pedagogy and will be another embodiment of the epistemological presence in a classroom. This question will be examined first in a context where we are acquiring or forming beliefs as learners (the discovery mode) and second where we are examining or revising beliefs we already hold (the critical mode).

In chapter 4, we have seen how truth and truthfulness are necessarily interlinked. Similarly, in section 4 of this chapter, the argument is that, if belief is grounded generally in matters of what we ought to believe, we must be equipped with the necessary habits, dispositions, and virtues to tackle our beliefs, specifically open-mindedness. If we seriously question whether we ought to believe what we believe, that is a necessary disposition or intellectual habit for us: to be open to considering alternatives to the beliefs we are acquiring, and to be prepared to discard beliefs we find to be incorrect. There is some psychological evidence that there are numerous inhibitors to open-mindedness and that it is rare and vulnerable (Peterson & Seligman, 2004, p. 159). But it is possible to teach it. However, if we consider such virtues as being fair or just, clearly we must be open-minded enough to examine evidence or our beliefs pertaining to a case where fairness or justice is required: open-mindedness, it might then be claimed, is fundamental to other virtues. Thus, as philosopher William Hare puts it, "Despite the fact that there is considerable disagreement about the presuppositions and implications of the concept, it is widely held that open-mindedness involves a willingness to form and revise one's views as impartially and as objectively as possible in the light of available evidence and argument" (1985, p. 3). Some of those disagreements can be examined through three topics, specifically when the person is acquiring and forming a belief (the discovery mode), critiquing and revising what we already believe (the critical mode), and the task of developing habits of thought congruent with open-mindedness (the procedural mode). Notice too, here, that open-mindedness is very different from being tolerant (but see chapter 11).

I. Dimensions of Belief

Many, but by no means all, of our beliefs are more or less rooted in evidence on the basis of which we can claim to know something, for we can believe things where the evidence is barely enough: hunches are beliefs. Our individual minds, however, are not filing cabinets with beliefs neatly stacked away; rather, our minds are cluttered with all manner of things: dreams, vague musings (that's a funny-looking dog), wonderings (will it rain tomorrow?), desires (I'd love to be able to ski), and imaginings (what would happen if...?). Our beliefs, too, can be manifest in our thoughts and words, and also, though not always, in our actions.

In chapter 2, we noted five features of belief.

1.   You cannot change your beliefs at will, as if you could choose to believe something one minute and its opposite the next. This is not a psychological

matter; it makes no sense to say, "Maybe we could change our beliefs in a minute if we tried a bit harder."

2. You can't believe *impossible* things—that is, things that are empirically impossible (Hitler is alive and well) or that seem impossible to you (there are fairies at the bottom of your garden).

3. You do not have to be conscious to have a belief, unlike with imagining: most of the things we believe are not simultaneously at the forefront of our thoughts.

4. Our beliefs are often, but not always, our achievements. We often have worked very hard to come to believe things: for example, 2 + 2 = 4 does not spring automatically into the thoughts or beliefs of a young child. To believe the truth of that equation needs work, whereas we have acquired many other beliefs just in our upbringing.

5. Finally, beliefs are different from other mental states, such as feelings and intuitions, or mental acts, such as intentions.

Yet how does this discussion about beliefs connect to teaching? Much of what we teach children is a matter of teaching beliefs about the world—its past, present, and future. Our curricula, at all levels of education, contain content knowledge—that is, beliefs that are true and for which we have evidence. Of course, we will on many occasions teach students and children to question beliefs, their own or other people's, and they may not be able then to make up their minds what to believe. The educational process is grounded in having students and children grasp ideas, facts, and considerations of all kinds that form in their minds as beliefs. So as we think about teaching children knowledge, we are in fact thinking first about teaching them beliefs.

We now need to push beyond these preliminaries.

First, it must be true that a person is the authority on what he or she believes. In this sense, belief is like pain. I know I have a pain—and while my doctor may feel my broken leg, she feels the broken bone, not the pain. Nevertheless, we frequently draw conclusions about what a person believes, not just from what he says, but from how he acts, just as we can tell a person is in pain if his broken shin bone is sticking through his calf. It follows that one cannot be mistaken about what one believes, though what one believes (i.e., the proposition) may itself be mistaken: just because I believe something does not make it true. Sometimes we may not "know what to believe" when presented with alternative possibilities, and, even "I don't know what I believe." And we tell other people that they "can't possibly believe that" but we are challenging the content of their beliefs, not the fact that they know what they believe.

Second, in the central case, any belief can be stated as a proposition: I believe "that" *p*. "There is now widespread agreement among analytic philosophers that belief is (roughly) a disposition, an affirmative attitude towards a proposition or state of affairs. To believe that p is to take it that p is true and that the state of affairs described by p obtains" (Chignell, 2010, p. 9).

As all propositions can in principle be true or false, so all beliefs are open to being examined for their truth, although in many cases that may be hugely difficult (e.g., my belief that what my horoscope says every morning will come true). So, to use Griffiths's canny phrase, "beliefs wait on evidence" (1967, p. 140), as "there could not be such a thing as belief, unless there were publicly intelligible standards of evidence and an actual tendency to use them: something like common sense, so to speak" (p. 142). Those standards of evidence, which will be examined in more detail in chapter 6, and the tendency to use them, are both intellectual and moral. We can thus always ask whether it is *appropriate* to believe this or that—to raise, in other words, the question of the ethics of belief, which we will turn to in section 3.

In sum, you can't just will yourself to stop believing something; you can't believe impossible things; having a belief does not demand that you be conscious of it all the time; beliefs are often achievements, and they are different from feelings. Finally, a person is the authority on what he or she believes, and all beliefs can be stated as propositions that open them up to questions of truth and falsity. These are formal attributes of the notion of belief, and they contain very little about the individual believer. How, for example, would one teach children to discriminate between the worth of different beliefs, for they are clearly not just one of a kind? Do people have strong beliefs about certain things, but weak beliefs about others? Presumably so: we all have beliefs that we regard as more or less important (see chapter 7). Roberts and Wood describe beliefs as having three worthy characteristics: "load-bearing, worthiness, and relevance" (2007, p. 156 ff.). This opens up the challenging issue of commitment to one's beliefs and to what one knows, which will also be examined in detail in chapter 8.

II. Connectedness and Complexity in Belief

Before examining the ethical questions, we must base all our questions about belief in the context of education and move into the more restricted territory of the curriculum, where the purpose of the enterprise is to have students come to hold specific beliefs and, of course, to test their truth or falsity. Yet beliefs taught in schools, as Hamlet said, come not in legions, but in battalions. We need therefore to examine both the interconnectedness and complexity of beliefs we hold, specifically those that are taught to children. The format of a curriculum in public education usually includes a list of learning objectives that describes content and method. The overarching epistemological objective is that children come to hold new beliefs about the world, to understand why they are correct, and to use methods of investigation or inquiry appropriate to those beliefs. In this section, the different dimensions of teaching new beliefs are described through samples from the Commonwealth of Virginia's Standards of Learning. We begin with Grade 3.

EARTH PATTERNS, CYCLES, AND CHANGE

3.8 The student will investigate and understand basic patterns and cycles occurring in nature. Key concepts include

a) patterns of natural events (day and night, seasonal changes, phases of the moon, and tides); and
b) animal and plant life cycles.

3.9 The student will investigate and understand the water cycle and its relationship to life on Earth.

Look at the epistemological features of the beliefs embedded in these standards.

1. The content of a belief is always *characterized by the concepts* in a language that constitute the belief. Standard 3.8 is rich in concepts that the student will come to understand—day, night, seasonal change, phase of the moon, tides, and life cycles, for instance. A concept is itself not a belief but an articulation of a phenomenon (life cycle) or object (moon) shared with all who speak the language. To say I know what a life cycle is does not necessarily commit me to holding any beliefs about it.

2. For understanding Earth patterns, cycles, and change, however, the concepts have to be framed in a coherent relationship, expressed in language as a belief—for example, "The energy from the sun drives the water cycle."

3. There are correct and incorrect uses of both beliefs and concepts. For instance, if a child says that "the water cycle derives the energy from the sun," the statement is not just an incorrect belief but displays misunderstanding of the concepts of the sun's energy and the water cycle. In acquiring new beliefs, therefore, students may be correct or incorrect about either a belief, the concepts that make up that belief, or, of course, both.

4. Once any concept or set of concepts is acquired, they are added to the individual's intellectual platform, or background (see chapter 1). This process, not logically or psychologically determinate as a process, occurs from the outset at the beginning of a child's life as he or she acquires language.

5. The acquisition of new beliefs and the concepts they contain demands not reciting definitions of concepts but *examining the truth of the beliefs* that contain distinct concepts as they are acquired through investigation. For example, a student could easily rote learn the concepts of "evaporation, condensation, precipitation" and define them accurately but, if faced with a puddle of water, have no idea how it came to be there. Watching a saucer of water evaporate under the sun, tracking the condensation from a steaming kettle,

or measuring rainfall as investigation of these concepts and their application itself enriches the dimensions of each of them.

This is manifestly a formal—some might say arid—account. First, it puts aside the huge variety of legitimate ways in which we use these concepts: for example, a student may know stories of the Man in the Moon, Jack and the Beanstalk, and other frames of imagining natural phenomena or cycles. The moon and moonlight have a significant place in romantic love stories and in horror stories. Think Harry Potter and his adventures. So the notion of correctness, as it has been used above, presupposes a particular epistemological context—for example, natural science. Second, nothing is implied here about *how* a student can be taught these new beliefs—that is, how a teacher constructs learning experiences so that the child investigates the world and comes to hold these beliefs. Third, the very aridity begins to suggest that something is lacking, namely how the individual stands in relation to these beliefs, which will be examined in chapter 8.

We have, however, indicated six elements in the teaching of beliefs, in this case in natural science: they were characterized by connected concepts, in a coherent relationship; their acquisition built background, though both concepts and beliefs can be incorrectly used and can be examined for truth. The Virginia Standards of Learning for sixth-grade English exemplify further the dimensions of teaching new beliefs, as it introduces complexity at various levels into what may have seemed a straightforward relation between concepts, investigation, and the acquisition of new beliefs.

The sixth-grade student will be an active participant in classroom discussions. The student will present personal opinions, understand differing viewpoints, distinguish between fact and opinion, and analyze the effectiveness of group communication. The student will begin the study of word origins and continue vocabulary development. The student will read independently a variety of fiction and nonfiction, including a significant number of classic works, for appreciation and comprehension. The student will also plan, draft, revise, and edit narratives, descriptions, and explanations, with attention to composition and style as well as sentence formation, usage, and mechanics. The student will also demonstrate correct u[se] of language, spelling, and mechanics by applying grammatical conven[tions] in writing and speaking. In addition, reading and writing will be [used as] tools for learning academic concepts, and available technology [used] as appropriate.

Sixth-Grade English

Additional dimensions of teaching beliefs, formally speaking, appear in this example.

1. The primary additional dimension of belief in the sixth-grade English frame that does not appear in third-grade science is the development of *the capacity to understand the beliefs of others* but not holding those beliefs oneself. The teaching objective is thus to have the student listen to the beliefs of others and understand them but not necessarily share them. The task is to learn how to entertain a belief and to hold it up for examination but not necessarily accept it as one's own—for example, by asking for further evidence to convince one of its truth.

2. That characteristic of understanding enables the differentiation of belief into two major types: a belief that is factual and thus based correctly in evidence, and a belief that may be based in evidence, but which people can honestly and seriously disagree about how the evidence counts—that is, use their judgment. These two dimensions require the development of language and thought that goes beyond merely descriptive analysis of phenomena, as in the third-grade natural science standard, opening up space for inquiry and beliefs about human intention and action, acts and consequences, hypothetical and categorical statements. Foremost, however, in this account, beliefs are rooted in the public world and public language. Group communication will involve negotiation on beliefs, on the concepts used, and on their meaning. In discussion and in making common judgments, we need to agree on definitions, as Wittgenstein (1971) pointed out.

3. Also required here is the development of the ability to reflect on and refine one's beliefs. Different from the methodology of investigation is the drafting and revising character of the work that is sometimes seen as merely technical—getting the periods, paragraphing, and quotation marks right. But, if such revision is thorough, it must involve thought about what is being written and expounded. In that sense, beliefs are open for change or modification.

4. The phrase "academic concepts" is presumably meant to imply the use of abstract concepts, rather than the concrete concepts of the third-grade natural science curriculum. We indicated earlier six elements in the teaching of beliefs, in this case in natural science: they were characterized by connected concepts, in a coherent relationship; their acquisition built background, though both concepts and beliefs can be incorrectly used and can be examined for truth. We can now add the significance of understanding the beliefs of other people, the difference between a belief based on clear evidence and a belief ▮ere judgment is needed, the development of reflecting on one's own be- ▮nd the development of understanding abstract rather than just concrete

Finally, to complexity and eighth-grade history and social studies standards:

ERA II: CLASSICAL CIVILIZATIONS AND RISE OF RELIGIOUS TRADITIONS, 1000 BC TO AD 500

WHI.4 The student will demonstrate knowledge of the civilizations of Persia, India, and China in terms of chronology, geography, social structures, government, economy, religion, and contributions to later civilizations by

a) describing Persia, with emphasis on the development of an imperial bureaucracy;

b) describing India, with emphasis on the Aryan migrations and the caste system;

c) describing the origins, beliefs, traditions, customs, and spread of Hinduism;

d) describing the origins, beliefs, traditions, customs, and spread of Buddhism;

e) describing China, with emphasis on the development of an empire and the construction of the Great Wall;

f) describing the impact of Confucianism, Taoism, and Buddhism.

(*History and Social Science Standards of Learning*, 2007 Department of Education, Virginia)

Clearly the level of complexity of the beliefs to be acquired by students through a curriculum rises through grade levels. As might be expected at the eighth grade, the level of complexity of the kinds of understanding that are to be taught here imply complex beliefs. Yet the complexity lies, according to this curriculum, in "describing" but not doing much by way of the analysis demanded by the sixth-grade English curriculum. "Demonstrating knowledge" is the requirement.

It does, however, illustrate some complexities. First, it is crucial for students acquiring new beliefs to understand the distinctive interrelationships of concepts in different areas of human action. Philosophers Hirst (1972/2010), Phenix (1964), and Oakeshott (1962/2010) have in different ways discussed the significance of understanding how concepts (and thereby beliefs) are connected within specific frameworks. For Oakeshott, human life can be understood through different "conversations," illustrated in his essay "The Voice of Poetry in the Conversation of Mankind." Hirst famously distinguished forms and fields of knowledge, while Phenix constructed the differences in terms of realms of meaning (see Further Reading).

If we examine the first eighth-grade curriculum statement with this in mind, it will be clear that in discussing the economy as opposed to, say, the religions of these different countries requires a set of concepts particular to that inquiry. Concepts like markets, bartering, trading, supply, and demand, which are in different ways interconnected in discussing a civilization's economy, are different from the interrelations of specifically religious concepts like nirvana, the divine, the afterlife, or reincarnation. Of course, there could be economic questions about a religion (how the religious institution finances its activities, tithes, land ownership, etc.), and there might be religious questions about an economy (e.g., is usury ethical?). But it would be crucial for students acquiring new beliefs to understand the distinctive interrelationships of concepts in different areas of human action.

These dimensions in the teaching of beliefs are formal, so they are not set out as a claim here that the growth in intellectual demands indicated in these examples are exemplars of conceptual development or that the formal dimensions have implications for pedagogy per se. However, if we are teaching students to know and understand things, we are teaching them beliefs. The rudiments of belief underlie the curriculum descriptions. A classroom with an epistemological presence will therefore imply teaching and learning in which:

a. new concepts and the correct and incorrect uses of those concepts through the framing of coherent sentences and statements are developed and acquired;

b. modes of investigation or inquiry relevant to those concepts, providing a platform for expanding understanding through those concepts, are acquired and developed;

c. learning beliefs demands developing the capacity to understand beliefs but not necessarily hold them oneself;

d. learners acquire and develop understanding of the distinction between factual beliefs and opinion-based beliefs and the role of judgment;

e. beliefs are articulated within the public language we have, and issues of fact and opinion are examined to illustrate the complexity of human actions and beliefs and how our beliefs may be described—for example, as hypothetical or categorical;

f. the capability to reflect on and revise beliefs in the light of that examination is seen both as a moral obligation (see section 3) and as a central requirement for living and flourishing within a constantly changing world;

g. understanding how all beliefs can develop complexity, especially within the different tasks of analysis and description, and for their coherence, will depend on understanding how there are different sets of concepts in addressing human practices or theories about those practices; and

h. these matters of belief will be clearly articulated and not be solely subsumed within curriculum content.

The direction of this discussion is to get at what teaching beliefs implies in the context of trying to get children to know things, below the level of describing any given curriculum. I have placed great emphasis here on the notion of belief, because of its connection to knowledge and truth and thus to the curriculum of the school. However, while it is very generally true that our acquisition of beliefs must imply that new beliefs latch on to those we already have in our belief platform, it is much more difficult to glean from this analysis a logic of curriculum and how it should be taught. One possibility, advocated by Hirsch (1999), is that we can chart a sequential step-by-step path to mastery of concepts and beliefs. Another possibility, advocated by Bruner (1977, p. 13), is of a spiral curriculum, in which concepts and beliefs are constantly revisited throughout schooling.

III. The Conscience of Belief: Ought I to Believe What I Believe?

Locke's *Essay Concerning Human Understanding* (1690/1979) begins with an overview of his task. In the brief section on method, he writes:

> It is therefore worthwhile to search out the bounds between Opinion and Knowledge, and examine by what measures, in things whereof we have no certain knowledge, we ought to regulate our assent and moderate our persuasions.
>
> *(chapter 1, section 3)*

His claim and his method is that we should not believe things for which we lack evidence, a sentiment very strongly put by Clifford (1877/1999): "It is wrong always, everywhere, and for anyone to believe anything on insufficient evidence." This may be called the "discovery" aspect of the ethics of beliefs, because it suggests content where we are acquiring new knowledge and forming new beliefs on the basis of evidence we have not heretofore entertained. But we should also examine evidence for the beliefs we already have, however firmly they are held. This may be called the "critical" aspect of the ethics of belief, because we are obliged to reconsider, revise, and critique our own beliefs, whether knowledge or opinion. In both the acquisition of knowledge and reflection on what we know and believe, there are ethical considerations apparent. A juror, in discovery mode, may listen to the prosecuting attorney carefully but not come to believe the defendant is guilty because the evidence offered does not support the conclusion. The juror next to her, however, listens and finds the evidence convincing as to the prisoner's guilt, but she ought to be in critical mode as to her own view of the evidence, because, say, she wasn't paying attention, or she finds the attorney's manner persuasive, rather than the evidence. Both modes are educationally, socially, politically, and morally important.

First, as we grow up, we free ourselves from our habit when young of believing that other people know things, such that we are in perpetual discovery mode: phrases like "young children are sponges" testify to this. But the critical mode signals that we have learned how to doubt. As C. S. Peirce (1877, p. 4) puts it, "doubt is an uneasy and dissatisfied state from which we struggle to free ourselves and pass into the state of belief." Doubt, as he describes it, is an irritant that can be solved only by inquiry, by "the settlement of opinion." However, Peirce describes the settlement activity, in terms of belief and doubt, in importantly interesting ways. He describes first the method of tenacity, as when we hold grimly to our beliefs, come what may, perhaps because we cannot cope with doubt, or despise reason, or simply prefer the satisfaction of "my opinion" (see chapter 8). Another way of describing those who cling tenaciously to unexamined beliefs is that they are intellectually intemperate (Quinton, 1987, p. 49): they are "over-ready" to believe, even gullible. But of course, we live socially, and unless we are hermits, we are going to hear other people's opinions that may shake our own. We are also, as Peirce reminds us, going to be more or less committed to the beliefs we have (see chapter 8).

Contrasted with the notion of tenacity in holding beliefs, however, is what Peirce calls the method of authority. He draws to our attention regimes, states, and systems of thought that can exercise a kind of tyranny over our thinking, practically and institutionally for the individual, for example, in the Inquisition or in Orwell's *Nineteen Eighty-Four*. This was not an original thought; both de Tocqueville in his famous *Democracy in America* and John Stuart Mill in his essay *On Liberty* warned of despotisms of convention or opinion. Modern media pundits can attract "followers" who then "intemperately" follow the beliefs that are put out without attention to their truth. In a modern idiom, "politically correct" thought can have a similar effect, even though, like some other dogmas, its intent is liberalizing. Yet this also can be an effect of partisan politics—for instance, when adherence to a particular political line becomes a so-called litmus test of acceptability or approval. That kind of authority can also occur in teaching—for example, when teachers insist on their viewpoint as correct and dismiss any deviation from it as eccentric or simply wrong—yet this, as we have seen in chapter 3, demeans the notions of both epistemological and moral authority. What, therefore, is implied in the notion of an ethics of belief?

The crux of the matter lies in whether we have a conscience about what we believe. We usually think of what we ought to do in terms of what we do, how we act, how we conduct ourselves. That can be equally true of what we believe—which is the domain of the ethics of belief. However, "the careful ethicist of belief will specify which type, if any, she means to be advocating, and whether one type has priority over the other" (Chignell, 2010, p. 5). There are three possible types of "ought": (a) *epistemological* ought refers to rules of knowledge, logic, and reason; (b) *moral* ought refers to how our beliefs are connected with the interests and concerns of other people; and (c) *prudential* ought is self-regarding only (p. 5). Putting the prudential type to one side, the difference between the other two can be put like this. The emphasis in the epistemological type will include not just those beliefs that do not impact other people (e.g., that the earth moves around the sun) but a general emphasis on just getting the evidence right. The moral type would be some kind of account of moral obligation to believe what is true—for example, because it impacts other people, or because it is bad for your character not to do so, across the range of justifications for moral behavior.

But the context discussed here is one of teaching and learning, not just social life, politics, or civil society in general. Philosopher Antony Quinton (1987) argues that the question of the ethics of belief, in discovery or critical mode is significant in teaching because the authority of the teachers compels students to attend to what teachers say and to accept it (p. 42). In discovery mode, too, teachers express beliefs on matters about which pupils have no opinions. So, when a class is first introduced, say, to slavery and the Civil War, the students will learn about these matters from a point of view. "This combination of institutionalized power with lack of resources for intellectual resistance to their influence imposes a particular responsibility on the teacher for the right ordering of beliefs they express in their professional capacity" (Quinton, 1987, p. 42).

Yet it is not just epistemologically important for teachers and students to get it "right." Children learning beliefs are learning about the world and, in so doing, developing themselves as individuals importantly, though not exclusively, through their teachers. The task then becomes to get children to see their own learning and development as a moral business, for them to develop a conscience about what they believe. The development of the discovery and the critical modes in children is effectively done within a moral classroom with an epistemological presence— that is, one in which the issue of "ought I to believe this?" is presented as both an epistemological and a moral matter.

The desirable dispositions, habits of mind, or intellectual virtues to be developed in children with respect to both modes include at least justice, fairness, temperance, and courage. That seems rather grand. But our sense of justice and fairness will give due weight to beliefs that are not our own. Temperance here refers in the main to the disposition characteristic of tenacity discussed earlier. Even when our beliefs are challenged, we may still want to cling to our beliefs. To reexamine our beliefs, fundamental or not, requires some measure of risk-taking, maybe intellectual courage. That reexamination may also become less psychologically daunting with practice.

But what then is the central point of this argument for the primacy of the moral in an ethics of belief? Quinton suggests two reasons, about ourselves and others. First, that we need to acquire better, more reasonable beliefs for ourselves— that is, to avoid the delusionary effects on us of false beliefs that will make our lives dysfunctional. This asserts the dominance of reason, because we can assume that people who hold tenaciously to erroneous beliefs do not regard their lives as dysfunctional, but they do not wish to examine what they believe. Second, that "this is a literally moral purpose because of the tendency our beliefs have to be communicated to others and also because of the influence they have on our conduct and thus on the welfare of others" (1987, p. 52). So, if we refer back to the opening paragraph of this chapter, with its description of how our lives comprise so many exchanges of beliefs, all communication of belief is appropriately subject to moral examination. Our lives can be changed by such exchanges, as when we say, "I had never thought of it like that before." Living in any community demands constant interchanges of beliefs, and when we make assertions, especially to those who are inclined to accept "authorities," we have a moral responsibility to them. This demands care; it is not a matter of upending other people's beliefs or mocking them. How we assert our beliefs also matters prudentially. "Paying attention to alternative views is a good strategy to discover our mistaken beliefs," which is both a moral and a prudential reason (Riggs, 2010, p. 177).

But engaging in critical reflection on one's own beliefs (as opposed to journaling about one's actions) is difficult along two parallel dimensions. First, its inherent difficulty for all of us is that we are facing changes that include, perhaps, the abandonment of beliefs and attitudes we have previously held. For this, there is, in general, little incentive and less motivation. Second, as our beliefs are a central part of our makeup, such difficulties are not merely matters of theory: as Belenky and colleagues would put it, they directly influence how we see ourselves, who we are. Self-protection can take many forms. In teaching freshmen undergraduates, it is a commonplace to find many individuals with fixed views about religion, politics, and many social issues. One form of self-protection embodying the resistance to open-mindedness comes from social determinism—for example, "My family are rich, so you would expect me to be a Republican," or "Marines don't think like that," both statements written by students in a recent class. Familiar to many teachers are attitudes of helplessness or class: "People like me don't go to college." To surround oneself with such cloaks provides an excuse, perhaps a reason, valid or invalid, for not facing up to the challenges that the ethics of belief present. But it is not merely social determinism or reluctance to take risks. For other students, there is an unattractive refusal to entertain other possibilities: it is as if they have gotten stuck, often as a result of high school work inviting their opinions, believing that their opinion is just fine and one need not engage in reasoned argument, or, God forbid, change one's mind. The concern in encountering too many freshmen with these views is that their schooling has clearly *not* had them face the moral question: ought I to believe what I believe? They have no conscience of belief. Students need to examine and be in awe of divergent opinions, views, pros and cons, or arguments, not just select a mast on which to pin their flag.

IV. Belief and Open-Mindedness

Following this examination of the characteristics of belief, how beliefs are built up with complexity and interconnectedness, and the questions in the ethics of belief, we can now examine open-mindedness, which seems to be both an intellectual and a moral virtue fundamental to the discovery and the critical modes of the acquisition of beliefs (see also chapter 12).

Several philosophers have contributed to our understanding of what open-mindedness is (e.g., Adler, 2004; Riggs, 2010). However, it is William Hare (1979, 1985, 2007, 2009) who is widely recognized as the philosopher whose corpus has most furthered our understanding of the virtue of open-mindedness: in his original formulation, he argued that a person is "disposed to revise or reject the position he holds if sound objections are brought against it, or, in the situation in which the person presently has no opinion on some issue, he is disposed to make up his mind in the light of available evidence and argument as objectively and as impartially as possible" (1979, pp. 8–9). Thus, as with truthfulness, open-mindedness is the property of a person. In Riggs's (2010) account, following Adler, open-mindedness is primarily an attitude toward oneself as a believer, rather than toward any particular belief, or the range of beliefs we hold (p. 180). It means that we are aware of our fallibility as believers, acknowledging the possibility that we are wrong. Yet there are some fairly standard ways in which we get muddled about the virtue of open-mindedness. First, it is important to see that open-mindedness is not in opposition to one's having strong beliefs, as if everything were always on the table. Being open-minded does not imply a paralysis of action, a continuous uncertainty because one ought to be open-minded about everything. Second, sometimes open-mindedness gets confused with tolerance, but a tolerant person might believe just one thing—people can do what they want and be very closed-minded about that belief (see chapter 12). Yet, in respect of acquiring or revising beliefs, open-mindedness is fundamental. Without this disposition, it is difficult to see how we can make any intellectual or moral progress. Belief and the virtue of open-mindedness are intellectually and morally integral, because having an open mind enables us to pursue the truth. This point may be put in different ways. Montmarquet (2000), for example, argues that open-mindedness is one of the virtues "*constitutive* of, and not just instrumentally related to, the project of free and responsible intellectual inquiry" (p. 140). In this view we change the notion of open-mindedness being fundamental to its being constitutive of belief—that is, inextricably part of it. One cannot, so to speak, do without it, especially, for example, when we have to consider questions of justice or fairness, because if we are not open-minded, it is difficult to see how our judgments can be fair.

Recall that psychologists tell us that the "importance of open-mindedness arises from the massive evidence that people are biased in favor of ideas that are already strong in their minds" (Peterson & Seligman, 2004, p.144). Open-mindedness might be not just fundamental but corrective. Though this closed-mindedness might be true of adults surveyed, questions arise for education. It is a sobering thought that 150 years of mass education has left us with a population that is predominantly closed-minded, which suggests that the role of education in closed-mindedness has been underrated. The task in schooling is not one of remediation. Education may have filled our minds with right answer conclusions, not interesting puzzles. The task is therefore not merely to give children a sense of certainty or the wisdom in holding strong beliefs, but to strive constantly for the consideration of alternatives as they grow and to lay down the habits of thoughts embedded in the virtue of open-mindedness in schooling. The teaching needs to be robust enough to have children grasp those alternatives and be able to explain conclusions that have taken alternatives into account and made a judgment, which is internal to open-mindedness, specifically in the sense of withholding judgment until avenues of inquiry have been examined. For that general outcome, closed-minded self-protection will not be needed. (For an excellent discussion of how the ethics of belief relate to the ethics of teaching, see Degenhardt, 1998.)

However, Siegel (2009) argues that, important though open-mindedness is as an intellectual virtue, we must recognize that people who are open-minded can also be incompetent in their reasoning and their critical thinking. Becoming open-minded, as he puts it, is "part of the journey toward becoming a critical thinker, not the other way around" (p. 32), which suggests that, in considering teaching, the development of both open-mindedness and critical thinking in the individual will be integral. Of course, as Forrest (2008) suggests, a person might be highly expert in critiquing the arguments of others but be closed-minded in respect of alternative arguments, a perspicuous feature of much political commentary. As critical thinking is a form of inquiry, Montmarquet's (2000) argument for a constitutive relationship between open-mindedness and critical thinking seems persuasive.

But if the distinction between a discovery and a critical mode of open-mindedness is useful, Siegel's argument seems strongly relevant to those who already have views that require examination—that is, in critical mode (referred to by Chignell, 2010, as "belief-maintenance" or "belief-relinquishing"), in which critical thinking is essential. In discovery mode (referred to by Chignell, 2010, as "belief-formation," p. 1), in which the initial grounds for open-mindedness and epistemic quality must be laid down by teachers and educators, the development of this disposition becomes critical in how the individual acquires and then examines beliefs. (See chapter 11 for a discussion of the critical thinker and the critical spirit.) Moreover, if we follow Riggs and see open-mindedness as an attitude toward oneself, its development will focus more on how the individual establishes an identity as open-minded, recognizing the fallibility of one's beliefs, rather than on the epistemic quality of one's capability as a critical thinker. Educationally, both seem critical if the child-learner is taught to see him or herself as in charge of his or her own moral and epistemological status.

Finally in this chapter, the task is to examine the two modes of open-mindedness but add a third describing the habits of thought needed. The three modes are:

1. open-mindedness in the context of forming a belief (the discovery mode)
2. critiquing, reflecting on and revising what we already believe (the critical mode)
3. the task of developing habits of thought congruent with open-mindedness (the development mode)

The discovery mode. There is profound moral importance in the fostering of open-mindedness in children. To begin with, many of the beliefs we hold as teachers and that we convey to children are likely to change under new circumstances, new discoveries, and new attitudes. For this, children have to be prepared.

The challenge can be well illustrated through the eighth-grade information-based curriculum described earlier. There is no particular reason why that curriculum, as it stands, could instill or develop open-mindedness, because there is nothing much in the content to be open-minded about. So the first criterion in the discovery and acquisition of new beliefs that encourages open-mindedness must involve *consistent consideration of alternatives* to ensure the learner appreciates that there are different ways of looking at events, eras, and cultures. No such controversies or alternatives appear in that eighth-grade curriculum outlined earlier. For example, in each civilization discussed there are substantial controversial issues—for example, the Indian caste system that Gandhi attacked. Why could the curriculum not outline some of these controversies? Through that trajectory of learning, children can discover that knowledge is, to a greater or lesser extent, provisional.

The term "discovery" matters here. To discover something is an achievement, though it can be done by accident. (Learning by discovery has a long and muddled history in educational thought.) But the intentional *procedure* for setting out to make a discovery is one in which alternative scenarios or interpretations are examined and discarded, then reexamined and modified in the light of the purported object of discovery, a procedure not necessary in just gathering information. This is at the core of any theory of inquiry, particularly in Dewey's theory, with its "emphasis on the situational, the transactional, the open-ended, and the social" (Schön, 1992, p. 122). The classroom situation in which the development of open-mindedness is a target is one in which teachers and learners participate in the sophisticated procedure of exchanging ideas in the open social context of the classroom. Discovery mode, however, demands the entertaining of different approaches and different sets of beliefs beyond the trivial. For example, in a classroom we might argue about whether a whale is a fish or a mammal, but the controversy, if there is one, does not get far beyond definitions. But a much tougher, non-trivial discussion for an elementary classroom might be whether we should make margarine out of whale oil, which would provide a practical context in which the pros and cons can be elaborated, alternative policies and commitments developed, all of which, for most children, will be a discovery. Equally, in William Hare's (2007, p. 208) example, the activities of Christopher Columbus provide, for a classroom, a different kind of voyage of discovery, away from the glib certitudes of patriotism.

Manifestly the constant examination of alternative explanations or interpretations presents teachers with various types of challenges, dependent on the content. Forrest (2008) examines the difficulties in exploring sensitive topics of controversy when a student might be a person "acutely affected as a result of having been directly involved and/or having experienced the reality to which the controversy substantively refers" (p. 83). She uses such examples as teaching *The Merchant of Venice* when there are Jewish students and providing abortion statistics in health education programs. A second type of pedagogical problem arises when a teacher wants to reach consensus after discussion of alternatives, for example in having children examine the relationship between the American pioneers and Native Americans, but then search for consensus judgments on what was "right." This is not, of course, to argue, that everything should be open-ended, but divergence of view should be encouraged, notwithstanding the pressure for class unity, not least because that would respect the epistemological presence.

The critical mode. The critical mode is one in which we critique, reflect on, and revise what we already believe. In practice, the development of the discovery and the critical modes may run together. However, we develop attitudes toward how we hold our beliefs. At one end, we might be skeptics, distrusting on principle anything claimed by anyone; more sensitively, like Francis Bacon, we could adopt a general principle of systematic doubt. At the other end, we might have beliefs for which there is not, and cannot be, evidence—for example, in the realm of blind faith as opposed to a faith that is constantly troubled, searching for reasons. And everything in between. (The most subtle and developed account of reflection as applied to professionals is Donald Schön's [1995] analysis of reflective practice as knowing-in-action, reflection-in-action, and reflective conversation with the situation.)

The promotion of open-mindedness will be far more easily facilitated in a classroom with an epistemological presence where the spirit of cooperative inquiry, rather than knowledge accumulation, is dominant. Riggs's view of open-mindedness—that is, open-mindedness as a personal property—is particularly pertinent here, and it takes us back to the quote from Belenky and colleagues at the beginning of chapter 1. Children cannot begin to approach such questions as "What is truth? What is authority? To whom do I listen? What counts for me as evidence? How do I know what I know?" with any rigor without having the epistemic quality of Siegel's discussion, but the reflective capacity underpinned by open-mindedness. The closed-minded resistance of many of us can be preempted by teaching children early how to handle reflection on their beliefs and articulating to them what open-mindedness is—in other words, opening up for them epistemological secrets. There are dangers: some children may feel rewarded just by changing their minds, by adopting a flavor-of-the-month attitude toward what they believe. Such children will believe anything you tell them as long as they get an A. The central task of the critical mode is to engender confidence in one's beliefs alongside the commitment to reexamine them, not merely when challenged, but as a moral responsibility.

The development mode. What then are the habits of thought that need to be addressed in the development of open-mindedness? Paul and Elder (2009, p. 21) suggest five problems of egocentric thinking, which are common to the development of critical thinking and the open mind. Those pertinent to the discovery mode in open-mindedness are (a) innate egocentrism, where "humans do not naturally consider the rights and needs of others. We do not naturally appreciate the point of view of others nor the limitations in our own point of view"; (b) innate sociocentrism, which assumes the views of my family or my peers or my culture are correct; and (c) innate wish-fulfillment, believing what "feels good" where believing what puts me in a good light, no change required and no need to admit I was wrong. More relevant to the critical mode are (d) innate self-validation, where a person has a strong desire to maintain beliefs he or she has without wanting to examine the evidence and (e) innate selfishness, where what I believe (right or wrong) gives me power or personal advantage of some kind.

Paul and Elder's use of the word "innate" here seems to be too strong, especially when used of socio-centrism, because it does not seem obvious that we are born with these tendencies, though manifestly our culture and upbringing may instill them in us. That apart, it is not difficult, even in the elementary school, to see these as obstacles to the development of open-mindedness. Positively these obstacles show, respectively, the need for an epistemological presence in classrooms, where teachers work constantly at:

1. The notion of knowledge as provisional and the development of a strong sense of alternatives to counteract the egocentrism;
2. The consistent construction of alternatives;
3. Reinforcing constantly the characteristics of being open-minded;
4. Helping children find validation and success in the development of the dispositions and habits of thought of open-mindedness; and
5. Undermining displays of the self-protection characteristics outlined earlier.

In each of these, any of us may have such cognitive weaknesses as non-evidential belief, overconfidence, bias, or rushing to conclusions (Siegel, 2009), all of which can defeat the development of an open mind.

Missing here is an account of judgment, for judgment is the quality of balancing competing kinds of claims—for example, from different virtuous possibilities—and understanding their complexity (see chapter 6). Judgments can be correct but their implementation a disaster. However, making good judgments is not something that can be taught, though wise and experienced teachers can prod students into examining and reexamining their judgments such that such self-reflection in the critical mode does become habitual. Good judgment arises from constant reflective practice, again, an achievement of one's own initiative, and that is a substantial element in the virtue of impartiality, to which we now turn.

6

EVIDENCE, IMPARTIALITY, AND JUDGMENT

> We can never survey our own sentiments and motives, we can never form any judgment concerning them; unless we remove ourselves, as it were, from our own natural station, and endeavor to view them as at a certain distance from us. But we can do this in no other way than endeavoring to view with the eyes of other people, or as other people are likely to view them.
> —*Adam Smith,* A Theory of Moral Sentiments *(1759)*

The connection between knowledge and virtue has been examined so far through establishing criteria described as public and professional knowledge and examining those virtues specifically connected to one or other of the six features of knowledge identified. In public knowledge, truth has been linked to the virtue of truthfulness. Similarly with the criterion of belief, as the core of public knowledge, a person will need to be virtuously open-minded if he or she is to either acquire new beliefs or examine those he or she presently has. The third criterion of knowledge, the evidence condition, demands impartiality; this is the condition of knowledge usually described as justification for what one knows—that is, on what grounds A *believes* p to be *true.*

Sections 1 and 2 of this chapter expand the brief account of evidence, warrant, and justification given in chapter 2 by first discussing philosophical approaches to the justification a person needs if he or she is to be said to know something—in this case, a proposition. In particular, I explore the relationship between justification and judgment, suggesting that the type of justification appropriate will rest on the context of the assertions being made. However, such justifications and judgment raise immediate questions about objectivity and subjectivity. Section 2 thus describes three separate kinds of differences between the objective and the subjective—the ontological, the epistemological, and the perspectival (Dancy & Sosa, 1992, pp. 310–312), with comments on how these distinctions occur in curriculum. Any account of assertions being objective or subjective, however, fails to get us into the perspective of the agent, especially whether he or she has examined evidence impartially. Section 4 will then contain an explication of impartiality as an intellectual virtue, its intimate connection to objectivity, and the role of individual judgment in coming to impartial or non-partial decisions, essential in the examination of evidence. The questions faced in the discussion of judgment raise questions of the individual's perspective and thus will lead directly into part III, where the focus is on personal knowledge. Manifestly the development of judgment is a central feature of the classroom with an epistemological presence.

I. Approaches to Justification in Knowledge

Philosophers have discussed for centuries what are the necessary and sufficient conditions for the statement that A knows p. Some have followed Plato's original line and argued that knowledge is the height of mental achievement—in his view, higher than belief or opinion. Others have followed David Hume's eighteenth-century skepticism about knowledge, except with regard to empirical statements, and A. J. Ayer (1952) notoriously wrote *Language, Truth and Logic* to argue that no statements other than empirical or analytical statements had meaning: moral, religious, aesthetic statements were mere expression of emotion. A complete survey of how philosophers have tried to give an account of what knowledge is has to be left to one side (but see Ayer, 1957; Williams, M., 2001; Woozley, 1966). But let us pick up from chapter 2. A believes that p is a *necessary* condition of A knowing p, but this one criterion is not *sufficient,* at least because A can believe that p where p is false. A person who thinks he or she knows that p must believe p, but of course he or she may be mistaken. Similarly for A to know p, on this account, he or she must not only believe it; it must be true. But the belief condition and the truth condition are not enough either, because a person may have a true belief (e.g., that Spain will win the World Cup), but he or she cannot be said to know it before the event. So if we are searching for necessary and sufficient conditions for knowledge, knowledge cannot just be true belief. So, while most would agree about the first two conditions (belief and truth) as necessary to knowledge, the claim is that they are not sufficient. The search for justification follows: A knows that p; p is true; but how does he or she know? How can someone justify his or her assertion that he or she knows p? While most philosophers believed this third condition was necessary, establishing exactly what it is has proved highly contestable.

Some stressed that A must have evidence for p—that is, the "knower" must be able to produce evidence or data supporting his or her claim to know. So, for instance, if we think of forensic evidence produced in a murder trial, DNA for instance, to support the attorney's claim that Joe Bloggs murdered Jane Doe, this data is clearly connected to support the truth of the claim. The evidence matters. We can see that this should be true of all scientific and historical explanations where it might be thought they will provide a definitive answer, even though, as Phillips (1987) points out, contemporary science recognizes the significance of interpretation, though it still aspires to be value-free. Philosopher A. J. Ayer (1957) suggested that the third condition should be understood as the "right to be sure," which backs off the need for evidence as such and covers, so to speak, a much wider range of social and personal life. Neither the view represented by Hume (see Noonan, 1999) nor that represented by Ayer have won assent, especially since Gettier (1967) showed that the three conditions as established simply could not produce the necessary and sufficient conditions for knowledge, the elixir philosophers were after.

Yet this led to some speculation as to whether the search for a third condition was even appropriate; maybe this type of justification account was, so to say, like an examiner's view of knowledge, with the social context of knowledge not unlike an examination hall (see Williams, 1973, p. 146). That is, this requirement seemed to turn the realm of knowledge into some kind of quiz where in response to every assertion interlocutors or conversationalists are constantly asking, "How do you know that?" The account of knowledge thus distorts the human conversation where there is continuing exchange of beliefs and knowledge, a social fact that the search for necessary and sufficient conditions seemed to neglect.

Moreover, the tough-minded conditions for evidence neglect that we hold our beliefs in manifestly different ways—for example, uncertainly, vigorously, or defensively. Nevertheless, out of the wreckage of the third-condition debate appeared a quite new approach. Philosopher Ernest Sosa explains: "we have reached the view that knowledge is true belief out of intellectual virtue, belief that turns out right by reason of the virtue and not just by coincidence" (Sosa, 1991, p. 277, quoted in Sosa, 2009, p. 24–25n). This rejects the third condition as solely a matter of evidence and opens up what is called virtue epistemology. In writing of the virtue epistemologists, Roberts and Wood (2007) write: "All these philosophers accept the general model of knowledge as adequately grounded (warranted, justified) true belief and seek a conception of such grounding or some supplement to that grounding, that enables them to specify the logically necessary and sufficient conditions for any beliefs being a case of knowledge" (p. 9). There are two main alternative views.

First, several philosophers (e.g., Sosa, 2009; Greco, 2010) interpreted the third condition in terms of the *reliability* of the person claiming to know. If someone says "I know p, on this argument," what we want to know is whether the person is reliable—in other words, whether he or she has certain moral or intellectual virtues, truthfulness for example, that would make him or her a person on whom we could rely for the truth of what was said. Axtell (2000) explains:

> To attribute an action or belief to the workings of an intellectual virtue is to identify its ground with an attribute of the agent that is still more stable and less fleeting than is a skill: Sosa requires that justified beliefs be generated by a genuine power or capacity or competence of the agent to arrive at truth, and it is such powers of persons that are identified with intellectual virtue.
>
> *(p. xvi)*

In other words, we are justified in saying that we know something if we have the "power, capacity, and competence" to arrive at the truth, and presumably if people who have such power, capacity, and competence share their knowledge with us, we too could "rely" on that person's power, capacity, or competence, and thereby on his or her judgment.

Second, other contemporary philosophers (e.g., Hookaway, 2000; Zagzebski, 1996) argue that it is not just a matter of reliability but of responsibility. As Hookaway, quoted by Axtell (2000), puts it:

> Justified beliefs are those that issue from the *responsible* inquiries of virtuous inquirers [my italics]. It is a mistake to put it the other way round: epistemic virtues are those habits and dispositions that lead us to have justified beliefs. The primary focus is on how we order activities directed to answering questions and assessing methods of answering questions; it is not upon the epistemic status of beliefs.
>
> *(p. xiii)*

In the reliabilist perspective, as Axtell puts it, virtuous character is defined in terms of successful and stable dispositions to form belief, whereas in the responsibilist perspective questions of epistemic status are "decentralized in favor of agency and inquiry" (Axtell, 2000, p. xiii; see Further Reading).

From this brief survey, which does scant justice to the excellence of decades of philosophical work, two conclusions may be drawn: (1) human beings can *reasonably* claim to have knowledge, but *reasonably* use different types of justification in different social contexts, and (2) on the many occasions in which we are acquiring knowledge in either discovery or critical mode, we will need to make judgments about the reasonableness of what is being asserted. Each of these can be dealt with in turn.

II. Justification, Context, and Judgment

Virtue epistemology in both reliabilist and responsibilist modes puts the agent at the center of justification, rather than the quasi-independent justification that comes from the discarded evidence condition. Those modes are hospitable to all agents, provided they decide and act reasonably, which will include attention to virtue. Our beliefs range over the whole of human experience, and if we take the agent as the justifier, in the infinitely varied social context of our conversations, we are likely to base our judgments, as agents, using different criteria of justification, *criteria appropriate to the context*. That we can reasonably use *different* criteria of justification is illustrated in the following examples.

1. A criminal court wants to know about the innocence or guilt of the defendant. The criterion of "reasonable doubt" emphasizes that, while jurors will consider the witness's veracity (and thus reliability), their main focus will be the evidence presented and how it connects to the crime.

2. A conference of scientists wants to know the precise details of the hypothesis, the experiment, the results, and whether it can be replicated. Members of the audience will no doubt take into account the wisdom, experience, and reliability of the presenting scientist, but they will likewise direct their attention primarily to the evidence.

3. Two patients in a doctors' office want to know what is causing the terrible pain in each of their stomachs. Patient Tom (who has had trouble with doctors before) wants all the pathological details of his rotten appendix and what alternatives there might be, which the doctor answers, no doubt, with the help of one of those charming plastic models perspicuous in doctors' offices. Patient Bill simply accepts his doctor's word for his problem, because, Bill believes, the doctor has responsibly done all the examinations and tests, in other words, made "virtuous inquiries." Both are differently justified in saying that they know they have appendicitis.

4. Patient Carlos has just been diagnosed with colon cancer, following various scans and examinations. He goes to the doctor who has Sosa's "power, capacity and competence," which make his judgment reliable. However, a patient diagnosed with cancer is frequently in a quandary about knowing what's wrong with him or her and what should be done and as often as not, has himself to make a judgment as to the desirable treatment. Typically, an oncologist will produce an analysis of the grade of the cancer, how aggressive the tumor is, and then offer a set of alternative scenarios, maybe surgery, maybe radiotherapy, maybe a bone marrow transplant, maybe just "watch and wait" and, depending on how serious it is, some indicators of life expectancy (e.g., "too early to tell," "six to nine months," or "make sure your affairs are in order"). The phenomenon of cancer is such that predictions can be very unreliable, though the oncologists themselves may not be. They give it, as we say, their best shot. So Carlos has to work with the knowledge as far as it goes: he is looking for "power, capacity and competence" and "virtuous inquiry," but that doesn't get him very far. At the end of the day, he factors in all kinds of issues about himself and his family, no doubt—and he may deceive himself on this. Even if he accepts the reliable doctor's judgment, a second opinion to the contrary throws him back on his own judgment.

5. Jill is the principal of a school and a woman of great character and commitment, with stable moral views and virtues. Parents and faculty see how equipped she is with practical reason based in her sense of who she is. So they always accept what she says is right—say, in coping with a troublesome child, because of the practical wisdom that emerges from whom she has become. They take the truth of what she says such that they then see the situation as she does: their justification for taking her view is her authority as a reliable and responsible person who is both competent and virtuous. Yet, given the social context of the school as an institution, they are being guided professionally, such that all kinds of justifications can reasonably be provided for

their taking her point of view—that is, what she sees as the case. Interesting here is the fact that, if they ask for evidence, Jill can probably only point to past cases that contribute to practical wisdom but cannot be knock-down evidence, as children differ in significant respects.

These different cases are not a typology of all possible ways in which we can be said to know things. But they do suggest that there will be different reasonable sorts of justification for different contexts, avoiding thereby any view of our knowledge as based on some kind of Platonic continuum (our senses, opinion, belief, and knowledge), on some scientific type of objectivity with palpable evidence, or into the reliabilist or the responsibilist camp. In the mind of the agent, the line between knowledge, true belief, opinions, and mere beliefs is invariably fluid. We cannot, in our social contexts, postpone commitments to taking any particular proposition as true. We often don't have the luxury of waiting on being completely convinced. None of this is to deny the significance of our beliefs being guided by a search for truth, but we do so, and make judgments, guided by what is reasonable.

Judgment and Justification

The second conclusion is this: judgment is integrally connected to what we come to believe. Of course, many of our beliefs become habits of thought unquestioned in our social life. Our judgments on events, other people, and the world in general can become habitual: Trojans should never trust "Greeks bearing gifts" given the experience of the Trojan horse. But frequently, and especially in discovery or critical mode, we have to make judgments. To make a judgment is to "arrive at a decision or conclusion on the basis of indications and probabilities where the facts are not clearly ascertained" (Abercrombie, 1965, p. 29). Mathematical calculations are either correct or incorrect and frequently require no judgment; knowing your mother's maiden name likewise. A necessary element in the acquisition or examination of knowledge will be the agent's capability to scrutinize the world, on the basis of an impartial disposition, which alone can lead to a sound basis for judgment, if not one that is wise, elegant, or clear. This is to emphasize, first, that all knowledge claims are made "from a point of view" that much knowledge is provisional, and the development of judgment is a crucial capability in coming to know and to explain to others in what Oakeshott (1962/2010) called "the conversation of mankind." Adam Smith (1759/1976) focuses on how we look at ourselves:

> We can never survey our own sentiments and motives, we can never form any judgment concerning them; unless we remove ourselves, as it were, from our own natural station, and endeavor to view them as at a certain distance from us. But we can do this in no other way than endeavoring to view with the eyes of other people, or as other people are likely to view them.
>
> *(III 1.2, 110)*

But this could not be true of everything on which we judge: Smith is describing the role of the impartial spectator, as if there were something called "an independent point of view" (see Sen, 2010, pp. 124–126), but we can still adopt an impartial view of the world without the metaphor of the spectator, which Thomas Nagel (1989) calls "the view from nowhere."

Of course, judgment must also be cognizant of three initial factors. First, to repeat, we can learn a little about the problem of knowledge from those young children who test our patience with interminable questioning. Human judgment and dialogue, the child is unwittingly pointing out, is necessary to evidence. Second, our beliefs should (see chapter 5) constantly change in the light of new evidence, so our judgment will be consistently tested. Third, some evidence we want may not be publicly accessible. That is, a claim to knowledge could arise from a person's private experience, so it is a matter of judgment on our part, not just whether that person is reliable or responsible, but whether that kind of justification is sufficient. However, before examining judgment in more detail, and the complexity of scrutiny and making sound judgment from an impartial point of view, it will be useful to get clearer about objectivity and subjectivity, the extent to which our judgments can be objective or, as some claim, that all judgments are merely subjective ("well, that's just your opinion") or, as some philosophers have suggested, "inter-subjective."

III. Objectivity and Subjectivity

"The first essential is that a conception of objectivity must establish a public framework of thought sufficient for the concept of judgment to apply and for conclusions to be reached on the basis of reasons and evidence after discussion and due reflection" (Sen, 2010, p. 62). My stance toward arguments about objectivity, subjectivity, and relativism is limited here to pointing them out and giving a point of view, but also insisting that these matters not be treated as epistemological secrets. We need to have children grow up understanding them, because these controversies influence every aspect of our lives, not just those of intellectuals, since ideas percolate through contemporary thought, influencing politics, art, education, and religion. These distinctions, though not familiar to many teachers, are not that complex and are part of the basic structure of what we know and who we are. "Any idea or problem or body of knowledge can be presented in a form simple enough so that any particular learner can understand it in a recognizable form" (Bruner, 1968, p. 44). But the sharing has to be much more than just telling. Clearer perspectives emerge when teachers and learners together share contemplation of, or actions upon, the world (its objects, theories, values, and other mental properties). *As subjects we look at objects, individually or together.* In terms of our concerns with belief, truth, evidence, commitment, experience, and identity, we must engage in shared contemplation (or conversation, or action, or transmission of information). Teachers cannot assume childlike naïveté, otherwise children will never grow out of it. This discussion of objectivity and subjectivity is simply a starting point for teachers, but it demonstrates the significance of how knowledge is viewed and by whom, an understanding to be nurtured in a classroom with an epistemological presence.

There are three ways we can look at the distinction between the objective and the subjective (see Dancy & Sosa, 1992, pp. 310–312):

> The objectivity and subjectivity of things (everything from mountains to dreams)
> The objectivity and subjectivity of beliefs and theories
> The objectivity and subjectivity of perspective

Objectivity and Subjectivity of Things

The first contrast relates to the existence of "things." All natural phenomena—for example, the sun and moon, the rocks composing the Grand Tetons, and the water in Lake Superior—can be said to have objective existence. Contrasted with these objective things are the subjective events in the world—my dreams, sensations people get at a rock concert, desert mirages, and human desires of all kinds. The subjective things have to be experienced by conscious human beings, in some respect, to exist at all, whereas the Grand Tetons would still be there even if everyone on the planet died this minute, and there was no one to see them. This use of the objective or subjective is labeled "ontological" because it is connected to the existence of things, not to how they are perceived.

Objectivity and Subjectivity of Beliefs and Theories

But, most of our time in life is taken up with thinking (in a general sense) about things, whether they are external and real to us (like the Grand Tetons) or private, internal experiences (like our dreams). So the second contrast of the objective and the subjective belongs within our views of what knowledge is, our beliefs and theories about the "epistemological." Our beliefs, our theories, our judgments, and indeed everything that it makes sense to call "a mental act" are the subject of this contrast, not questions of existence. Yet they are obviously connected. Searle (1999) puts it like this:

1. "Suppose external realism [e.g., that the Gulf of Mexico exists] is true. Then there exists a real world, independently of us and our interests.
2. If there exists a real world, then there is a way that the world really is. There is an objective way that things are in the world.
3. If there is a way things really are, then we ought to be able to say how they are.
4. If we can say how things are, then what we say is objectively true or false depending on the extent to which we succeed or fail in saying how they are." (p. 15)

So we can accept Haley's claim about Kunta Kinte not merely as true, but as objectively true, if there is sufficient warrant in the evidence, and that is how things were. Therefore when we say something is objective, we are claiming (rightly or wrongly) that what we are saying is true and that good evidence, warrant, or justification can be displayed, to which anyone who took the issue seriously would assent. When we are saying something is subjective, epistemologically, our claim is that either (a) the types of claims being made lie outside the possibility of evidence—that is, are rooted in personal experience—or (b) we are just stating a point of view without making any claim to knowledge. So the statement "I know Shakespeare is a better poet than Robert Frost" looks objective. It makes a claim independent of my personal preferences, but I could still say, "but I prefer Frost." The preference would be subjective, however, because we might think that aesthetic claims to knowledge can't be objective. On the other hand, if I say, "I prefer Frost to Shakespeare," then we would ordinarily say that this is just an expression of your preference and is thereby subjective.

Objectivity and Subjectivity of Perspective

The third contrast is an offshoot of the second. It is an attempt to distinguish claims or points of view that are, as Bell puts it, "non-perspectival" (and thereby objective) from those that incorporate a perspective (and are thereby subjective) (see Dancy & Sosa, 1992, p. 311). Here is a typical non-perspectival report of a police officer watching a suspect. "The subject was observed proceeding down the road, putting his right hand on the front driver's-side door of each motor vehicle as he passed." This is in marked contrast with the following perspectival report of the same police officer: "I saw this villain scurrying furtively down the road, checking each car door to see if he could steal anything." Or (non-perspectival) "Shakespeare is a better poet than Robert Frost"; (perspectival) "I prefer Robert Frost to Shakespeare." Obviously, the first seeks to be devoid of any kind of evaluative comment, and that includes obliterating from the account the actual observer. The second, on the other hand, puts the observer as the "subject" of the sentence.

However, philosophical argument rages around these two rather innocent descriptions of the non-perspectival and the perspectival. First, few now continue to argue that there can be any such thing as a claim to know anything outside a point of view. This includes the idea of the "impartial spectator" that Adam Smith put forward or, in another context, John Rawls's characterization of an ideal society based in justice (see Sen, 2010, especially chapter 2). It is a relatively trivial point to say that I see my son sitting there and I am seeing him from a point of view. Polanyi, as we have seen, spoke of nothing being objective (in the non-perspectival sense), because we become committed to the theoretical frameworks within which we hold beliefs about phenomena. Yet, some contemporary philosophers argue not merely that there can be no such thing as a non-perspectival view (as with the police officer) but that nothing *exists independently* of our linguistic description of it. There are no such things as "facts of the matter" (or, for that matter, the Gulf of Mexico), they say, only our utterances about them. This means, of course, that the notion of a "reality check" on anything at all is impossible. It would also deny such philosophers the possibility of wishing that things could be other than they are, because that wish admits an objective reality (Williams, 2002, p. 140).

Relativism. There is, however, one final consideration critical to these three contrasts (the ontological, the epistemological, and the perspectival). Teachers will confront relativist views daily from their students at all ages, even if they don't hold to relativism themselves. Some claim that the whole epistemological system within which anyone works, the weight that one gives to issues of truth, the very understandings that constitute all the epistemological elements that have been outlined, may be fine for this society, this culture, or this era in which "I" am. (Such claims almost never say "we" rather than "I.") But people in other societies, cultures, or eras, it is claimed, may not view these matters in the same way. Just as there is no totally "objective" perspective, so it is claimed, there is no "absolute" (i.e., overriding) epistemological system. All systems are *relative* to each other. None is absolute or dominant. Rather, an epistemological system is always de-pendent on the context—the society, culture, or epoch in which it exists.

This is an important claim because it is so familiar. Is it correct?

First, it could be regarded as true but uninformative. Of course, we can say, the epistemological system I am describing in this society is *in some sense* depen-dent on the society, culture, or epoch in which I am living, just as I said it was my view of *my* son sitting in the chair. But in what sense is the epistemological system dependent? To begin with, where else could it come from but the society in which one lives? But the emptiness of this way of putting it raises the question whether there are similarities in outlook, perspective, or epistemology in all or some societies. Relativism arbitrarily puts the emphasis on differences, rather than similarities. Why stress one rather than the other? Science would seem an obvious "international" language, with common criteria of truth and methodology. The problem is that relativists are not sufficiently discriminating. Surely there will be some cultural patterns—for example, in attitudes toward women or the upbring-ing of children—that are different, yet there are also cultural similarities in the upbringing of children, for instance, not least that natural parents are, in general, responsible for them.

Second, were self-respecting relativists to ask the question "Is relativism cor-rect?" they would find themselves in the *peritrope* trap. That is, asking whether it is correct, they are presumably appealing to some super-system in terms of which it can be judged, and for relativists no such system exists. Put the other way around, relativists are claiming that their view of epistemological systems is true for all sys-tems and they are therefore themselves claiming at least one overriding truth—of some non-relative kind. But that claim defeats the claim they're making. They are saying "All claims are relative excepting, of course, our claim that 'all claims are relative,' which is itself 'absolute,' applying to everybody." That, to say the very least, is a self-contradiction. Whether that will convince relativists is another matter! (For a much fuller account of relativism and its problems see Williams, 1985, chapter 9.)

Historically, we can see the attractiveness of relativism, especially in moral matters. Moreover, we need to separate relativism with regard to the past and former societies from our contemporary world. The problem may be not that there is no universal morality but that where we find differences with other societies (e.g., over human rights in China) we don't know what to do about them politically; a relativist shrugging of the shoulders won't do. Notice that "relative" need not be the same as the insistence that everything is "subjective." We could say that all epistemological systems are relative to societies, cultures, or eras, but, as a matter of fact, in societies X and Y (but not mine), people believe in moral and other absolutes, and those who don't may suffer the consequences. Without some such distinction between their relativist claims as distinct from a claim that all claims, wherever they are made, are subjective, relativists would have difficulty in explaining such phenomena as the rule of the Iranian Ayatollahs and their beliefs about the Koran.

In historical and social matters, we have witnessed the gradual erosion of the view of knowledge-as-certainty rooted in a tough-minded demand for evidence to be replaced by a much more skeptical view of the world (building on Bacon's principle of systematic doubt). In science, too, the "quest for certainty" has been seriously undermined in the twentieth century by such books as Thomas Kuhn's *Structure of Scientific Revolutions* (1996; but see Searle, 1999). Kuhn portrays the instability of science as a discipline producing knowledge that is fixed; rather, as with Einstein's and Newtonian mechanics, knowledge even in science is relative—in the obvious proprietorial sense—to particular epochs. Equally, relativism seemed anthropologically coherent from the massive human mobility beginning around 1500. Immigrants to America who disagreed about their Christianity but tolerated divergence sowed some relativist seeds. When colonial and imperial administrators from Europe did not own much land, they tended to allow the "natives" their own belief systems, not a novelty in human history but stretching back to Cyrus II of ancient Persia and to Ashoka in India (see Sen, 2010, chapter 3). This was to accept implicitly that it was "right for them." This was more a matter of morality and politics than epistemology at its initiation.

However, as a final problem with relativism, the relativist does run into some practical and moral difficulties. Do we really have nothing to say about Nazis who turned killing people into a bureaucratic industry except "Well, seems pretty terrible to me, but, you know, everything's relative"? As Bernard Williams (2005, chapter 6) has pointed out, it is not something built into morality that we should not interfere with other societies or that we should just accept what other societies do. We may be politically puzzled as to what to do, but that is not a consequence of moral relativism. None of this is to say that we should self-righteously ignore or take no notice of the moral experiences of human beings who happen to live in other societies and cultures or to have lived in other eras and think of ourselves as somehow morally superior, or, worse still, to demean their experiences by regarding them as merely of mild interest. Far from it. Approaching our lives from both a moral and an epistemological perspective, to dismiss as irrelevant the experiences of those societies is to cut ourselves off from important potential sources of wisdom and moral improvement, once we define cogently what counts as "another society."

The issues of relativism are therefore manifestly important in classrooms, especially in a country with as much national power, multiculturalism, and civic patriotism as the United States. But so, of course, are the differences between the disciplines and what the character of judgments are within them. So while the solution to the epistemological problem of objectivity in the arts may elude us, the range and complexity of our understandings have to be passed on to children, because the aesthetic motive is as powerful in its way as the moral motive. That is, a scientist, a historian, a mathematician, or a philosopher, like a painter, a poet, a writer, or a pianist, may be as much moved by the aesthetic in his or her work as by its pragmatic outcome. Elegance, form, style, and coherence are aesthetic terms all of which apply to most human activities, from making love to developing a mathematical theorem (see Eisner, 1979; Saw, 1971).

Similarly, is nothing about history objective? This is, of course, a hugely complex question. (Christopher Blake, quoted by Dray [1964, p. 39], thinks it is a silly question, like saying "Are stories interesting?") However, though history will not reveal "objective" fact in the ontological sense, that does not mean, as some authors and pundits think, we can just make it up. Facts about the past do not exist like the Gulf of Mexico exists. Within the epistemological contrast of objective and subjective, however, there are rules that must not be broken. Once a work appears, the community (historians and or the rest of us) will form our own judgments as to its truth—seen as a true interpretation. This is not objective in a strict sense, but it is not subjective either. We can call it epistemologically "inter-subjective" to convey that everyone who has a serious interest can make a judgment about it. Consensus among those who have examined it carefully, if we accept the theories with which they start, is sufficient for us to claim knowledge of and for that interpretation. Usually, we will have differing interpretations. Reaching those interpretations requires impartiality.

IV. Impartiality and Judgment

Impartiality is an intellectual virtue. For example, when 10-year-old Samantha's parents meet with the principal, her teacher, the guidance counselor, and the district psychologist to review her behavior problems and to discuss the relative merits of different actions they might take, they will be expected to be impartial. "A is impartial in respect R with regard to group G if and only if A's actions in respect R are not influenced at all by which member(s) of G benefit or are harmed by these actions" (Gert, 1995, p. 104). That these be all honest people, even that they be open-minded, is not a necessary part of their being impartial. We might, of course, anticipate that both parents and her teacher will support Samantha strongly, but the object of the discussion is to come to an agreed judgment. Frequently we think of impartiality as connected to such roles as the umpire, the referee, or the judge, where the intellectual capability to be impartial is a central description of the role (in addition to keeping time, for instance). Notice, however, that in Gert's formulation, the context must be one of the impartial agent making a choice among alternatives, in this case, which course of action will best help Samantha. Of course, if the context was, say, a Pentagon contract rather than a child's grow-ing up problems, the relevant officials are making an award and their actions are of clear benefit to one or another of the parties concerned; but we do not expect the umpire or referee to "give the game" to one or other of the protagonists. We should also remember that Mafia leaders can be impartial, though their judgments and decisions are immoral, so our assumption is that those involved in Samantha's future will be benign, but that might sometimes not be true.

We can put the intellectual virtue of impartiality another way. A is impartial in respect Q if and only if A's *judgments* in respect Q are formed by the examina-tion of alternatives in such a way that each alternative is given intellectual respect in coming to those judgments. By respect is meant giving each alternative dili-gent and due consideration. That does not imply accepting them. As an ideal, we would expect jurors in both civil and criminal cases to be impartial, and attorneys seeking to discover whether this or that juror is suitable will be especially inter-ested in whether the prospective jurors *can* be impartial. Equally, we would expect those involved in Samantha's case to listen carefully to contradictory viewpoints and weigh the issues impartially. Whether they can or not raises the question discussed by Jollimore (2006) as to the cognitive requirements of being impartial. He mentions this problem in respect of moral impartiality, but the problems are equally difficult in impartiality as an intellectual virtue. He notes arguments that no judgment or point of view can be detached from the situation, as it is impos-sible to adopt an unsituated point of view (see Young, 1990), and/or our emo-tions and commitments will always enter a judgment. Samantha's parents and her teacher may be in precisely this "situation." (For an extensive discussion of ethical objectivity, see Stout, 1990, passim, and Sen, 2010, especially chapter 5.)

If impartiality as an intellectual virtue means that in coming to a judgment each alternative is given intellectual respect, then like other virtues, it is to be seen as both an aspiration and a disposition. It refers to the way we think about those alternatives; the virtue describes a way of coming to a judgment, not an outcome of that thinking. Therefore, even those who are virtuous in respect of impartiality may have biases of which they are aware, may simply make mistakes, or may be obliged to make a judgment (as with Samantha's principal) of which they are un-certain. The implications of this account for teaching are complex: can we teach judgment? It is clearly not like the timing that a tennis prodigy would bring to the game. It would seem important to be less concerned with the outcome than developing the habit of mind, the disposition to be impartial.

Critical to this account of impartiality as an intellectual virtue is the act of judgment that is the primary outcome, since it implies a decision, of the exercise of the virtue. Yet judging is, as Ryle (1949) would put it, a task-achievement verb. That is, we can see not only the outcome of a judgment but the task involved in making a judgment. An account of impartiality is therefore incomplete without some analysis of judgment. First, while there are certain common elements to judgment, any judgment is necessarily context-bound. Making judgments about where to send your children to school, or, as executor, how your intestate grandmother's possessions should be divided are very different contexts requiring judgment based on "the facts of the case." (There is a perhaps old-fashioned use of the word, in which one would say of someone that he or she lacks judgment or, of course, that he or she has excellent judgment. Roughly, there is an implication here about experience giving a person a certain intellectual quality.)

But a person's judgment (task sense) leads to a judgment (achievement sense). The conclusion is the outcome of an episode in which inferring, estimating, and evaluating the evidence is conducted. It is not difficult, if we think of Samantha's case, to imagine all kinds of possible and probable outcomes that have to be taken into account; facts may not be all that clear, so inferences may be needed. We may need to interpret what may be not clear and even almost unintelligible: in some cases, as with the intestate grandmother, we may have some memories of what she once said she wanted. We would then need to check with other family members, friends, and others, if we are to arrive at a judgment of quality, just as the principal might want to talk to Samantha's previous teachers, because judgments, like all other conclusions, can be hasty, ill-considered, unfair, or downright stupid. The judgment that arises from the disposition of impartiality may turn out to be a mistake of some kind, but it will have examined alternatives and been assiduous in comparing and evaluating those alternatives. Judgment can be suspended—that is, a decision or conclusion may not be reached and the matter left open. We heed the maxim *not* to rush to judgment, especially when our concern is impartiality. In the paradigm case of a judge, a formal judgment may take some time.

However, in terms of the application to education, one of the most fascinating (and groundbreaking) books about judgment for any educator is psychologist Minnie Abercrombie's 1965 work *The Anatomy of Judgment*. Her argument is as follows:

> In receiving information from a given stimulus pattern we select from the total amount of information available, (that is, from the complex of the stimulus pattern in its context) and from our own store of information. The receipt of information therefore involves making a judgment, but in many cases (as for instance in seeing familiar things) this is done so rapidly and automatically *(i.e. habitually)* [my italics] that we are unaware of the extent

of our personal involvement in the act, tending to regard the information as given. In such cases we might obtain alternative selections from the information available.

Many factors of which we are unconscious influence our judgments, both in cases where we are not aware of making any (as in seeing) and in those where we are (as in evaluating evidence from an experiment)... we might make more valid judgments if we could become conscious of some of these factors.

(p. 172)

Abercrombie's work was conducted over five years with medical students in London, England. Such students would have been highly intelligent and successful in high schools, both because only a small number of any age cohort in Britain at the time could gain entrance into universities and because medicine was regarded as a highly prestigious career path. Thus, while full of information from biology, chemistry, and physics, the students found difficulty in going beyond the information given. Abercrombie sought to bring an epistemological presence into her class through creating discussion groups in which her guidance was minimized and dialogic space was open, thereby having students think about themselves as knowers and thinkers. Each group of students, annually, engaged with several topics—for instance, understanding observer error in using instruments, descriptions and inferences, the use of words (What is "normal"? What is "average"?), classification, and evaluating evidence. In each of these cases, a controlled test showed that those students who had taken Abercrombie's course made "much sounder judgments" (p. 158).

There are, however, some critical elements to a student's development of better judgment. First, Abercrombie's course challenged what students thought they saw with their own eyes. "Knowledge of the external world obtained through sight is conditioned by one's own mental processes, and this shook the students' previously held belief in the concreteness and permanence of physical things." Second, the pattern of teaching through lecture was abandoned; whereas students had relied on what was "correct," they now found difficulty in changing the views they had acquired, and, to a large degree, were frightened of change itself. Third, students were initially highly dependent on authority, whether of experts or the teacher, and the process of weaning them from that dependence created some classroom hostility. Crucial, for our purposes, is the fact that these elite students should arrive from high school at the university with these very weak intellectual characteristics, similar to Perry's (1970) later work with Harvard students. They knew a lot of stuff, but not much about knowledge.

Students thus appeared to enter university, in general, with fixed views, with commitments that x is the case, to search for the "right answer," and to have developed this attitude through constant exposure to authority in the classroom that ignores the epistemology and fails to take students constantly into the realm of systematic doubt. This is both because of the pedagogical situation—for example, the teacher as the dominant factor in the classroom—and because of the way the information is given, tested, and frequently forgotten. Left behind is an intellectual mind-set that resists doubt at the very time when the young mind should be open and in the search for knowledge. Without open-mindedness, a search for truth, and the ability to see the world impartially (examining each alternative conscientiously), it is difficult to see how students can make cogent judgments. At the crux of Abercrombie's experiments is that students had to test their views against those of other students, to open themselves to challenges and serious inquiry in open dialogue. Of course, just as the medical students were fixed with the perceptions they treasured and found change difficult, so teachers have to examine the models of childhood they work with that influence what they think children are capable of.

V. Toward the Epistemological Presence: Preliminaries

We have now reached the point at which the different characteristics of public knowledge have been explored in terms of their relationship to truthfulness, open-mindedness, and impartiality. This is an appropriate juncture at which to articulate, in a preliminary way, the central features of the classroom with an epistemological presence where children or students will reflect on who they are, how they interact with their teacher(s) and their companions, and the character of their beliefs and of the knowledge they are examining. They will come to understand the relationship between their public and private personae and how much or how little of their lives is within their control. Classroom encounters will be infused with moral attitudes and questions, even in the teaching and learning of science and mathematics. They will have a teacher who understands the dimensions of his or her moral and epistemological authority.

The students can expect to confront three primary types of questions: about what the beliefs are within the subject matter they are learning, how they reveal themselves in how they learn, and how both questions are embedded in the search for truth. They will therefore come to understand the difference between public and personal knowledge. They will constantly be involved in dialogue among themselves, becoming confident enough to understand the messiness, the ambiguity, and the provisional character of much that is called knowledge. That will yield questions, teaching, and discussions in which there are no hidden secrets, in which different interpretations are welcomed and demanded. In particular, students will develop a conscience about their beliefs, welcome the puzzles and uncertainties the search for truth brings, and, be confident in being open-minded, making judgments between alternatives, and placing high value on accuracy and sincerity.

The search for truth will bring moral and epistemological encounters. Discussions may yield personal animosities that will need to be revealed, but the careful development of truthfulness will also create a profound atmosphere of

or vice
versa

mutual trust. The classroom can embrace a balance of competition and cooperation, without any competition being for extrinsic goods, because the search for
truth is seen as its own reward. Such a classroom will develop a kind of intimacy, in
which coming to know other people becomes an understanding of not just their
personality, but what drives them, what they believe about the world. Teachers and
learners will support each other in the struggle to be virtuous, especially in regard
to the challenges of truthfulness, open-mindedness, and impartiality. Central to
such an experience will be to understand the limited value of opinion—that is,
one in which certainty is expressed, rather than sought for. Children will still
develop strongly and soundly held views, but they will recognize the possibilities for error. Questions about what is good and right, interpersonally or in the
quest for truth, will inhabit the classroom, not merely be occasional visitors. The
educational development of the child is one that embodies both knowledge and
virtue, properly understood, and that produces criteria for judgments about both
teaching and learning. Above all, the child in such a classroom reflects on him or
herself as a person learning and is confident to take initiatives in that learning.

PART III

Virtue and Personal Knowledge

Introduction

Personal knowledge consists of three elements: experience, commitment, and identity.

An individual's experience, first, is located in time and space, culture, family, generation, education, even epoch or era. This may be called the *historical individual,* and that aspect of a person's experience describes individuality of memories, intentions, intuitions, understandings, perceptions, and introspections and reasons. To this notion of experience as a source of personal knowledge will be linked the virtue of integrity, not as a synonym for honesty or uprightness, but integrity as wholeness.

Second, to repeat, it is "a non-negotiable fact of human nature that human beings live by believing" (Roberts & Wood, 2007, p. 193). However, a distinctive aspect of belief is how individuals holds their beliefs—that is, the levels of commitment for the *belief-holding individual,* which opens up a critical feature of human life—the will and in particular the virtue of courage.

Third, the human individual creates an identity or, to some degree, has one shaped for him or her. This is not something constructed in youth and then fixed through to old age. Identity describes, differently from the historical individual, the *self-conscious individual,* incorporating metaphorically the stages of life that Shakespeare describes in *As You Like It.* One's identity is whom one sees oneself as, and identity is closely integrated with the virtue of self-knowledge.

The articulation of these three "individuals" is a device to focus on the three elements of personal knowledge and, of course, they overlap. Memory, for example, is here examined under integrity, but it could equally well be examined under personal identity where, perhaps, it has a more logical home. But, as Warnock

(1987, pp. 61–62) puts it, "It is the concept of myself as the recipient and posses-sor, the systematic organizer of experiences, that is central. Memory could neither exist, nor be valued, if this center of experience, the familiar self, did not exist." However, unlike public knowledge, where the criteria of truth, belief, and justi-fication have been established philosophically for some decades, this account of personal knowledge is idiosyncratic, and other philosophers might emphasize dif-ferent characteristics. The account given here springs directly from the questions posed by Mary Belenky and her colleagues (see chapter 1) that urges us to ex-amine the person who is a knower or seeker rather than simply the formal condi-tions of knowledge: "Our basic assumptions about the nature of truth and reality and the origins of knowledge shape the way we see the world and ourselves as participants in it. They affect our definitions of ourselves, the way we interact with others, our public and private personae, our sense of control over life events, our views of teaching and learning, and our conceptions of morality" (Belenky et al., 1986, p. 3).

Chapter 7, on the historical individual, begins with a focus on the voice and the eye. The significance of the voice, especially in feminist literature, draws our attention to ways in which people can be silenced and, positively, the idea that we need to find our voices to find out who we are. The voice is not a single instru-ment; it is always part of the orchestra of conversation in which many voices, each with its own timbre, tone, and emphasis, find space in the dialogues of human life. In chapter 1, we noted the case of Virgil from which the notion of what we see things as emerged, and here we examine not only the potential for error when we use sight as a source of our personal knowledge, but also the intellectual control we exert over what we see. But specifically, there are three capabilities that power experience, memory, intuitions and understandings, and reasons and motives. This account of experience as a feature of the life of a human being is connected to in-tegrity as a virtue, which, following David Norton (1995), is seen as having three main features: (1) the integration of separable aspects of the self into a consistent whole, (2) "wholeness as completeness," by which integrity is distinguishable, for example, from fanaticism or monomania, and (3) a deeper kind of honesty, with which integrity is not to be equated. The epistemological presence in the classroom will require articulate voices, discriminating eyes, and an emphasis on the integrity as wholeness of the child as seen in the three types of capability that power experience.

The second aspect of personal knowledge can be examined through the no-tion of the belief-holding individual. In chapter 5, we noted the significance of the conscience of belief, and this chapter extends that discussion, examining how difficult we find changing our beliefs or altering our misconceptions of reality. Commitment to what we believe is, morally speaking, dependent on the worth of the belief: we cannot admire a commitment, say, to exterminate Jews. The place of commitment, however, is articulated by Michael Polanyi (1962/1974) in his attack on the idea that science is objective. He argues that the scientist becomes committed to the beliefs about the world that he or she has: indeed, commitments become passions. This is of considerable importance for the epistemological presence in the classroom, because as children acquire beliefs (the discovery mode) and examine their beliefs (the critical mode), they will need to avoid the various types of flaccidity and rigidity that imperil commitments that have moral worth and clarity. Yet we can control what we believe: the beliefs we have we can choose to accept or reject. Believing is, with some qualifications, a matter of will. It is therefore argued in chapter 8 that courage is the intellectual and moral virtue congruent with commitment. We can be committed to beliefs yet lack the intellectual courage to examine them. On the other hand, we frequently take risks in what we believe, not necessarily in terms of what others might think, but because they upset our equilibrium. Nowhere is this more apparent than in questions of encouragement, when we seek to put courage into people, a task essential to the development of the confident child in a classroom with an epistemological presence.

Finally, in chapter 9, we turn to the self-conscious individual, raising those questions of identity central to understanding oneself. Identity can be personal, social, and within a political order. If children and students are to develop a coherent sense of self, they must expand the horizons of their language, cultivate an imagination about themselves, continuously reflect on what they value and what is of most worth, and set their dignity and self-confidence as autonomous selves within the framework of autonomy and rationality. Distinctive of personal identity is autonomy—that is, the ability to manage one's life. However, a person's identity is also complicated by the roles that the individual plays, and there is a distinction of importance between a philosophical and a sociological conception of a role. The sociologist's use of the word "role" must be distinguished from the philosophical use that is focused on a role's obligations, its rights and duties, specifically the teacher's role in a moral space and a political order. Particularly important for education, too, is a teacher's identity as a citizen, and whether or not it is a role. However, identity as a source of personal knowledge creates a major challenge: that of knowing oneself. Clearly other people assist us in the creation of our identity, an especially important dimension of teaching. But the account of self-knowledge makes it a matter not of beliefs about oneself, but how a person constitutes him or herself. Our self-knowledge is thus not a matter of applying the criteria of knowledge to our self-knowledge, but that *self-knowledge is the process of constituting ourselves through understanding who we are, and it is that understanding that will require intellectual and moral virtues.*

7

EXPERIENCE AND INTEGRITY

The Historical Individual

> The existence... of personal and social knowledge which the subject cannot even adequately express, let alone justify: these things do not stand opposed, in some mysterious way, to a rational and scientific picture of what the world is like.... The role... of the reflective and self-conscious in human affairs is indeed a serious issue, but it is not to be thought of in terms of replacing weather-magic with meteorology.
>
> *(Williams, 2006a, p. 52)*

Polanyi (1962/1974) wrote that human beings "must inevitably see the universe from a center lying within ourselves and speak about it in terms of a human language shaped by the exigencies of human intercourse" (p. 3). He is not denying that there is external realism (Searle, 1992), but he is emphasizing the place of the individual in how we view the external world, a rather different vantage point from Adam Smith's impartial spectator. This argument in his book *Personal Knowledge: Towards a Post-Critical Philosophy* introduces us to personal knowledge, and it will recur throughout this part III. We begin with experience and the historical individual: It was noted in chapter 2, first, that experiencing something is not just about objects getting in touch with our senses, as if the sudden warmth of the sun on our skin on a spring day was the paradigm of experience. Second, though we can share an experience with others, like watching an eclipse, flying across the Atlantic, or being in a house (or a classroom) together in a power outage, few experiences are the same for everyone. Third, "Nobody has... *an* experience without bringing to bear on the raw materials of an encounter with the world the cultural resources that allow him to turn it into *an* experience" (Ryan on Dewey's view of experience: 1997, pp. 337–338), a fact that complicates any teaching task. Fourth, our experiences seem private, unverifiable, and, as such, privileged; yet this is not necessarily so—if we are in conversation, in a dialogic space, and we are committed as responsible people to facing up to Belenky and colleagues' questions, we can examine another person's experiences with them (and vice versa), but there has to be that space, a characteristic of the epistemological presence in a classroom. Experience, however private, can be shared. Finally, the historical and cultural identity with which a child has been brought up will in turn influence how he or she sees the public knowledge encountered in classrooms. As John Dewey put it, "No one would question that a child in a slum tenement has a different experience from that of a child in a cultured home; that the country lad has a different kind of experience from the city boy, or a boy on the seashore one different from the lad who is brought up on inland prairies" (1997, p. 40).

Knowledge of ourselves and our knowledge of subject matter will become interdependent, whatever the variety of our backgrounds. One classic danger in teaching is to ignore the children's real-world experiences and provide for them ersatz experiences that they understand are unreal. Children, as human beings, develop their own voice through such public modes as dance, song, art, poetry, music, science, sports, and politics, and from the background of their family or culture, they contribute to the human conversation, interpreting and reinterpreting their own experience. A conversation both invites givers and rewards receivers. It is no surprise that the question facing the ordinary person "To whom do I listen?" contains the implicit question "Which voices are worth hearing?" (Belenky et al., 1986).

In this chapter, the task is to examine what one might call the organs of experience: the *voice* in dialogue, in conversation, and in the articulation of experience; the *eye* in perception, in how we see things *as;* and, less important epistemologically, the *ear* as the listening vehicle. In section 3, the focus shifts to an examination of those human capabilities that power experience—that is, memory, perceptions and introspections, intuitions and understandings, and reasons and motives; and how this range of mental phenomena are located in a classroom with an epistemological presence. Finally, in section 4, experience is connected to the virtue of integrity, in which integrity is portrayed as personal wholeness to which our experiences contribute positively or negatively, not as a synonym for honesty.

I. The Voice as an Organ of Experience

Words like "dialogic," "interlocution," and "conversation" presume the use of the human voice. The voice is not simply the words we speak or write, any more than a person is simply a human body. The words, as Wittgenstein put it, only create the rough ground on which the voice can begin to move. All voices are individual. The vast range of possibilities that the human voice provides is a startling reminder of its power: compare Luciano Pavarotti, Lena Horne, Martin Luther King Jr., Michael Jackson, Anthony Hopkins, Ray Charles, Winston Churchill, Rod Stewart, Stephen Hawking, Franklin Delano Roosevelt, Adolf Hitler, and Alex Haley's griot. The human voice is not just expressive in terms of emotion, music, or poetry; it is the physical vehicle of speech in a language through which we convey our experience, wants, needs, ideas, and musings to others, precisely, oratorically, or rhetorically. "The whole of us, it would seem, is included in the compass of the human voice" (Rée, 1999).

Manifestly, the power of a voice can be a vital instrument in political power in different dimensions, but people's voices (*vox populi*) can be silenced by tyrannies, only to explode when regimes fall, for example in Eastern Europe in the 1990s or in the Mideast in 2011. Classrooms, too, can silence individuals: there certain voices, often those of boys or young men, can drown out or silence the voices of girls or young women. It was Carol Gilligan's (1982) book *In a Different Voice* that illuminated this educational problem for women. In 1986 there also appeared *Women's Ways of Knowing: The Development of Self, Voice, and Mind* by Mary Belenky, Blythe Clinchy, Nancy Goldberger, and Jill Tarule (1986) from which the quotation with which this book opened is taken.

In the research of Belenky and colleagues, the experiences and self-understandings of women are intimately connected to how they view the world epistemologically and how they view the strength of voice that they have or do not have. The women interviewed were a heterogeneous group—of different ethnic, academic, social, and class backgrounds—the target being to "describe... epistemological perspectives from which women know and view the world" (1986, p. 15). The place of the voice was not anticipated as these researchers began their work. They were surprised by how frequently women interviewees used metaphors of voice, not sight (as in Descartes or Plato), to explain their epistemological perspective. The authors therefore "adopted the voice and silence metaphor as their own" (p. 19). Five main epistemological categories emerged in this research: *silence, received knowledge, subjective knowledge, procedural knowledge,* and *constructed knowledge.*

Silence is "a position in which women experience themselves as mindless and voiceless and subject to the whims of external authority." Such women frequently define themselves in terms of a geographical space, and they find conversation difficult and have not recognized having any experience of it at school (Belenky et al., 1986, p. 34). These are the ranks of the silent girls in school classrooms. *Received knowledge* is the perspective "from which women conceive of themselves as capable of receiving, even reproducing knowledge from the all-knowing external authorities, but not creating knowledge on their own." *Subjective knowledge* is the perspective "from which truth and knowledge are conceived of as personal, private, and subjectively known or intuited." *Procedural knowledge* is "the position in which women are invested in learning and applying objective procedures for obtaining and communicating knowledge." Here a sense of benign authority and the power of reason influence women who are knowledgeable. They engage in conscious analysis, tending to see things as problematic, which can sometimes lead to the silence of uncertain thinking as opposed to that of fear. They fall into two distinct categories: separate knowers, whose commitment is to rules, and connected knowers, with commitment to relationships. The *separate knower* is a doubter who listens to reasons, examining positions rather than the people who articulate those positions. Discourse for the separate knower is adversarial and antagonistic, not reconciliatory. The *connected knower,* on the other hand, builds on the subjective, pays great attention to conversation, and is procedurally interested in how other people think—how they arrive at conclusions, as it were, from their perspective. They are nonjudgmental, are forbearing, and prefer to work in collaborative groups. They do not work within the intuition of the subjective knower: "Connected knowing involves feeling, because it is rooted in relationship; but it also involves thought" (p. 121). Many women teachers are separate or connected knowers.

Constructed knowledge is a position in which "women view all knowledge as contextual, experience themselves as creators of knowledge, and value both subjective and objective strategies for knowing" (Belenky et al., 1986, p. 15). Three women in Belenky and colleagues' research were "all articulate and reflective people. They noticed what was going on with others and cared about the lives of people about them. They were intensely self-conscious, in the best sense of the word—aware of their own thought, their judgments, their moods and desires. Each wanted her own voice and actions to make a difference to other people and in the world... all three had learned the profound lesson that even the most ordinary human being is engaged in the construction of knowledge." "To understand," as Jean Piaget (1973) said, "is to invent" (see Belenky et al., 1986, p. 133). Putting on one side the matter of constructed knowledge (see Phillips, 2000), the portrait of the "ordinary person" offered here is presumably an account of what parents and schools must want for their children, of both genders, because it embodies the educational ideal of intellectual autonomy.

What can we learn from this research as educators? First, the need is paramount to create a classroom with an epistemological presence, strongly monitored to facilitate the historical individual's (the child's) "world-as-I-see-it and articulate what I see." The voice of the skeptic, the expert, the paternalist teacher, or the social obstacles (peers in the classroom) that prevent a child from achieving a strong, independent voice can be as destructive to epistemological autonomy as the metaphysical notion that the words we utter have within them concepts that are fixed immutably. Our voice is the source and medium of our utterances, figuring in the expression of our interests (Gould, 1998, p. 62). You can hear how interested or uninterested people are in what they are saying, but you may be uncertain whether they simply seem to be interested—a common experience of teachers listening to children. Second, this account should be read and understood by women teachers and especially student teachers, as it can offer a significant prop in self-explanation, self-knowledge, and self-identity, especially considered as a person and/or inside a role.

Indeed, Gould (1998, p. 63) continues: our voices are "damaged when we have to say what we have no interest in saying," akin to the "damage done to our minds by pursuing intellectual problems *whose connection to our real interests has been severed from the outset.*" The significance of this remark for the educational process cannot be underestimated: "connection to our real interests" implies the connection to the voice that speaks from our experience, not, once again, from simulated experience. So without the voice articulating our thoughts and ideas, our capacity for self-reflection is grossly inhibited, as it is couched in only secondhand experience.

We should add, too, that the historical individual takes part in different types of conversations, for which there are different rules and standards, as well as traditions. Harré (1983) argues that "fundamental human reality is a conversation, effectively without beginning or end, to which, from time, to time, individuals may make contributions. . . . The structure of our thinking and feeling will reflect, in various ways, the form and content of that conversation" (p. 19). Oakeshott, too, following his early book *Experience and Its Modes,* sets out the ideas of differing traditions and conversations:

> As civilized human beings, we are the inheritors, neither of an inquiry about ourselves and the world, nor of an accumulating body of information, but of a conversation, begun in the primeval forests and extended and made more articulate in the course of centuries. It is a conversation which goes on both in public and within each of ourselves.
>
> *(1991, pp. 490–491)*

To take part in any conversation, we must learn the conventions. The extent to which the historical individual is enabled through education to reach the intellectual autonomy needed for participation in old and new conversations is dependent on the purposeful development of an individual's voice through which his or her contributions can be articulated. Conversations are in particular modes, particular languages, and to those conversations the personal experience of the individual can contribute. Children in classrooms must learn how to converse.

II. The Eye as an Organ of Experience

Yet human knowledge has also depended, especially in philosophy and in science, on the "eye" and on the language and metaphors associated with it—point of view, insight, perspective, and, of course, the impartial spectator. The fundamental tasks of science are observation and experiment—the investigation of phenomena.

However, first, like the shibboleth that the camera never lies, human perception is consistently open to error. Abercrombie (1965) noted the significance of observer error in her students' inability to read X-rays effectively. Chabris and Simons (2010) carried out a remarkable experiment. A film was made of a group of players throwing a ball about, and subjects were asked to count the number of passes. In the middle of the film a man dressed as a gorilla walks between the players, beats his chest, and walks off. After the experiment, subjects were first asked, "How many passes?" and then, "Did you see the gorilla?" The almost unanimous response from the subjects was "What gorilla?" When the subjects were shown the film again, they usually expressed total surprise at having missed the gorilla. Too often, we see what we are looking for and ignore what we are not looking for.

So, second, it is not simply that we cannot have a theory-neutral base for viewing the world; our perceptions are highly selective. "Visual perception . . . is distinctly voluntary and subject to intellectual control" (Rée, 1999, p. 52). Missing for Abercrombie's medical students is looking at the slides with a spirit of inquiry, rather than a search for the right answer. We can be confused, as the gorilla example illustrates, but we can also see things the way we want. If we differ about the evidence before our eyes, therefore, there may be more than a clash of rival theories: rather an absence of cognitive control. Those who didn't see the gorilla had 20–20 vision. The eye dominates our talk of our sense-*impressions.* Certainly Plato's Myth of the Cave developed in *The Republic,* built entirely on sight and how people see the world, was a massive influence on Western philosophy.

Third, the distinctions of knowledge Belenky and colleagues deploy might be true not only of voice but also of sight, specifically in terms of the relation to authority. Hans Christian Andersen's fable of "The Emperor's New Clothes" reminds us of such problems. Everyone agreed that the Emperor had new clothes, even the impartial spectator. But, of course, the Emperor was naked, as the boy pointed out. As teachers, we should cultivate the sights, insights, and voices of children who see the world outside the dictates of authority and shout "Look at the King!" We should also listen for that voice in ourselves and learn to watch the world with care and caution. We have to be able to see it (whatever "it" might be) for ourselves, and with it, the limitations of the human perspectives on which we must draw for knowledge. The challenge, once again, is to develop the "voice" and the "sight" in children such that they are confident in what they say and see, bringing their experience to bear on human problems. However, while it is useful to examine these two organs, acknowledging the ear too, "our primary sense organ is not our eyes or ears or fingers or nose or tongue: it is our body" (Rée, 1999, p. 328). Thus, the experiences children have as historical individuals, though not private, are their own; their perspectives (what they see things *as*) need to be brought into the conversation of the classroom; and to develop self-understanding of their experiences, they need to develop their sight, trust it, and articulate what they see with a strong voice. Saying what one thinks is a major step toward knowing what one thinks. That is why a child's silence is such an educational challenge.

III. Human Capabilities That Power Experience

Teachers therefore need to recognize the range and depth of a child's experience, as it comprises everything the child has encountered and how he or she understands the world. There are several mental capabilities through which we understand the world and specifically our own experience of it, including ourselves. This range of human capabilities powers our experience; it includes our memory, our intuitions and understandings, and our reasons and motives, all of which are educable and each of which contributes to our personal identity, which are the topics here (see chapter 9). Perceptions and introspections have already been discussed under "seeing things *as.*"

Memory

Calling a memory to mind is a recapitulation of experience that the historical individual possesses. The importance of memory for us as individuals cannot be underestimated. "The things I have to choose between would not be as they are if my past had been different," writes philosopher Mary Warnock (1987). "My consciousness of my self in the present, as a person with choices to make is a consciousness inseparable from what has happened to me. My present cannot be divorced from my past, neither can my concept of self be separated from my awareness of what I was in the past. The person and 'his' past are one and the same" (p. 63; see also chapter 9).

John Sutton (2010) identifies three categories of memory: habit, propositional, and recollective. Memory as habit is displayed primarily in skills—at any level, but in such obvious cases as Roger Federer's hitting a tennis ball, executed with intention and attention. Propositional memory consists of all the knowledge we have underlying our general knowledge of the world. Recollective memory includes all kinds of memories that we can bring to mind: where we were when Kennedy was shot, for instance, or the brouhaha at my sister's wedding.

Memory can be viewed as a physiological faculty of the brain. We talk of it as playing tricks on us, or losing it, or committing "things" to it. We forget things, as in "my memory is getting awful." Many elderly people can remember incidents from their childhood but not what they ate for breakfast—long-term and short-term memory. There are "feats" of memory, photographic memories, and "total recall." The verbs that describe memory, however, are "remembering," "calling to mind," or "recollecting," which describe the epistemological, not the physiological, aspect of memory. Critically, we can be mistaken about what we remember or recollect in two main ways. First, where we imagine our participation at an event, say, when we were not actually there, but call it something we remember, an assertion usually open to evidence by witnesses. Second, where we misremember something—that is, we don't imagine that we were there, rather, say, we confuse the event with another like it. As we saw in chapter 5, we can be mistaken about our beliefs, and that extends to what we believe when we remember. So we can stand corrected about what we think we remember.

If we can be mistaken in this way, then the basic assumption is that what we say we remember or recollect is in fact true. What we remember (or misremember) in propositional memory is a belief we have about the past. So, as both Warnock and Sutton suggest, our memories are a source of knowledge about the past, and often about ourselves as the agent. Such memories can be happy, distasteful, or poignant, and there are those we would rather forget; but they can also be simply false. While logically we cannot remember anything from the future, our recollective memories of others can often act as examples for us to follow or as examples warning us what not to do. Remembering, in the propositional or recollective sense, is particularly human: it "is a core instance of the general, flexible human capacity to think about events and experiences which are not present, so that mental life isn't entirely determined by the current environment and the immediate needs of the organism" (Sutton, 2010, section 2).

But the place of memory in the experience of education seems, in general, to be a limited one. Two matters are important here. First, schooling experience is, too frequently, undertaking the task of *memorizing*. It is the deliberate act of committing propositions (e.g., Pythagoras's Theorem, multiplication tables, why the Chinese built the Great Wall) to memory for recall in a test. Remembering is rarely a task as such; events happen, we learn things, and later we recall them, or bring them to mind, or we do not, though we can of course say, "I must try to remember this," and create mnemonics to help us. But, because memorizing is a task, it has a beginning and an end. Once the task is over, with its achievement or failure, we have no particular reason to make what has been memorized something that we remember, unlike the brouhaha at my sister's wedding. Of course, some memorizations stick, like multiplication tables, or the recitation of a poem, for which there are no doubt good educational reasons, but it makes little sense to clutter children's minds with piled-up memorizations.

Yet, it seems obvious that, when students just have to memorize stuff, it is more likely to be remembered if the stuff has emotional impact. We are more likely to remember beliefs, or to recollect, when we have some emotional investment in the truth of the propositions or events in which we have taken part—when, to use Gould's phrase, the connection with our real interests has not been severed. In remembering, we have "a general capacity for the constructive simulating or imagining of specific events remote from immediate circumstances" (Sutton, 2010, section 1.2). Our memories feed our conception of our future: just as Roberts and Wood suggested that beliefs are what make the individual, and that includes recollections and memories.

A second problem is whether there are things we could not forget, such as philosopher Gilbert Ryle's famous example, "the difference between right and wrong" (Ryle, 1958). That, presumably, is something we want children not to forget. First, "it (the difference between right and wrong) is, for instance, inculcated by upbringing rather than imparted by dictation. It is not a set of things *memorized* and is not, consequently, the sort of knowledge of which shortness of memory is the natural enemy" (p. 149; my italics). We do not, outside some very special explanation, remember to be truthful. Second, when we come to understand the difference, we are not acquiring a capacity to do anything or to have come to believe a set of propositions. "To have been taught the difference is to have been brought to appreciate the difference" (p. 156), and that implies a changed person. Third, if I forget that it was Lincoln who spoke of government of the people, by the people, for the people, I am not changing as a person, though if I no longer care about what happens to my children, say, then I am changed. When we say to a person, "You have changed," it is not because he has forgotten (or remembered) anything: something has shifted in his value-system. So, finally, it is Ryle's use of the word *appreciate* that should trigger the educator's concerns here. "The notions of *learning, studying, teaching* and *knowing* are ampler notions than our academic epistemologies have acknowledged," he writes. "They are hospitable enough to house under their roofs notions like those of *inspiring, kindling and infecting*" (p. 154). What is true of right and wrong could also be true of much that is taught, if, to use Roberts and Wood's phraseology, children come to love knowledge, to care about it, to embrace it—or, at least, particular aspects of it. The experience of curriculum is something we might then not forget.

Intuitions and Understandings

"We hold these truths to be self-evident, that all men are created equal, that they are endowed by their Creator with unalienable rights, that among these are Life, Liberty and the Pursuit of Happiness." Self-evidence is a form of intuition. Some philosophers have held that our intuitions are the source of our morality: self-evidence means that we just "see" what is right or good. For others self-evidence means "that the truth of what is affirmed derives from the rules governing the terms which are combined... [for example] 'a square contains some right angles'" (Peters, R. S., 1966, p. 102; see, e.g., Moore, 1903; Ross, 1930). Of course, in trying to work out a practical moral theory, reliance on intuition is risky. First, people disagree about what is self-evident (e.g., promise-keeping in Peters's example), and, second, people can have all sorts of daft intuitions for which justification is not required. But the question of self-evidence, though that is an important topic in problems of justification, is not germane here to the notion of experience.

Our intuitions may be self-regarding, self-actualizing, social, or intellectual. Typically intuitions are described in terms of the sight metaphor, but other parts of the anatomy may be involved: "I feel it in my bones" or "I have a gut feeling." First, many of these intuitions are *self-regarding*. We have to learn to anticipate dangers, and we develop our intuitive capability as part of and through our experience. We take actions, often self-protective or avoiding actions, to some sensed danger. Second, there are *self-actualizing* intuitions. Young people thinking about teaching as a career have much the same kind of intuitions about themselves. They make such remarks as "I see myself in a classroom": Recruiters will want to see that intuition actualized and tested, because many a would-be teacher's intuitions prove unreliable when faced with classroom reality. Third, there are *social* intuitions, often ascribed more to women than to men. People rely on their world experience and sensibilities to understand the actions and motives of others, intuiting possible outcomes and happenings. "This will end in tears" sounds like a prophecy, but it is most often intuitive about a social situation. Finally, there are purely *intellectual* intuitions. For the scientist, an intuition may lead to a discovery, but it may also lead nowhere; it has to be tested. An intellectual intuition is like an insight, rooted in expertise, in which ideas are rearranged, often against the grain. An intuition by Robert Warren led to the discovery of the *Helicobacter pylori* bacteria by Barry Marshall and Robert Warren and overthrew the surgical treatment for stomach ulcers in favor of treating the patient with antibiotics, which won them the Nobel Prize in 2005.

Understanding differs from intuition. It has, of course, an ordinary sense, synonymous with "I know what you mean," that need not concern us here. Understandings can also be categorized under the four general categories for intuitions: self-regarding, self-actualizing, social, and intellectual. The plural "understandings" convey that an individual will have all manner of understandings that govern experience: she understands football, her parents, what good recipes are, the Beethoven Violin Concerto, *Waiting for Godot,* and much else. To have an understanding, however, requires neither the ability to rehearse a set of propositions that are connected to each other, nor that these propositions be true. Rather there are levels of understanding, as Roberts and Wood (2007) point out, but each level involves *"grasping connections* or *fitting things together"* (p. 45), a connectedness that characterizes an understanding. Understandings in this holistic way pervade all aspects of human life, especially when people love each other and when understandings do not need to be articulated.

Both intuitions and understandings therefore have no necessary connection with truth, but they consist in and shape beliefs that usually become manifest in actions or attitudes. They also begin to develop as a language is learned. They are therefore educable. Required of teachers is the ability to help children shape their intuitions and their understandings, because an understanding, given its lack of a necessary connection with truth, is likely to be idiosyncratic. Intuitions and understandings are our own. They become embedded in our experience of the world and contribute to our knowledge of it. The teaching task is how we create from a curriculum, and the school experience, ranges of understanding as the bases on which intuitions are formed: in other words, *how can curriculum become the child's own?* This is not just a theoretical matter. A classroom with an epistemological presence must be hospitable to all the different kinds of intuitions, understandings, and misunderstandings a child has and to the successes and failures of the child realizing these intuitions and understandings in action.

Reasons and Motives

There are reasons, and there are *my* reasons; there are motives, and there are *my* motives. The educational task is to close the gap between the two, making reasons and motives the child's own also. That is a bizarre way of putting it, but it picks out the need to help children be both rational and reasonable and not leave them, in the ancient phrase, leading an unexamined life. As we know too well, there are bad reasons for, and bad motives in, actions. A murderer acts out of greed (his motive) because he needs his victim's cash (his reason). Indeed reasons and motives are always open to moral appraisal, and the educational task is, formidably, to instill right reason and right motives (which begs an ethical question or two, which we can leave on one side here). For the moment, however, the personal sorting out of one's reasons and one's motives are the experiential basis for our lives and our actions, which are themselves open to moral scrutiny.

There are numerous ways to avoid or to bungle the use of reason. The person who falters in the search for truth is content with falsehoods or inaccuracies. The closed-minded person often is unable to face the rigors of reason, content with saying "Well, that's just your opinion" and thereby abandoning reason. Reason demands the examination of bias—hence the importance of being impartial. Commitment to reason needs to be a primary disposition in a person's life. We learn to use reason with practice. As infants learn language, they learn basic rules of social life—such as taking a means to an end, and that effects have causes—such that they acquire the capacity not just to lurch from one experience to another, but to choose. Immediately choice is real for the child, so are reasons for choices. The task of family upbringing leading to education then becomes one of linking reasons to choices—that is, deliberating about them. So, many an American parent says to a child, "I think you should think about why you made a bad choice there."

Developing the use of reason will be in (a) making choices, (b) having good reasons for those choices, and (c) developing those dispositions and virtues that enable the child to make choices that connect to the ideals and principles he or she is beginning to hold. Education can contribute, but the child must make these his or her own. Ten-year-old Melanie is an interesting example here. As her awareness of animals grows, she begins to link the cows she sees in fields with the beef on her plate, the pigs she saw on the farm with the breakfast bacon, the chickens in her grandfather's yard with the barbecue, and the ducks on the pond with the occasional dinner treat and the toys in her bath. She makes a choice to avoid meat. But in the process of developing her principles, making choices and working out reasons for them, she can make many mistakes, not in how she presents her emerging principles to her family, but in a lack of discretion about nonhuman life. Cows and tsetse flies are to be treated alike. Destroying a hornet's nest is on a par with training dogs to fight. She is being unreasonable, though not irrational. She has not yet started to discriminate in the complex problems of the relationships between human and nonhuman life, in which issues of danger, the balance of an ecosystem, the use of pesticides in the development of crops, and the human treatment of animals all are on the table in the forum of reason. This is a matter not of persuading her to abandon her principles, but helping her use reason to face up to the complexity her principles display. But these are *her* reasons, and her personal experiences as her awareness of animals grows are critical in their development—as, of course, is her exposure to sensitive parents and teachers. The world of reasoning invites passions, not merely to the topics, but to the use of reason itself (Peters, R. S., 1972). Any hearty conversation shows that.

Education insofar as it inculcates a desire to search for truth must ipso facto be committed to rationality, as truth cannot be found, except idiosyncratically, in our feelings or intuitions. Yet our choices are rarely, if at all, devoid of emotion: we have motives for believing or acting in certain ways. We can be subject to emotion, as when a wave of anger flows over us such that we do things we will regret, if we have appraised the context in a way that provokes our emotions. Reason and emotion will always be around in asking such questions as "Why is this a good reason? Why is this a bad motive?" which of course become commonplace in a classroom with an epistemological presence. (See Further Reading.)

The core implication of considering memory, intuitions and understandings, and reasons and motives is that, in a classroom with an epistemological presence, the child takes *ownership* of the curriculum. By that, I mean that the child becomes involved such that the memories (not the memorizations) of the classroom encounter are vivid and long-lasting; that his or her intuitions are respected and valued, especially in terms of the self-actualizing intuitions; and that reasons do become his or her reasons and motives for learning. These reasons and motives are not just instrumental, say, to pass the test, but a part of who he or she is. The lived curriculum then becomes the moral and epistemological property of the child, not the documents available on state websites.

IV. The Integrity of Experience

In 2001, Robert Hanssen, a senior member of the FBI, was arrested on charges of espionage that had continued for over 20 years. His sole justification was that he needed the money. Yet he was a devout Catholic, attending Mass at 6:30 AM during the week and belonging to a select Catholic organization, Opus Dei. He had six children, who went to private Catholic schools in Vienna, Virginia. He secretly videotaped his sexual life with his wife, which he shared with a friend. He lavished money and gifts on a Washington prostitute. He was tried and sent to prison for life without parole, avoiding the death sentence for treason through a plea bargain. Greed, betrayal of wife and country, promiscuity, and religious devotion are features of what seems to have been not just a double, but a triple life. A thoroughly unintegrated, some might say disintegrated, personality. Hanssen lacks each of the three main features of Norton's description of integrity:

> As we use the term here, "moral integrity" has three-dimensional meaning. In the first place it means integration of separable aspects of the self—notably faculties, desires, interests, roles, life-shaping choices—into a consistent whole. Second, it implies "wholeness as completeness" by which it is distinguishable, for example, from fanaticism or monomania. The third dimension may be preliminary described as a deeper kind of honesty.
>
> *(1995, pp. 82–83)*

Yet it is tempting to think that Hanssen's case is just an aberration, a highly extreme example of human experience. Yet, Jackall (2009) describes business managers who regularly attend church and would regard themselves as devout but use unethical practices in their work. Children who leave home for boarding school often experience a different life there from that at home: family and school values are sometimes in strong opposition, and the individual is obliged to live within each. We can often be placed in different roles, with conflicts between their embedded values. They can contribute to a loss, or a lack of realization of, personal integrity.

However, when a person knits together memory, intuitions and understandings, and reasons and motives in his or her experience of life—how he or she understands and practices it—that person has the virtue of integrity. It is commonplace to use integrity only in Norton's last dimension, in which it is used primarily of politicians, lawyers, and bank managers (see Carter, 1997). A view of integrity, as with other moral positions, is normative and derived from a point of view. Norton's book *Democracy and Moral Development* powerfully articulates an Aristotelian perspective, which is the platform on which this view of experience and integrity is built.

Norton is interested in identifying the connection between politics and virtue in what he calls a developmental democracy. He sets out a very strong statement of the educational purposes of a democracy—namely, "that the purpose of politics and government is enhancement of the quality of life of human beings; that the central agency of such enhancement is the initiative to self-development in individuals, and that the paramount function of government is to provide the necessary but non-self-suppliable conditions for optimizing opportunities for individual self-discovery and self-development" (1995, p. 80). Enhancement of the quality of life does not mean material goods, better health, or any of the usual political prescriptions for happiness. Rather, in the Aristotelian tradition, such enhancement means the "accession by human beings of moral virtues" (p. 81), which are dispositions of character. Such virtues are personally useful, valuable in themselves, but also of social utility. "The possession of (these) virtues is to the credit of persons who possess them: it is the result of their own initiative" (p. 81). The job of government is therefore to remove as many obstacles as possible to that self-development. But the process must be one of self-discovery, searching for experiences that are intrinsically rewarding (see previous section), because self-discovery can occur "in the context of preparation for vocational choice, or of preparation for any of the other life-shaping choices" (p. 82).

Each of Norton's dimensions picks out a different aspect of the relation between experience and integrity. First is the integration of separable aspects of the self—notably faculties, desires, interests, roles, life-shaping choices—into a consistent whole. Why is this first dimension of integrity valuable? First, at a basic level of existence, conflicting desires are painful. The process of socialization of the young child is, in part, one of reducing those conflicts, characteristically in biting the nipple that feeds him or her (Bowlby, 1988). These become magnified through childhood into the making of choices, life-shaping and otherwise, which indicate what one values. Second, the resolution of conflicting desires cannot just be imposed, because the desires will still be in place. Such conflicts, such lack of coherence among values in this individual are not merely painful, they are dysfunctional, because of the psychological tensions they create. A person who hates his or her job spends the work day in a cloud of anxiety, alienation, and profound discontent. All such attitudes, beliefs, and affects influence job satisfaction (Weiss, 2002) and thus mental health, for individuals satisfied with their jobs have a fit between the activities and values of the workplace and the basic values in terms of which they live their lives: "Meaningful work and meaningful living," as Norton describes it (1995, chapter 4).

The second dimension is "wholeness as completeness" by which integrity is distinguishable, for example, from fanaticism or monomania. Animal-loving Melanie, for instance, in her self-discovery could become fanatical. By that is meant that the individual has an interest that not only dominates other interests and values but excludes them. The fanatic therefore is a person whose values are stunted, because they are crushed by the power of the one value that overwhelms him or her. Notice here that the fanatic does not seem to make a choice and is in some respects passive in the face of what seems to be an obsession (nonclinical sense). We talk of hobbies or interests "taking people over." It betrays a lack of balance among values. Again, Bernard Williams (1985) suggests that the source of ethical conviction is not a decision but that it "in some sense comes to you" (p. 169). You cannot decide, so to speak, to be convinced. In Melanie's case, her would-be fanaticism could be explained in terms of how her love for animals, so to speak, sweeps over her.

One of the most interesting features of education and teaching is why students like Melanie develop propensities and interests toward certain subjects rather than others. The quality of teaching is often offered as an explanation, but the gist of arguments for liberal education lie in being brought up to appreciate the range of human endeavor—an appreciation for many different conversations and traditions—a view that must rest, as we think about this from the viewpoint of the historical individual, in an argument for "wholeness as completeness." What we want, in the liberal education tradition, is not to squelch special interests, but to have them set within the framework of the individual experience of the range that life can offer and to ensure that how a person values his or her specialism does not lead to a quest for a hierarchy of value among human pursuits. Above all, this will make choices more informed.

The third dimension may be preliminarily described as a deeper kind of honesty, Norton suggests. By this, he means something like Polonius's injunction to Laertes "to thine own self be true." This is not, of course, self-esteem. Nor is the remark neutral about what the self contains, but it seems to be a weaker dimension of integrity, though we can recognize the direction of it. Moreover, who the self (the child in front of the teacher) is can be cloudy and uncertain, and we may be very unclear about that historical individual's identity, especially as childhood moves into adolescence and the sweet, charming eight-year-old becomes a lazy, idle, good-for-nothing adolescent. But the questions of self-knowledge and identity are discussed in chapter 9. The second aspect of experience, how we hold our beliefs, is explored in chapter 8.

8

COMMITMENT, COURAGE, AND WILL

The Belief-Holding Individual

> True courage requires freedom, and freedom is best cultivated by an education that awakens critical thinking.
>
> *(Nussbaum, 1997, p. 55)*

The belief-holding individual within the realm of personal knowledge is to be regarded not just as holding justified true beliefs, but by the extent of his or her commitment to those beliefs. How then do we regard such commitment? First, "tenacity with respect to one's own epistemic acquirements is natural and good" (Roberts & Wood, 2007, p. 183). Generally, a person of commitment is seen as morally admirable, as in "he has the courage of his convictions," or "he knows where he stands," although such an evaluation will be tempered by judgment about the moral or intellectual worth of the commitment. Second, strong commitment can bring about moral or ideological blindness that makes the search for truth difficult if not impossible for persons so wedded to their beliefs. Third, a belief-holding individual can be an uncommitted person, an intellectual agnostic, a fence-sitter, the person who does not know what to think, not to be confused with a person who deliberates carefully and cautiously.

For educators, such commitment is a serious matter. If it is correct that adults, as the research (Peterson & Seligman, 2004) indicates, are so committed that they ignore counterevidence, even that it serves to entrench their perceptions, what has been the role of education in the development of such blind commitment? If it is the case that commitment to beliefs can block off reason, and that it cauterizes the serious entertainment of alternatives to one's beliefs, then we may wonder how adults got to be so dysfunctional intellectually, to use Quinton's phrase (see chapter 5). This is not just a failure to behave impartially in coming to a judgment; rather, an intensive, strong commitment to beliefs is the obstacle to ever thinking impartially. Empirical studies could no doubt resolve how such formed commitments become so immutable and impervious, but it would not be difficult to construct one hypothesis. Children are constantly required in schooling to *get the answer right,* the correctness being determined by whoever is responsible for the tests by which they are judged. They therefore in most circumstances reject any "wrong" belief, and clinging to the ideal of the right answer (true or untrue) becomes a habit. The interminable request of freshmen students in my experience is "What do you want us to do?" and university teachers, let alone schoolteachers, are not reluctant in requiring "right" answers. Why then should we be surprised if, once possessed of right answers, the learner clings to the ideas those answers contain? Because he or she has been validated through getting things right, examining or changing held beliefs becomes psychologically difficult. Of course, children learn from families and cultures too, but the key here is not that adults should not be committed to strong beliefs, but that they should always be able to assess alternatives: to be committed, in other words, to the search for truth as *primary* to a commitment for the truth of the specific beliefs held. This can be nurtured, as we have seen, through the establishment of an epistemological presence in a classroom or a seminar room. In section 1, Polanyi's account of personal knowledge provides a basis for exploring what commitment is, and its intellectual and moral character. In section 2, the varieties of commitment to beliefs—that is, the different ways in which we can be said to hold our beliefs—help us to define the educational challenges, using the difference between the discovery and the critical mode as a framework—how do we help children to be "judiciously" committed to beliefs without their becoming dogmatists, and/or how do we convey the idea of knowledge as provisional, without their becoming intellectual agnostics? But this is in part a matter of the will, and in section 3 the articulation of the various aspects of will embedded in commitment to beliefs provides the basis for examining the immensely interesting virtue of courage and commitment in section 4. Not often noticed in education and teaching is the connection between courage and encouragement and how to foster courage in children, which is the topic of the final section.

I. Polanyi and Commitment

In discussing the epistemology of science, Polanyi argues that knowledge of theories (i.e., an integrated bunch of propositions) in practice cannot be cut off from the individuals who are the knowers. His focus is primarily the work of the scientist and, only to a lesser degree, the "ordinary person" pursuing truth. That basic argument needs to be repeated here. There is no such thing as objectivity in science, he says, and the ideal of strict objectivism is absurd (see Polanyi, 1962/1974, chapter 1). We have no objective theories, only theories to which we are committed. In the process of argument (both one-on-one and across the centuries), our theories (yours or mine) are challenged by rival theories to which other people are committed. The ideal of objectivism (i.e., that scientific facts are value free) cannot handle the necessary human element of judgment that we make about such theories in the light of which we become committed. If we are to be responsible people concerned about the truth, we must understand the significance of our knowledge of ourselves and the appraisals and the judgments we make, because they are interdependent with our public knowledge claims. We cannot disentangle our personal judgment from our understanding of theories (and thereby also of any proposition) and from our commitment to them as we make a claim. In this way Polanyi describes a relationship between the individual and the way he or she sees the world—that is, through the theories to which we are committed. "When we accept a set of presuppositions and use them as our interpretative framework," he writes in an unusual metaphor, "we may be said to dwell in them as we do in our own body" (p. 60).

To believe something, in this account, is to commit oneself to its truth (Polanyi, 1962/1974, p. 298), or, as Roberts and Wood (2007, p. 184) phrase it differently, "Beliefs are, after all, some kind of commitment to the truth of the believed propositions." But that is not subjective. Rather, personal knowledge, in his sense, transcends the disjunction between the subjective and the objective (Polanyi, 1962/1974, p. 300). To explain this, he contrasts our beliefs with our appetites (hunger, thirst, sex, etc.) that are entirely manifested in our subjective feelings. The act of discovery—acquiring new beliefs—combines three elements: first, a sense of satisfaction (akin to a subjective feeling), second, a submission to the standards and rules (of language or method) embedded in the structure of what is believed, and, third, universal legislation (i.e., that a belief that is justified true knowledge is true not just for me, but for everyone: it is universalizable). "Commitment is a personal choice, *seeking* and eventually accepting something believed (both by the person incurring the commitment and the writer describing it) to be impersonally given" (p. 302; my italics). The commitment is embodied in Polanyi's term "submission": "No one can know universal intellectual standards except by acknowledging their jurisdiction over himself as part of the terms on which he holds himself responsible for his intellectual efforts" (p. 303). Embedded in those rules and standards are traditional ways of going on—as ways of seeking truth—and the work of those who have gone before us and upon whose shoulders we stand.

However, committing oneself to a belief is for Polanyi a necessary part of "the act of knowing." But it is not just a subjective feeling but, in some cases, "a *passionate* contribution of the person knowing what is being known" (my italics). For Polanyi, everything that one knows, to a lesser or greater degree, demands the seeker's activity, not merely in the discovery or the critical mode, but in what one believes. Commitment is therefore to be seen as responsible assent, rooted in responsible judgment; responsible here referring to both the intellectual and the moral (see Polanyi, 1962/1974, chapter 10). But commitment to a belief does not make it true, and people's judgments will differ about the truth of assertions, even though all are committed to the beliefs they hold. Yet the central feature of commitment binds the personal to the universal, the personal to the public—through one's submission to rules and standards and to the universalizability of one's belief.

This is not the forum to enter a more detailed account or critique of Polanyi's work or to note the similarities with Dewey's account of knowledge. From this very brief review of what is a very complicated and at times obscure argument, there are some persuasive elements. First, this view of personal knowledge is a strong account of the necessity of individual interpretation of ideas and theories, hence the impossibility of Adam Smith's detachment. Second, individualism is held firmly in place by being always put within the rules, standards, and methods either of ordinary language or of the specific languages of disciplines and rules of logic to which, in respect of the search of truth, the individual must submit. Third, Polanyi foreshadows issues about both the conscience of belief, already discussed in chapter 5, and the account of knowledge given by virtue epistemologists, because of his emphasis on the notion of responsibility in respect of one's beliefs. Polanyi thus obliges us to attend strongly to the personal in knowledge, carefully distinguishing it from subjective opinion through his insistence on the rules and standards that "dwell" in us, a notion that in the modern idiom, we might describe as internalizing.

However, the major puzzle that confronts us as educators after this glance at Polanyi is this question of commitment, of how we hold our beliefs. After all, Polanyi's notion that commitment to beliefs involves passion may be true of scientists at the frontiers of knowledge or, indeed, of Monday morning quarterbacks, but it cannot be correct to assert this in terms of everything we can be said to know—for example, one's mother's maiden name. We therefore need to give an account of the various ways in which belief-holding individuals hold their beliefs, and that will open up the virtues of the will within which the virtues and vices of commitment can be examined. To such commitments, we bring such personal qualities as determination, carefulness, concentration, self-restraint, patience, and conscientiousness, but also courage. Such qualities are necessary if we regard the purposeful acquisition of some of our beliefs as our achievements, for which, in a general sense, an effort of will is demanded, and as a result of which these are beliefs to which we become committed.

II. How We Hold Our Beliefs

Roberts and Wood (2007) approach the question of how we hold our beliefs through an examination of a trait of intellectual character they describe as firmness. They distinguish between what they call flaccidity and rigidity, identifying these as the poles of the commitment continuum. Putting the details of their excellent characterizations to one side, Roberts and Wood describe flaccidity of four types, three of which are important here. The first is roughly that of the rambling mind, without order, as though it were filled with ideas that are constantly in motion: "less a house than a pile of lumber" (p. 186). The second is a young person fascinated by ideas, but wearing the appropriate intellectual clothing, so to speak, every time he or she comes across a new set of understandings or theories: he or she flits from system to system with the promiscuity of a butterfly, and we may hope that he or she will settle somewhere. The third is the person who seems simply flummoxed by the world, always thinking that his or her self-descriptions are always open to change, that the whole basis of identity is contingent and fallible, an account that Roberts and Wood extend in their discussion of Rorty (pp. 189–191).

At the opposite end of the commitment continuum is rigidity, of which Roberts and Wood discern five types: "dogmatism, doxastic [i.e., pertaining to beliefs or opinions], complacency, stolid perseverance, perceptual rigidity, and comprehensional rigidity" (2007, p. 194). *Dogmatism* is the "disposition to *respond* irrationally to *oppositions* to the belief: anomalies, objections, evidence to the contrary, counter-examples, and the like," exemplified by Nyhan and Reifler (2010) in their study of the failure of individuals to take on board corrections to their political beliefs. Interestingly, Roberts and Wood suggest that "dogmatic persons cannot know very clearly what they believe, because of the contrariety between the beliefs they hold dogmatically and their means of defending them" (p. 198). *Doxastic complacency,* on the other hand is "laziness in belief formation" (p. 198). This can be a failure "to know when and how to examine [one's] beliefs or to be willing to do so" (p. 199). Such people can't be bothered. *Stolid perseverance* is not exactly pursuit of a lost cause: rather it picks out a certain kind of blindness to the value of what one is doing, a person trapped in a set of habits and attitudes seemingly immutable.

Perceptual rigidity can be described as the possession of people who are "blind" or "deaf" (p. 202) to other ways of perceiving the world. They have established perceptual categories, and, presented with alternative categories, they are unable or unwilling to use them. Perceptual rigidity may be described, in part, as a lack of intellectual curiosity, together with a sense of comfort about the categories with which one is familiar. Recall the scenes toward the end of the movie *The Bridge on the River Kwai*. Colonel Nicholson has fought against immensely difficult odds to build the morale of what remains of his regiment in the harshest conditions of a Japanese prisoner-of-war camp in 1944. He has done this by persuading the camp commander to use the British soldiers' expertise to build a bridge that will, of course, facilitate the movement of supplies for the Japanese Army. When British commandoes arrive to blow up the bridge, Nicholson does his best to thwart the attempt. In so doing he suddenly (and in the movie dramatically) realizes that he has been blind to the implications of "helping the enemy," since he has been rigidly (and with extraordinary bravery and commitment) focused on troop morale, survival, and the achievement of building the bridge, totally blind to what is not far short of treason.

Finally, Roberts and Wood describe *comprehensional rigidity*. This they describe as having two aspects: "a lack of acquaintance with and practice in the categories of the alien framework" and "an emotional discomfort with the alternative ways of understanding" (2007, p. 205). Some academics, for instance, refuse to take postmodernism seriously and get very angry at this frame of understanding (see Peters, M., 2008). Educationally, Roberts and Wood seek "an intellectual adventuresomeness that works against rigidity" (2007, p. 205). The dispositions that would work against such rigidity include "basic respect for others," "generosity of spirit," "intellectual industriousness," and "love of knowledge," the latter of which includes the search for truth (p. 206).

Of these five characteristics of the person of commitment Roberts and Wood have described, none are obviously the property of young children; we must therefore assume that they are acquired in the course of growing up, which, of course, includes formal education in schools. A classroom with an epistemological presence will be an arena in which how children hold their beliefs can be tackled positively rather than remedially. Of the five types, only stolid perseverance is sometimes a feature of young children's actions, where they persist in the face of obstacles and adversity on a course that is usually a lost cause ending in tears. We as teachers need therefore to provide experiences that seek to preempt the development of these undesirable dispositions of rigidity. Combating the development of dogmatism would be a persistent attempt through education to present "anomalies, objections, evidence to the contrary, counterexamples" as a matter of course. Undermining complacency is a matter of challenging the development of bad work habits (i.e., laziness) and creating dialogic space for individuals to be challenged. Perceptual rigidity can be constantly preempted by continued grappling with other, unfamiliar points of view and stimulation of the imagination through entering into other worlds, not merely learning about them as in the Grade 8 curriculum described in chapter 5.

To repeat, while teachers may have all kinds of strategies that mesh with the *problems* these kinds of dispositions create, a view of a classroom with an epistemological presence is that these experiences have to be framed openly and clearly as contributing to the *positive development* of habits of mind to preempt the development of undesirable forms of commitment. In particular children must become familiar with these weaknesses, early and often, otherwise they will not have the motivation, incentive, or will to grapple with them. Teachers and students need to be highly self-conscious—or gradually become so—as they work in both the discovery and the critical mode: it is not enough to say, "Mrs. Payton taught us this." The pedagogical problem then becomes one of getting children to have a conscience about getting the answers right but to have a more powerful conscience (and incentive) to ensure that they examine all reasonable alternatives to get into the habit of a commitment that is not susceptible to these intellectual weaknesses in commitment to beliefs. It will thus be useful to discern what is meant when we say of a person that he or she "holds" his or her beliefs rigidly, loosely, strongly, or intensely, and what that implies for educational practice.

"Insofar as we are rational in our beliefs…the intensity of belief will tend to correspond to the firmness of the available evidence" (Quine & Ullian, 1980, p. 16). The notion of intensity here signifies the level of commitment to the belief, but this can be true only of those cases in which, indeed, there is enough evidence. Crude distinctions can be made between what I will call the trivial, the substantial, the ideological, and the disciplined types of beliefs. For example, my *trivial* beliefs are those such as the sun will rise tomorrow, and an army of other beliefs I hold about the world and our place in it. They demand little evidence and are, so to speak, part of the bric-a-brac of our existence. Of course, any such belief might rise to the level of a substantial belief if its truth was in doubt. So, what marks off a *substantial* belief from a *trivial* belief in this account is when the evidence can be challenged. For example, substantial beliefs would be those on such matters large, like climate change, or small, such as whether my great-grandfather really was my grandfather's parent. Into this *substantial* category would come most of our beliefs about the historical past where interpretations are constantly being made such that our commitment to any one belief must, given Quine and Ullian's firmness of evidence problem, be provisional.

Our *ideological* beliefs are commitments of a quite different kind: they are part of what Roberts and Wood call "understandings" (2007, p. 212 ff.). First, there are questions of our moral beliefs—that is, whether one sees the world primarily in terms of obligation, duty, and principle (as with Kant): or whether one follows Aristotle, with an emphasis on human flourishing through the variety of moral beliefs. Second, if one has religious beliefs, these may or may not shape one's moral ideology but will almost certainly be influential in what one believes about the world. Third, there are our political beliefs that often are our moral beliefs writ large. Is our primary emphasis on individual freedom or social justice? Are we libertarian capitalists whose fundamental belief is that government should not interfere with the market? Or are we socialists who believe that capital must be restrained through central government planning? Such ideological beliefs are less open to evidence for the truth of what is asserted and, as we have seen with Nyhan and Reifler's research mentioned above, those who hold their ideological beliefs may not be influenced by evidence that undermines their validity.

Finally, the *disciplined* character of beliefs picks out procedural rules, not appropriately described as a process. This might be in games or sports, in conventions of behavior (e.g., in sailing), or of course in intellectual disciplines (Polanyi's rules and standards once again). It might be objected that these are not beliefs in the ordinary sense. But all such procedures, including those in a law court or a classroom, are not mere ways of going-on. In games, for instance, the procedures are determined not just by the purpose and the shape of the game but by what is fair, what penalties are given for infringement of the rules. Games have traditions, sets of usually unwritten beliefs about what is appropriate conduct. Procedures, like institutions, incorporate specific values to which proponents and participants adhere and to which, as beliefs about what should be done, they are strongly committed.

The implication of this analysis is that, contrary to Quine and Ullian's claim, across the spectrum of belief, intensity of belief is more likely on what I have dubbed ideological and disciplined matters than on the trivial (for which the evidence may be complete) or the substantial (for which there is masses of evidence open to different interpretations). Nor is this undesirable in general, however much we may disapprove of those ideological beliefs we do not share, because a strong commitment to leading a moral life according to, say, a commitment to one's duties and obligations is presumably desirable. People do change, however. There are atheists who are born again, and there are religious people who abandon their religious beliefs. Strong commitments can shift, provided they are not protected by dogmatism, complacency, or perceptual or comprehensional rigidity.

The appropriateness of the intensity of our beliefs therefore rests on their content. The overall educational problem is straightforward. How do we en*courage*—put courage into—children to enable them to face themselves and their beliefs, and how do we dis*courage* them from surrendering to Roberts and Woods's five bad habits of commitment, especially if their cultural or family background is one in which constant repetition of unexamined or false beliefs or assumptions about the world is the staple of conversation? To that we will turn after an examination of how commitment and the will are connected, because to be courageous is an act of will.

III. The Will and Commitment to Belief

Melanie has been attracted by things scientific, both through family encouragement and through being well taught, but also through watching Animal Planet and programs that spark her desire to learn more and to investigate. But doing science is not just bird-watching at the beach; it is tough work in terms of the homework required, the mathematics, the reading, and the lab work, all of which calls on her determination to succeed at the subject as well as the intellectual requirements of carefulness, accuracy, and being conscientious. However, she can't be intellectually undisciplined if she is to succeed in learning something more and extending her scientific repertoire. She must, as Polanyi indicates, submit herself to the rules and standards, the requirements not simply for conceptual understanding but for learning, and she needs self-control: she needs the willpower to "buckle down" in high school and, advisedly, "pull all-nighters" in college, which implies overcoming all kinds of distractions and temptations. Moreover, quite apart from exterior ways in which her emotions might be involved—for example, when her friends constantly tell her science is crap, which really annoys her—she will be developing the kind of passionate commitment Polanyi describes, which will spawn other emotions: disgust at a weak performance, elation at completing a project.

Melanie thus provides for us the four elements of the will as elaborated by Roberts and Wood (2007, p. 64 ff.). Present here is "a set of recognizable phenomena which roughly speaking involve the will" on Mary Warnock's account. "What they have in common is their relevance to situations of initiating and carrying on actions and getting things done. To investigate these would be to investigate the will" (see Pears, 1963, p. 15). Roberts and Wood (2007) locate the will firmly as a "central epistemic faculty" and propose that "its proper formation is crucial to intellectual character" (p. 60). The qualities described above, of course, could all be deployed for evil or non-moral ends. We thus always need to know about the object to which the will is being directed—for example, when we are attracted by the search for truth. However, Roberts and Wood also distinguish four functions of the will: "(1) attraction, desire, concern, attachment, etc.; (2) choice, effort, and undertaking; (3) willpower; and (4) emotion" (p. 64). Melanie embodies each of these.

Recall that virtue epistemologists argue that, just as actions are virtuous, so can beliefs be virtuous. One problem about action that has been of philosophical concern since Socrates is how to explain why a person who knows he ought to do x does not do it. So, it would appear, the person lacks the will. Aristotle discusses at length specific forms of failure to carry out what one thinks is right under the concept of *akrasia*. But could weakness of will relate to belief? Could someone try to believe something but fail? "Try as I might," a person might say, "I just can't believe it." A father who has lost his son at sea, in Williams's example, just can't accept the truth of the fact (1973, pp. 149–150). But, as Williams points out, it is not the belief we are "trying to believe," it is the truth of what is implied in the belief. It does not make sense to say that the father can't believe it because he is not trying hard enough: he can't accept the truth, a common feature of experience for those who mourn.

Roberts and Wood's first element of the will describes what motivates an individual such that his or her will is evoked; this might be attraction, desire, concern, or attachment. We pursue things that attract us (e.g., knowledge); we desire states (e.g., a happy marriage); we are concerned (e.g., we care for our dying friend); and we get attached to objects and pursuits (e.g., golf), all of which put demands on our will. The educator presumably puts the search for truth and the personal development of the student at the center of his or her desires and concerns and is engaged in helping the student do the same. These are the sources for the object to be pursued as a matter of will. For Melanie, it was the engagement with science.

The second element—matters of choice, effort, and undertaking—describe individual determination and such other qualities as persistence, perseverance, courage, and doggedness that are characteristic qualities of endeavor. Yet there are also qualities of attentiveness, such as carefulness, concentration, conscientiousness, and other qualities, such as vigilance and deliberation, necessary in one's undertakings (see Sockett, 1988). These might be regarded as qualities of heed (see Ryle, 1949). Here Melanie has to bring these resources of the will to bear on her love for science. Notice that these qualities are not freed from the quality of the task or the achievement. "I tried really hard on this essay" is laudable in its way, but always insufficient, because a work must be judged in terms of the application of the rules and standards.

The third element, willpower, is at least a matter of control of oneself, for which forbearance and self-restraint, patience, and endurance, and some other specific qualities, such as punctuality and tidiness, are the obvious qualities required. Of course willpower extends also to persistence and perseverance. But the matter of personal self-control and knowing oneself well enough to understand one's strengths and weaknesses is at the heart of willpower, extending its reach across all aspects of the will—as the nomenclature indicates. Melanie has to withstand the various temptations out there in order to develop the self-control embedded in good study habits.

The fourth element, emotion, points to significant features of the will that Roberts and Woods don't make enough of. First, they are right to say that emotion always has a cognitive core. That is, when you get angry, jealous, delighted, or overcome, you have appraised a situation in such a way that this is the emotion you feel. Such emotions are common in human experience, so much so that we comment when people don't display them: "You don't seem very pleased with the award" or "He doesn't seem too upset at her death." This indicates immediately that an emotion is a cognitive-affective affair, with, once again, familiar signals, floods of tears, screeches of delight, eyes flashing with anger, even perhaps, turning green with envy. Melanie is alive with passionate commitment. But where there is a cognitive core, there is also reason and rationality. Some emotional responses can be described as irrational, as when a jilted man kills his lover and then himself. It would be hard to describe that behavior as unreasonable. But, if instead of killing his lover, he demanded recompense for the gifts and flowers he had given her, we would regard that as unreasonable—at least in principle. However, the "rational passions" are aroused when people care about the truth and search for it. R. S. Peters (1972), in his brilliant but much-neglected essay "Reason and Passion," describes how the elements of a search for truth—checking sources, constantly searching for alternative explanations—are driven by the passion for reason. And, he suggests, these concerns, especially relevant for Melanie, are

> more precise articulations of the more generalized passions which begin to exert an influence when reasoning of a less precise sort gets under way, when children's curiosity leads them to ask for explanations, when their early delight in mastery gradually takes the form of the determination to get things right, and when primitive obstructiveness passes in to the love of order and system.
>
> *(p. 226)*

Commitment is thus expressed through the four characteristics of the will: "(1) attraction, desire, concern, attachment, etc.; (2) choice, effort, and undertaking; (3) willpower; and (4) emotion" (Roberts & Wood, 2007, p. 64). The extent to which any individual is committed to any particular type of belief is thus a matter of strength of will. Yet in each of these, any of the five weaknesses of rigidity— "dogmatism, doxastic [i.e., pertaining to beliefs or opinions], complacency, stolid perseverance, perceptual rigidity, and comprehensional rigidity"—may be apparent, as may the three indicators of flaccidity: the rambling mind, the promiscuity of beliefs, or the person who is simply flummoxed by the world. The extent of commitment can be illustrated through the example of courage.

IV. Being Committed: Courage as an Intellectual and Moral Virtue

We rarely think about our moral beliefs when we act. The picture Kohlberg offers of moral actions' being a constant set of dilemmas solved by reasoning is not an authentic view of moral conduct, although it is manifestly one small part of it. For most people, one might say, the problem is not one of not knowing what to do—that's obvious—but rather how can we gear ourselves up to do the (moral) thing. That is not to say that we all grow up with a bunch of moral intuitions about right and wrong, but to make the point about the phenomenology of people acting (or not acting) morally, which is a classic problem of the will.

However, the problems of the virtue of courage can be made apparent in Melanie's fascination with science. All virtues are frequently exercised against obstacles of one kind or another in the world, and in Melanie's case the obstacles are not simply of her own making. First, she is eclectic in her scientific interests, but she really prefers the biological. In this she has to brave her physics professor father's disdain for biology as being a weak science and her mother's totally immature and irresponsible attitude ("whatever makes you happy, Melanie"). Moreover, as a bright student, she is being pestered by her English teacher, who wants to wean her away from science and engross her in literature. Standing up for what she is interested in requires some mild forms of courage; after all, both father and teacher are in a position to make life difficult for her. Not all parents and teachers are benign. But second, having made the choice of her interests, she has to turn her interest into an undertaking, which certainly requires devotion, but once again demands effort. She loves the generalities of science but is seen by her teachers as not very good at it. The problem is that her view of her undertaking does not mesh with the official view of the school. Her biological interests have matured into a total involvement with animals and their lives. She has come to resent the ways in which animal biology is taught, because her interest is animal lives and behaviors and she has use for biology only insofar as it helps her understand them. Often in her classrooms, she has to take major risks in speaking up for PETA (which she has joined), making herself objectionable to teachers and some students. As her undertaking has deepened and not matured in a predictable way (e.g., to be a veterinary surgeon or high school biology teacher), she is facing constant challenges.

Of course, her preparedness to be courageous in these ways puts immense strains on her willpower and her emotions. She is trying to forge what seems to her a moral and intellectual path that goes against the grain of formal schooling. Faced with written assignments of a typical kind, she bravely sets her answers in the framework of her developing ideological beliefs about the sanctity of animal life, risking her grades. Biologists, she is finding, can be extremely hard-hearted, not least because her teachers have gotten used to university experiments on monkeys, cats, and rats, which strikes her as uncivilized. Her willpower is unconcerned with matters like punctuality or working hard; she is already a driven student.

Rather she has to summon the will to continue to take risks with ideas, to "think outside the box" in search of arguments that she presents to her teachers. The emotional aspect of her will keeps her going. That is, she feels a profound respect and love for members of the animal kingdom, and all people can say of her that she wouldn't hurt a fly.

"True courage," as Nussbaum (1997) remarks, "requires freedom" (p. 55). What is striking about Melanie—and there is no need to assume she is a rare belief-holding individual child—is that she has a freedom of mind. That is, she is liberated from the conventional views of her circle of friends and family. If we understand freedom and liberty in broad terms as "freedom from," then Melanie has not been constrained by those conventions but addressed moral problems in her own way. The courage, in other words, is primarily intellectual, not physical. This is not, to use the trivial expression, "thinking outside the box," but using the passion of her commitments to construct a world of moral purposes driven by a free intellect. This is not therefore an exercise in divergent thinking, as if it were just a process. What kinds of intellectual freedoms a classroom with an epistemological presence will demand will, to some degree, depend on the age and maturity of the children.

But courage is not, of course, a prerogative of children. In his foreword to Vivian Paley's (1986) book *Boys and Girls: Superheroes in the Doll Corner,* Philip Jackson wrote:

> The fundamental requirement is courage. Vivian Paley is courageous. She excels in the capacity to look at herself as a teacher in an unflinching way. . . . Reading of her occasional blunders as a teacher and of her efforts to correct them, all fully admitted and wholesomely confronted, we are encouraged to face up to weaknesses of our own.
>
> *(p. iii)*

Notice here Jackson's use of the word "encourage," where Paley's example stiffens our sinews. Melanie's experience invites the question "What do we do to encourage children?" Clearly her father (and her mother) and some of her teachers discourage her from pursuing what she is manifestly interested in—and the reactions of students (there's Melanie on her hobby-animal again) also serve to sap her will, to drain the courage out of her. To be more precise about this, we need to explore further the range of what encouragement is (see also Sockett, 1993, pp. 70–77).

First, traditions going back to Plato in *The Laches* connect courage only to the physical. Shakespeare's Henry V addressing his troops before Agincourt—"Once more unto the breach, dear friends, once more"—vividly illustrates this view of courage and the task of the general addressing his troops before battle. Yet, for all the brilliance of Shakespeare's portrayal of this form of encouragement, courage is manifestly applicable to all kinds of actions and beliefs that issue in actions—physical, intellectual, and emotional, or personal, institutional, social, and political. Yet courage, surely, can be described as such only in the context of some fear or danger that has to be overcome. The difficulty with this condition is that we normally are happy to label people as heroes who, for instance, jump into a river to save a person drowning, though the individuals often act spontaneously without thought of the dangers involved: hence the claim "anyone would have done it," which is, of course, nicely self-effacing but wrong. Yet this spontaneity picks out an important condition, namely that in the normal case, of course, practical reason is heavily involved, in facing either immediate danger or long-term goals. To ascribe courage to a person, therefore, does demand that the person see the situation as dangerous under some description: for people do extraordinary things without realizing the dangers—and those acts, while perhaps thoroughly laudable in terms of the goals, cannot be described as courageous in terms of motivation. Finally, courage is not found merely in a specific instance or episode but can be manifest over a long period. A school principal, hired to "turn it around," may have nasty confrontations with teachers and students and frightening forays with the faculty. She may develop a kind of fearlessness (see Roberts & Wood, 2007, p. 218). In pursuit of her long-term goals, she may no longer see particular situations as dangerous or frightening, but we would still be inclined to credit her with the virtue of courage. In pursuit of long-term goals, the agent may no longer see particular situations as dangerous or frightening, but we would still be inclined to describe his or her activities as courageous.

Thus courage will become a disposition, a stable virtue that is now part of the individual's character, because, as Roberts and Wood analyze all virtues, there are characteristic patterns of motivation instantiated in that disposition, but we do not need to let the life-saving hero be the paradigm of a courageous act. A courageous response is always a personal commitment. But, as indicated earlier, the central feature of commitment binds the personal to the universal, the personal to the public, through my submission to rules and standards and to the universalizability of my belief. The personal commitment to a courageous act or belief is the virtue of the individual, but it is always in the context of "how to go about things." This might seem obvious in the examples of courage described, but surely, are not people who face an unpleasant death from an inoperable cancer just locked in their own personal struggle? Not so, I think. In any culture, there are appropriate frameworks for dying. There are expectations and conventions that, as we get older, we recognize in the lives and deaths of others. The framework of choice for the dying person is, in other words, socially determined not in the weak sense (that everything is socially determined) but in a strong sense that there are ways in which the friends and family expect the choices about dying, where they are possible, to be made. Courage is the classic example of commitment, precisely because it is developed and exercised against the grain, against fear and danger.

Roberts and Wood (2007) put it nicely in terms of the fear the intellectually courageous person overcomes:

> We sometimes fear knowledge—for example, self-knowledge, knowledge of criticism of our pet views, and especially of our own works, and knowledge of facts that are painful to us. We fear others disagreeing with us; we fear

challenges to our views; we fear looking bad in front of our colleagues and students. We fear being harmed in the course of intellectual practices—say, being beaten up by a playful chimpanzee or infected with a disease in the course of experimentation with microbes.

(p. 219)

V. Encouraging Commitment

In 1757, the British admiral John Byng was court-martialed and shot. In a naval battle off Minorca against a French squadron, after losing some of his ships, he had decided not to pursue the enemy. He was accused of personal cowardice in the face of the enemy, and the draconian naval laws of the time demanded capital punishment across the ranks. The king refused a royal pardon, though opinion in the country was solidly for Byng. In Voltaire's play *Candide,* there is a scene in which a British soldier is being shot, a clear reference to Byng's death, and Candide says, "In this country, it is wise to kill an admiral from time to time to encourage the others" (*Dans ce pays-ci, il est bon de tuer de temps en temps un amiral pour encourager les autres*).

"Pour encourager les autres." Though Voltaire is being sarcastic, the force of the term *encourager* here is important to note, because it conveys the idea of putting courage into someone, in this context with the fear of death. Indeed many a sailor has found the internal resources to fight because they were terrified of either being, or being seen as, a coward, as Shakespeare's Henry V understood. We use the word "encourage" in varied ways, some of which do not reflect this central force of the word. "I am encouraged by your interest in my paintings," as an artist might say, has nothing to do with courage, but with hope. "I encourage you to continue" is a help designed to boost confidence. But, "encourage" is also similar to "embolden"—that is, to give someone the confidence to tackle a difficult task, to take a risk. But this risk need not be where the situation is publicly and objectively terrifying, as is the plight of any sailor; it can be where there is risk from the personal viewpoint of the agent alone.

I have indicated earlier that our educational system fundamentally rewards right answers to the extent that we develop comfort in having things correct and that this habit of mind then becomes a carapace for all our beliefs, a protective shell within which our lives are not to be disturbed by inconvenient facts. In the search for truth, encouragement is an intellectual and pedagogical strategy, not an exhortation (come on, Mrs. Long's class!). That strategy will have certain critical elements, all connected to the goal of having children make judicious commitments to what they believe and not hold these beliefs dogmatically or rigidly.

Encouragement demands (a) a context in which students search for the truth, not for the right answer, (b) the teacher setting an example of facing up to uncertainty in the struggle for truth, (c) a dialogic space that protects divergent thinking and fosters student interaction as a basis, (d) a framework of assignments congruent with a search for truth, and (e) diagnosis of individual students' fears and phobias to get the encouragement tailored to specific challenges.

First, to repeat, a classroom with an epistemological presence and without epistemological secrets will be dominated by the search for truth.

Second, in the quest for the right answer, the teacher is the intellectual arbiter, the authority on what is right. So the teacher asks students questions to find out who has the right answer to the question. That constantly reinforces the right-answer habit. An alternative is for a teacher to abandon that right-answer framework, and the habits and expectations that go with it, by *never (or rarely) asking children a question to which the teacher already knows the answer.* The encouragement here lies in the teacher's providing a strong example of grappling with uncertainty and being brave enough to tackle it. This intellectual modeling places a much greater range of obligations on teachers and a versatility of mind on which the contemporary curriculum seems to place little demand (see chapter 12).

Third, that stance would create the dialogic space needed in the classroom that must be strongly protected as an arena for ideas, not answers. Crucial here is that the space is not filled with hot air—either from teachers or children. It must be purposeful and geared to the search at hand and be a supportive and *encouraging* atmosphere. The test example in chapter 1 on why the Great Wall of China was built illustrates that a serious search for truth here would encounter numerous possibilities and alternatives, which children can discuss—for instance, that there would need to be a distinction between what the emperor thought he was doing and what the function turned out to be. Freshmen students, in my experience, seem to learn as much from others in their small groups as they learn from me, the teacher, for two reasons at least: First, in engaging with complex ideas, say, Mill's essay *On Liberty,* students will share different perspectives and negotiate understandings. That experience itself generates puzzles about understanding Mill, but also about the areas of human freedoms that he espouses and how the demands he makes are to be understood in contemporary America. They are gradually developing in this context the ability to play with ideas and to frame alternatives. Second, the right-answer habit is being broken up: reading a text becomes a matter not of memorizing Mill's view, but of engaging with it, of beginning to see reading the text as an exercise in companionship with the author on the subject of liberty. To read the transcripts of the medical students' engagements in Abercrombie's (1965) studies illustrates the power of group work, not just for learning, but for commitments examined and changed through taking risks. However, the curriculum also must be framed as a search for truth, which was the burden of my complaint at the Grade 8 curriculum in chapter 5. It is salutary to note that contemporary curriculum control and the frameworks of assessment militate against such careful, diligent work.

Fourth, to encourage students and children to take risks with ideas, assignments must provide challenges congruent with that target. In school and in some university teaching, we are likely to use tests that test only memory or assignments that demand recapitulation—for example, "How does Mill define liberty?" There are at least three pedagogical problems lurking in this injunction. First, there are certain assignment types that rarely provide for a context of risk-taking—for instance, "Do you agree with Mill...?" Second, risk-taking has to be informed by content. Children and students thus have to understand that risk-taking is a matter not of imagining some weird and wonderful possibility, but of using the rules and standards as the crutch upon which ideas can be generated. Assignments thus have to be very carefully framed and read. Third, while the group is significant in the dialogic space, the individual student must remain of paramount concern.

Finally, therefore, encouraging a commitment to hold beliefs intellectually in the ways described is a matter of individual endeavor. While it is possible to build confidence for a group (witness Henry V), the development of confidence in each individual is essential. First, each individual has his or her own idiosyncrasies, phobias, preoccupations, desires, and problems. There are no cookies to be cut in classrooms. Second, we know too well of dropout rates from high school and from college or university, let alone those who drop out mentally but still attend. We know that many mature students who return to study had lost confidence in their schools, were low-achievers, and have found personal confidence in other pursuits that enable them to tackle studying again. Built into taking risks with ideas, and making commitments, has to be a self-confidence that can be fostered only by teachers, one student at a time. Confidence will emerge from having the right kinds of experiences in learning, and all experiences can build up in a student a sense of wholeness, a sense of purpose and integrity.

This presupposes that children will develop a clear sense of identity, and for that, the virtue of self-knowledge is critical if (a) they are to have integrity of desires and values and wholeness as completeness and (b) they are to develop the will to pursue those desires and values by committing themselves appropriately to their beliefs and to their actions.

9

IDENTITY AND KNOWING ONESELF

The Self-Conscious Individual

The moral cast of the man lies below the level of the speech–act.
(Williams, 1973, p. 217)

Three "individuals" lurking beneath the framework of personal knowledge have
so far been identified: the historical individual existing in time and space, the belief-
holding individual, and his or her commitments, and it is to the self-conscious
individual that we now turn. Of course these are not individuated people, nor
are they a complete picture of the differing individuals we might be, but they
are elements of each and every one of us in respect of our personal knowledge as
persons, not just as human beings. (Infants don't hold beliefs, but they are persons.)
The argument in this chapter is that individual personal identity is contributory
to human flourishing, which demands that the agent has self-knowledge. The
question of personal identity is, roughly for the moment, about who I am as a
self: knowing that self, whatever its characteristics or quality, is integral to personal
identity and to its development.

Two preliminaries to the notion of identity: First, there is the philosophical
question of identity as sameness—for example, a person possesses a battle-ax used
at the Battle of Hastings in 1066. Of course, since then, it has needed several new
heads and several new handles; ergo is the ax still the one that had been used at
Hastings? This invites a set of questions about human idiosyncrasy—for example,
on people with multiple personalities, on transsexuals, and on the Jekylls and
Hydes of this world, as well as on people whose traumatic experiences change
them such that we might ask whether this is the same person. However, these
types of problem about identity need not concern us. Second, there are differing historical and contemporary conceptions of identity. For example, a crucial
concept in early modern England was that of an office—not a place with a desk
where one worked, but a social position with moral obligations. Over half the English population in the sixteenth century held offices, each of which was entered
through "taking an oath of office." Charles I had broken the oath of office as a

king and acted as a tyrant, and so he was executed. To understand that period, as with all studies of history and culture, we need to beware of taking the presuppositions of our modern view of identity and trying to understand the sixteenth century in our terms rather than theirs (Condren, 2006). The thoughts about identity here are therefore couched in what we may call (grand abstraction again) contemporary Western civilization.

In section 1 of this chapter, the account of personal identity rests on that of a person. "Person" is a normative concept describing someone worthy of respect as a human being, and it thus differs in meaning from that of "human being" *simpliciter* and differs again from "self," each having distinctive links to personal identity. If children and students are to develop a coherent sense of self, they must expand the horizons of their language, cultivate an imagination about themselves, continuously reflect on what they value and what is of most worth, and set their dignity and self-confidence as autonomous selves within the framework of autonomy and rationality. In section 2, the sociologist's use of the word role is briefly distinguished from the philosophical use that is focused on a role's obligations, its rights and duties, specifically the teacher's role in a moral space and a political order. Finally, in section 3, the account of self-knowledge makes it not a matter for criteria of knowledge but how a person constitutes him or herself. It is a virtue itself but descriptively implies other intellectual and moral virtues, such as honesty and courage. Self-knowledge, of course, also makes hugely different demands on persons in roles defined by moral purposes. For instance, the difference between the moral demands of bricklaying, while not negligible, and those of teaching are qualitatively different in respect of moral demands.

I. Persons and Personal Identity

Personal identity may be seen in two distinct ways. There is, first, the "socially defined fact of personal identity, in which the particularity of personal embodiment plays a part" (Harré, 1983, p. 27). That person over there is Bill Smith, which identifies Bill as a person with a body. Those of us who know Bill know him as wise, good, and friendly (his personal qualities) and as father, bricklayer, and Manchester United supporter (his roles). Even if we were looking at an infant Bill Smith in his stroller, we could still describe his temperament (e.g., "He's a bit moody today") and his social definition ("That's Melanie Smith's son, isn't it?") Matters of identity thus have this central element of social definition: this surfaces as an educational problem when children acquire stereotypical definitions of their social identity as students in classrooms—for example, as the class clown.

This social definition is distinct from the personal sense of identity through which "a person conceives of him or herself as a singular being with a continuous and unique history" (Harré, 1983, p. 27), though manifestly both senses of identity interact within the framework of our lives. It is this sense of personal identity that is the theme of this chapter, because it is located within our discussions of personal knowledge and how, from the inside, so to speak, we see the world. This is a particularly fertile field for educators and teachers, because how the child or the student conceives of him or herself is central to his or her self-concept, not just as a learner, but as someone beginning to locate him or herself in a framework of history (the historical individual), belief (the belief-holding individual), and self-development and beginning to ask not just "Who am I?" but "Where am I going?" However, social identity and personal identity matter in teaching students, because the teacher is contributing to the development of both. (Piaget, Kohlberg, Perry and others have contributed much to our understanding of development, but I will not discuss issues of development here. See Further Reading.) In the classroom, his teacher knows Bill Smith, the eighth-grader who seems a good kid, terrible at math, good in group work (as the teacher fixes his social identity), but that teacher must often wonder "what's going on in his head" (his personal identity). It is there that Bill is working away at who he is and where he is going, for which he needs teacher understanding and support, although how he truly sees himself is his to share or to protect.

Person and Self: The Person

In what follows, a distinction is made between identity as a *person* (Harré's social identity sense) and identity as a *self*. We are thus working with two interlocking but distinguishable concepts—person and self. As we have seen, for Harré, the person "is the socially defined, publicly visible embodied being, endowed with all kinds of powers and capacities for public, meaningful action" (1983, p. 26). Powers and capacities would include such things as using language and being self-aware as distinctive of human beings. This complex account, however, is unfinished. First, the normative concept of person carries with it the idea of intrinsic moral worth of the person: "the most urgent and powerful cluster of demands that we recognize as moral concern the respect for the life, integrity, and well-being, even flourishing, of others" (Taylor, 1989, p. 4). Upfront in understanding personhood, therefore, we need a strong sense of respect as being integral to it (see Downie & Telfer, 1969; Peters, R. S., 1966, chapter 8). Second, we need to recognize a more political way of looking at persons, emphasized in political and social conversation, as having rights as a way of upholding their dignity as persons. The worldwide discussion on human rights is driven by a sense of respect for every individual and the respect to which he or she is entitled (see Clapham, 2007, chapter 2). So, the question of whether Rover, the retriever, is to be regarded as a person is a matter of judgment of his moral worth, but, as a dog, he has no rights, though his owners (or should it be caregivers?) have duties to him. Yet the treatment of dogs commonly involves use of sterilization and euthanasia, procedures that, if not unthinkable, are at least exceedingly rare with persons qua persons, not to say controversial. Human beings as a class are worthy of respect as persons with rights. In addition to Harré's account, therefore, the "person" is located in a moral space, in Taylor's (1989) words, and in a political order, such as a democracy where a person has rights. (But see also Harré & Secord, 1972, especially chapter 6: "An Anthropomorphic Model of Man.")

Questions of how persons should be treated in general, how their liberties or rights should be restricted by law, and how conventions can provide a framework for the activities of persons (or what they should be able to do to their dogs) become matters of moral and political debate. The abortion debate is about at what stage a fetus becomes recognizably a person and therefore subject to evaluation of moral worth. The debate can get very clouded with talk of the "right to life" and the "woman's right to choose," which are sociopolitical slogans for serious and complex matters. The death penalty introduces a different range of issues, but that debate focuses on whether the state has the right to take a person's (note the word) life. Some advocates jump over the moral problems in the moral status of personhood by describing a murderer as "subhuman" and as "having lost the right to life," which invokes different kinds of moral and political evaluations but are attacks on the persons being treated as such. We also use the word "humane" in describing how governments and others deal with other people. As usual in political/moral discussions, people emphasize different principles: in debates on illegal immigration in the United States, "humaneness" has to be weighed in the balance with "retribution for those who break the law." Public life therefore is full of questions of how persons are to be treated, what rights they have, and what punishments are appropriate. But centrally, to regard human beings as persons is to see them as worthy of respect, which was not the way Hitler regarded Jews, gypsies, and other groups of human beings.

Person and Self: The Self

Yet if person is a socially defined, embodied human being with all kinds of capacities and rights in a moral space and a political order, how do we understand the notion of the self? First, it is highly likely that my description of myself would be much more complicated than any description that could be offered by my spouse or my friend, however close and long-standing our relationship. This is not to say that people "keep things to themselves" (i.e., to their selves), though they do, but no one can experience the world of my experiences exactly as I do. As we have seen in chapter 7, people can share their experiences, but, as we know from what we as individuals think, imagine, desire, remember, dream of, fantasize about, we don't, fortunately, share these with other people. This is also true of memory (see chapter 8), even though at its core "memory is the essence of personal identity. Figuratively speaking, memory is so much what makes him a certain person that, when provided with certain memories, he cannot doubt who he is" (Williams, 1973, p. 14). Without "private" experience being possible, of course, psychotherapy would make no sense, because the basic target of psychotherapy is to help a person understand his real self, which is either not known to him or suppressed through trauma. Yet it would also be intolerable socially if people were constantly rehearsing all their inner imaginings, dreams, and so on, not because it could become excruciatingly tedious, but because there would scarcely be time for ordinary life. Our "private" world is the world of our selves, and ou descriptions depend on our self-knowledge so that, as in the earlier quo from Bernard Williams, "Self-deception, which is one thing that the accurate agent must avoid, is a homage that fantasy pays to the sense of reality."

However, our self-descriptions apart, "What I am, as a self... is essentially defined by the way things have significance for me" (Taylor, 1989, p. 34). What has value for me? Where, ultimately, do I stand? "To know who you are is to be oriented in moral space—what is good or bad, what is worth doing and what not, what has meaning and importance, what is trivial or secondary" (p. 28). But what are the conditions and the capacities needed for this?

First and foremost, we need a language. "The limits of my language," Wittgenstein proposed, "mean the limits of my world" (1922, proposition 5), a philosophical statement given practical application by a former Israeli foreign minister, Abba Eban, who said of a British general that he was a man of few words, fortunately just enough to contain the thoughts of which he was capable! My language is used publicly, but also in what I think. This includes background knowledge. Thinking about one's self demands a language (see Hirst, 1972/2010, pp. 53–65), and the conversations of our lives, our social discourse, influence what we think. Language and thought are reciprocal, but thought without language is impossible. Wittgenstein's use of the word "limits" here is significant for educators: while it does not imply that those with limits of language are in some kind of deficit state, it emphasizes that the teaching task is to enlarge the language(s) for children to enable them to choose in terms of their location in a moral space and a political order. If a child cannot enter human conversation in all its different modes, that will place limits on how the child can come to answer these critical questions of self-definition. (The development of language is, of course, a major topic in child psychology; see Further Reading.)

Second, that is not merely a descriptive or an expressive language, but the language of imagination. Self-definition includes the what-if. Typically young children try out all sorts of possible futures. This year Samantha wants to be a pilot; next year, a vet; next year, a stay-at-home mom. Life without limits becomes a life with horizons. Necessarily, horizons contain ambitions, and ambitions are soon tempered by reality, the reality of what is required in terms of effort and knowledge to realize those ambitions. The educator must work for children to develop the imaginative capacity to imagine new horizons, to realize what they might become—in moral terms.

Third, as we develop a sense of self forming a critical element in our personal identity, we are bound to confront questions about what is worth doing, why we should do some things but not others, and what aspirations are of value, given our temperaments and desires. We confront, in other words, the question of what is the kind of life we want to lead. This is a matter of not merely imagination, but the establishment of directions, even principles of procedure. But unless children and students have a sufficient breadth of understanding of the world and the kinds of conversations that provide a home in which aspirations can mature, personal identity will have no opportunity to flourish.

Lest this seem too formal, consider Aisha. As a child growing up in rural Pakistan, at age 8 she saw her future as being like her mother and grandmother, caring for her husband and her children and eking out a modest rural existence. Her schooling was limited, but then she grew up speaking two or three local languages and had some English taught to her in the sparse formal context of her primary school. Opportunity came when she was 14 and her uncle, who had emigrated to the United States some years before, sponsored Aisha's father and family. As immigrants they were stunned by the wealth and the opportunities of their adopted country. While the family's coherence suffered somewhat from culture shock, Aisha's relatively short period in American schools opened up her imagination to what she might do. She was not a different self at 18 as compared to age 8. Yet she was, in another sense, a new self, because her self-definition was now able to embrace horizons with opportunities there for the taking. As an undergraduate, her memory of her family's poverty was constantly with her, and her initial focus for a career was one that would be financially rewarding—for example, as a lawyer, only to realize, through taking a philosophy major, that moral issues and her increasingly dominant concerns for others should guide her life; a different kind of emphasis in her self-definition thus appeared. After graduating, she started to work in nonprofit organizations and within a couple of years was back in the Swat Valley from which her family originally came 15 years before, in the role of a field worker for a human rights organization.

While the self is usually a coherent unity, William James distinguished the material me (the empirical self of the body), the social me (the recognition I get from others), and the spiritual me (everything in my consciousness) as an account of personal identity (see Hollis, 1977, pp. 92 ff.). Taylor (1989) also describes a three-point axis to our personal identity: "our respect for others (built into the normative realization of others as persons and as, in some sense, equals), what makes a full life (questions about worth), but also personal dignity" (p. 14). Aisha's orthodox commitment to Islam gave her the respect for others, so deeply engrained in her consciousness as to be invulnerable. But, given the contrast in living between her now American family and her relatives back home, she became driven by the issue of human rights and specifically the dignity of the individual. Dignity is important, as it expresses our self-definition to others, usually in nonverbal ways. Taylor suggests this is built into our very comportment—"the very way we walk, move, gesture, speak" (1989, p. 15)—how we appear to other people. This is not our social identity as a person, but a projection of our self. Dignity can be expressed erratically, even become warped. Minor insults used to result in duels as a matter of honor. Aggressive young men take revenge when they think they have been disrespected—"dissed"—the insult being to their dignity. Yet dignity is also profoundly linked to confidence in who we are, our self-confidence. The educational problem is too often that children and students become highly self-confident when, to put it slightly cruelly, they really have little to be confident about. Self-confidence is empty without self-consciousness. Dignity, of the kind Taylor mentions, can too easily become an act, under which can lie deep uncertainty. People sometimes do understand their self-confidence as an act, even a bluff, but many self-confident people lack a developed self-consciousness, indeed a fear of what the future holds for them. Facing infringements on their rights, they may passively accept their fate.

Yet there is a final element to personal identity and to the gap between the observed social person and the individual self. Hollis (1977) says, "An autonomous man acts freely by definition. He acts freely, only if he has good reasons for what he does (and no better reasons for doing something else). He has good reasons, only if he acts in his ultimate interests. His ultimate interests derive from what he essentially is. What he essentially is depends partly on what is essential to his being any person and partly on what is essential to his being that particular person" (p. 101). What "he essentially is" describes the self and is the "strict criterion" of identity for persons. Essentially, at least, a person is free, free to decide who he or she is, determining his or her ultimate interests and acting rationally in their light. Autonomy and freedom are thus constitutive non-negotiable elements of the normative self. When a person lacks autonomy and freedom, he or she cannot realize him or herself. The slave's personal identity as a self is so constricted that his or her own wants and desires are crushed and disallowed. The silent women in the Belenky and colleagues' study (see chapter 7) are, so to speak, locked out in terms of enriching their understanding of themselves. Neither the slave nor the silent woman has autonomy, except in some very limited sense and under harsh constraints.

So "our basic assumptions about the nature of truth and reality and the origins of knowledge shape the way we see the world and ourselves as participants in it. They affect our definitions of ourselves, the way we interact with others, our public and private personae, our sense of control over life events, our views of teaching and learning, and our conceptions of morality" (Belenky et al., 1986, p. 3). The intimate links between person and self is where public knowledge and personal knowledge come together for teachers and educators. If there is an epistemological presence in the classroom, it will be a place where "these basic assumptions…shape the way we see the world and ourselves as participants in it." But if children and students are to develop a coherent sense of self, they must expand the horizons of their language, cultivate an imagination about themselves, continuously reflect on what they value and what is of most worth, and set their dignity and self-confidence as autonomous selves within the framework of autonomy and rationality.

"When I was a child I spoke as a child, I understood as a child, I thought as a child; but when I became a man I put away childish things" (1 Cor. 13:11). Putting on one side the religious interpretation of this and the subsequent phrases, is becoming a man creating a new self? Sheldon (2006) suggests that old age is a process of both change and development, as we encounter new challenges up to and including how to die. So "the issue of our condition can never be exhausted for us by what we *are,* because we are always also changing and *becoming*" (Taylor, 1989, p. 47). Indeed, it would be odd, so to speak, to disown our childhood, because that would at least suggest some kind of loss of integrity as wholeness and the point made by Warnock (see chapter 7) about the integrity of a the historical person's past and present. Even if I am "born again," in any sense, that is only an achievement against a historical past self. Besides, if my experience is similar to other people's, images of my childhood are a constant in my mind and in my mind's eye.

II. Person, Role, and Teaching Purpose

> Tinker, tailor, Soldier, sailor, Rich man, poor man, Beggar-man, thief.
> —*Children's counting rhyme from 1695*

Tinkers, tailors, soldiers, and sailors are what we think of as social positions or roles people occupy, albeit lowly in the scheme of things. Rich men and poor men are not roles exactly, but they do describe a status in terms of wealth, whereas the beggar-man and the thief are occupations without being social positions or roles. Sociological theory would usually regard all of these as roles, simply because role (a) picks out a class of people with certain attributes, (b) has certain expectations and behaviors attached to it, and (c) can also be a way of picking out functions in a social system, as viewed from the outside, criteria applicable to each of these six characters (see Downie, 1971, chapter 6). It should also be said that there is no particular reason why a person acting in a role, viewed like this, need be aware that he is, indeed, in such a role.

It might, first, be argued that a person is no more than a bunch of roles. That is, Bill Smith is father, bricklayer, and Manchester United supporter (and much else), and his personal qualities of practical wisdom and friendliness are manifest in the roles he plays. This view is problematic because Bill's roles can conflict. He has to decide between going to see Manchester United or taking care of his infant son. In which role is he doing the deciding? Behind the roles stands the person. It might, second, be argued that being a person or a moral agent is itself a role, especially given Harré's account of a person as "socially defined." Downie (1971) points out various criticisms of this: Bill Smith would then be seen as playing the role of both bricklayer and moral agent simultaneously, which again cannot address role conflict and is, in Ryle's (1949) terms, a category mistake. There aren't two roles here: there is Bill the bricklayer, who is a moral agent deriving from his personhood, not from his role. We therefore have to insist on the notion of person not being itself a role: rather the person plays a variety of roles, in which activities his personal qualities—wisdom, friendliness, and so on—are apparent. "Moral agents are always acting: sometimes they act simply as persons, sometimes as persons in certain roles or capacities" (Downie, 1971, p. 133). Of course, what a person actually does within a role is dependent on what the demands of the role are. The role of the president of the United States, for instance, is embodied both in the oath of office and in the conventions and constitutional limits that are always to be interpreted by its occupant. The office is thus invested with the personal qualities that each occupant brings to it.

In chapter 3, in discussing the teacher's contractual, moral, and epistemological authority, it became apparent that the teacher's role comprised rights and duties of a particular kind. Apparent so far is the inescapable fact of the teacher's being a person and a self, a moral agent, with powers, capacities, and competencies; with moral ideals, and with virtues and dispositions. Manifestly teachers have different personal characteristics and qualities, though the role may put a premium on what those characteristics and qualities are. However,

> One of the greatest challenges in teaching is to survive misconceptions of teaching. We use the word "survive" because such misconceptions cannot be overcome in any final sense. Some regard the teacher as a trained techni-cian carrying out the dictates of policy-makers. Some treat the teacher as an economic resource, fabricating "human capital." Others regard the teacher as an instrument of political and cultural change. Still others assume that the teacher's charge is merely to conserve extant custom, knowledge, and belief.
>
> *(Hansen & Laverty, 2010, p. 234)*

Each of these is *a* conception of teaching and its social purpose, and each could be framed within a sociological analysis of the teacher's role or function. The "trained technician" view has a particular history, stemming from the successes of the natural sciences, parasitic on which is the putative success of psychology and sociology whose "findings from research" can be handed down to the teacher-technician to implement. Since, in this view, values must be separated from facts, decisions about ends are to be made by policy makers acting on behalf of the public who owns the schools. In the second "misconception," politicians and industrialists want schools to produce engineers and entrepreneurs, not archae-ologists: the function of the schools cannot be ignored in a knowledge-based economy. Third, other politicians and activists take the fact that the school must, at some level, be an agent in political and cultural change, and seek to demand the changes they want. From the political right, the Texas School Board changes the social studies curriculum. Others want prayer in schools. From the left, only social justice within schools will produce the political and cultural change. Finally, schools have traditionally had the function of conveying the "wisdom of the past," and this is seen by many to be a losing tradition. Like the technician-teacher, it contains an implicit view of the teacher as scholar. Hansen and Laverty are de-scribing these as misconceptions, against their own vivid conception of teaching invested with moral purpose and educationally intrinsic, not instrumental, ends.

Democratic disagreement on "what the schools are for" and thus how teaching should be conceived will reflect the protagonists' values and emphases. These are not, I think, misconceptions about teaching: they reveal debates and differences about the purposes of schooling—and the teachers within the institutions. To say a view of schooling is a misconception is to find an epistemological fault, but the purposes of schooling are debatable only within moral purposes. After all, the socializing purposes of Harold Mann's common school did not contain misconceptions about teaching. The schools simply had very limited educational purposes—witness McGuffey's Readers. To understand the role of the teacher and how his or her personhood (not personality) is embodied in teaching with educational purposes, I need to describe what the purpose is. Moreover, as with Dewey, any account has to be framed within the political order of democracy.

a. The fundamental requirement of the democratic life is that, as far as possible, people act freely and are able to choose how they can live their lives autonomously as moral agents.

b. We require a democratic polity, not because it is perfect, but because, as Karl Popper (1962, chapter 3) would have put it, its systems prevent those who want power from doing too much damage.

c. More positively, a democratic polity provides the political basis for human flourishing.

d. Being free, being able to choose, being autonomous, and being moral agents are not natural endowments of the human being.

e. We need a social and political environment, and institutions, in which these capacities and dispositions can develop and be fostered.

f. We need to be educated in such a way that we acquire the dispositions and attitudes, as well as appropriate knowledge and skill to become free, autonomous, choosing moral agents, if we are to realize these ambitions for human beings and their lives in a democratic polity.

We need, in other words, to be educated as persons. These requirements underpin *all the different possible kinds of curriculum—traditional or progressive, ancient or modern.* This is true even of strictly vocational programs, say for military pilots, because through any kind of program one's personal identity is being enhanced. But the pedagogical requirements for attaining these kinds of goals and purpose with children are clear and uncomplicated, which is not to say they are not disputed. How these criteria are to be interpreted and what weight individuals will place on each is open to democratic discourse.

First, as children and students are working their way to mature adulthood, they are simultaneously developing as persons and, as such, as moral agents. The schoolteacher, apart from family members, is first in line with the social responsibility for this, whether teaching advanced chemistry, shop, football, or initial literacy. One cannot disassociate who the child is becoming as a person from the subject the child is learning, because the subject itself is contributing to the child's identity, but also because the person is the ontological basis upon which hang all kinds of achievements, roles, and positions.

Second, we know enough about human beings to know that a major mode of learning is by example. The teacher must therefore embody moral agency for the children to emulate, even while teaching children to develop their own moral agency. But we run into danger, I think, if we imply that teachers are static rather than dynamic in the development of their own personal identity through and within teaching. Schools are places where teachers, as professionals and as persons, learn. The idea of being a self-conscious example to children should also extend to colleagues. For that to be successful, there needs to be a community that supports leadership by all, if such exemplification is not to be derided or accusations leveled that it is being used for personal gain or self-approval. Teachers are examples, not just on matters of respect, but as learners.

Third, the parameters of the educational role of the teacher can be derived from both the nature of personal identity and the development of self, as I have explored it, and the situation of persons within a moral space and a political order. However, this is not just a concentration on the child rather than the subject, to use that misbegotten contrast. Rather, which subjects and which disciplines should be encountered at different ages is also a matter of personal identity—but with a particular purpose. It is to inculcate the types of conversations and languages through which decisions and choices can become well-grounded. When we speak of a liberal education as concerned with the development of the well-rounded person, to use that cliché, we are seeking to provide for the development of the child or the student's mind, to provide a broad basis for the development of wants and desires as persons and as selves, as well as providing an identity with intellectual, social, and political issues necessary for democratic citizens. That is a development of personhood and of self as the individual constructs that identity.

Finally, as our views of education are rooted in a democratic society, teachers also contribute to the development of the child as a citizen. Citizenship implies loyalty to the democratic community. The American tradition, unlike many others, is vehemently patriotic, with the Pledge of Allegiance being the most outward and visible sign of that commitment. Schools in this society are expected to reinforce what are called American values, specifically that of national loyalty. Teachers therefore have an unspecific role as cheerleaders for the nation that it would be socially and professionally difficult for them to disavow. In this narrow sense, most, if not all, teachers teach citizenship. Yet three specific challenges have to be faced. First, the professional role demands that a teacher provide a model of a "concerned" citizen. At any educational level, as the demands of knowledge demonstrate, alternatives need to be understood. The broad axes of decision-making, issues of freedom and equality, can be exposed to children at any age, without specific political bias. Second, the teacher should describe and/or support models of participation—for example, in having children think about their less-fortunate contemporaries and act for them. Finally, the demands of knowledge should create an inquisitive spirit for children emerging as adult citizens. That is, policies and practices should be subject to scrutiny in classrooms. Teachers should not be wary of showing children examples of real evil, as in slavery or the Holocaust, or of the dire effects of natural disasters, as in Haiti. Teachers are ultrasensitive to political and parental complaints: they face politically charged demands to teach the myths and legends, and some facts, from the country's history. Yet school and college are probably the only venue in a child's life that can approach the conditions for a balanced political discourse. Of course, teachers need to know where they themselves stand, whether their stance is justifiable or precarious. In this respect, among many others, they need self-knowledge and knowledge of their role.

III. The Challenge of Knowing Oneself

Personal identity then is of two kinds: social identity (in which individuals are seen as persons) and self-identity, in which the self-conscious individual locates him or herself in a moral space and a political order. Schools, I have argued, are vehicles for helping the development of both forms of identity, specifically because, though the curriculum is described in terms of subjects, the student is developing his or her identity through the conversations within disciplines, in Taylor's webs of interlocution, in Kazepides's dialogues (2010), or in the kinds of conversation Oakeshott embraces. None of this can be attempted or achieved without self-knowledge. However, insofar as knowledge of any kind in the public realm demands the three conditions—namely A believes that p; p is true, and A has justification for p, then we might want to operate with those conditions as we seek knowledge of ourselves. Moreover, we would expect the virtues of truthfulness (chapter 4), open-mindedness (chapter 5), and impartiality (chapter 6) also to be characteristics of the self-knower. Of course, understanding oneself will also demand knowledge of one's experience (chapter 7) and the levels of one's commitment, requiring both courage and integrity-as-wholeness (chapter 8).

Self-knowledge has a long and distinguished history in philosophy, notoriously in Descartes's "Cogito, ergo sum" ("I think, therefore I am") that lays the ghosts of skepticism—because here, Descartes says, is one thing of which I have certain knowledge—my own existence. The objects of self-knowledge are our mental states, our sense impressions, and our desires. Some philosophers, in particular Ryle (1949), have argued there is no such thing as self-knowledge, as it is just one case of knowledge in general. However, there are some fundamental philosophical points to make about self-knowledge, given that it appears to be as much subject to questions of ordinary truth as any other sort of knowledge, precisely because it contains the word knowledge.

I suggested in chapter 5 that we are the authority on and cannot be mistaken about the beliefs that we have, though we might be mistaken about the content. I believe that Bill Smith is the king of France (but there is no king of France, so he can't be). So we could say first that what we *know* about ourselves cannot be gainsaid. However, while we can admit this is true of belief, it is clearly wrong about public knowledge incorporating criteria of truth independent of my say-so. But there is also something odd about my saying that I have beliefs about myself. For the question then is what are the beliefs about? For example, it is surely redundant to say I believe that I believe that Bill is the king of France. We don't peer inside at our beliefs, as if they were objects of our attention, introspectionists notwithstanding. We just have beliefs.

It is clearly the case, however, that a person who has self-knowledge is in a special position vis-à-vis the beliefs that underpin his public or personal knowledge, because, literally speaking, he observes situations and interprets them against whatever small- or large-scale theories he has. This might be true of anything external to him—that is, the way he regularly forms beliefs. Or it might be his self-monitoring of the way he thinks, for example, about his children's upbringing and how he treats them. Here, once again, we run across the notion of "seeing as." But when he comes to "view" what he knows, he is not observing anything, not even in his mind's eye, which is a weakness of introspectionism. What he appears to do is to examine his beliefs or other mental states. "For conceiving a belief or intention (etc.) as my own requires treating it as *open to change.* [my italics] What is special about the method of knowing one's own states, on this view, is that we are each *agents,* relative to our own states: we are uniquely able to constitute ourselves" (Gertler, 2008, 1.2.1). This suggests that our self-knowledge is not a matter of applying the criteria of knowledge to our self-knowledge, but that *self-knowledge is the process of constituting ourselves through understanding who we are, and it is that understanding that will require intellectual and moral virtues.*

However, this does not mean to say we are marooned in our own thoughts. "Self-knowledge," writes MacIntyre (1999), "both presupposes and is presupposed by our self-ascriptions of identity. . . . But genuine and extensive self-knowledge becomes possible only in consequence of those social relationships which on occasion provide badly needed correction for our own judgments" (p. 95). Self-knowledge, he writes, is a "shared achievement." An attempt to transpose general criteria of knowledge to self-knowledge is mistaken: they do not apply. Rather our self-knowledge is how we build our identity as persons and selves, not always (but not never, either) bounded by the demands of truth in the public sense and that it is framed in terms of our relations with others. The remark "You can be such a fool," if it does not elicit a right hook, will pull a person up short and make him focus on him or herself. Thus the description of personal identity and self-identity, on this "constitution" argument, is achieved through examining our beliefs and seeing that our identity is within our control as agents and becomes the vehicle for determining who we are and where we are going, but it is also in play, so to speak, within the network of relationships that we have. If that is plausible, then dispositions to be open-minded, to listen to the advice of others, to see oneself as learning, are also virtues necessary to self-knowledge.

However, the conditions of developing our identity still demand the use of reason, especially the core virtue of honesty or truthfulness (see chapter 4) and the avoidance of deceit (i.e., self-deception). If I fail to be honest with myself, which is bound to influence my actions one way or another, I am also misleading others and failing to recognize that obligation. Self-knowledge demands moral appraisal of oneself, operating in a moral space and a political order.

The primary way in which we examine our beliefs and our selves, our wants and wishes, needs and desires, is through moral self-critique in service of developing our personal and social identity. If we examine this requirement for teachers and their self-knowledge, we can describe two distinct lines of inquiry, suggested by Oakeshott (1991, pp. 70–78). In self-reflective thought, he suggests, there are requirements of self-disclosure and requirements of self-enactment.

1. *Self-disclosure* would describe my practical interactions with other agents (children in classrooms, faculty in lounges, parents in conferences) and how they took place. So reflection here would be to review my actions, intentional or unintentional, especially how my moral self is disclosed in these public interactions. For example, in examining my altercation with Bill Smith in my eighth-grade class today, as he was not concentrating and just playing around, I will need to try to trace how I appeared to him and to the class, the language I used (encouraging, discouraging, supportive, or hostile). This would also give me insight into how my educational values of both a general and specific kind played into that altercation. The purpose, of course, is to learn as a teacher.

2. *Self-enactment* is deliberation on and examination of those moral sentiments and virtues, principles and commitments to which I aspire, which I enact, and which are at the core of my personal identity. In this self-conversation, so to speak, I am not here concerned with Bill and his problems. My review of self-enactment does not demand a focus on practice to make the examination coherent or cogent. Rather, I need to examine rigorously my motives in teaching, my ambitions, and my ideals. My altercation with Bill might trigger my interest, say, in the work of Nel Noddings on caring. To deepen my personal identity in this respect is achieved through exposing the limits of my knowledge and understanding, translating them into horizons through reading, and extending my conversations of whatever seems suitable for this pursuit.

However, there is an important caveat for teachers to this twofold direction of inquiry in search of self-identity. Such rigorous thought may make the occupation of teaching less attractive. I may conclude that teaching is not a good fit with my temperament and talents. I may decide I really don't like working with children. I may feel in my efforts at teaching I see more in terms of failure than success or that I do not have the mental resources to summon what I think is needed to cope with the plight of some of the children I teach. Self-reflection is therefore not self-congratulatory: it can be frightening and demand the kind of courage outlined in chapter 8. My commitment to teaching, in other words, can collapse if I am sincere and honest with myself. Neither guilt nor shame has any place in this direction of inquiry—though they might in other sorts of inquiry. Teaching as a moral activity demands putting oneself on the line in so many ways, in particular in supporting children not just as you correct their math, but supporting them to figure out who they are and where they are going. That is a tough business.

In either of these inquiries, self-deception must be avoided—as the Delphic oracle's motto "know thyself" implies. Julia was head of a math department in a suburban high school and was a student in a program on which I taught. After a two-week workshop, she came to me in a state of some distress. She felt she had deceived herself over 19 years into thinking that her tough, no-nonsense approach to the students showed her excellence as a teacher. She realized she had turned into a martinet, she had turned her math teaching into "rule by fear," and while she had all the formal successes (AP successes, etc., college-bound math majors), she had simply erected this role-identity, thinking it matched her self-identity, and had suddenly come to realize how false it was and how she had been deceiving herself all this time. She was not, she decided, that kind of person as she had begun to investigate on the program the moral base for her professionalism. The point here is not the courage she showed in being candid with herself (admirable in itself), but the fact of her self-deception over 19 years. Of course, too, once she understood the gap between her practice and her personhood, the challenge of rebuilding her teaching identity became immense. Self-deception incorporates fantasies about oneself and how others see one, but only serious inquiry will purge it.

But Julia points also to another danger in a teaching role. How do we become sufficiently self-aware to ensure our teaching stays dynamic? Teaching (whatever its potential variety) can easily be routinized; indeed, teaching demands the establishment of habits of conduct and routines that make classroom work possible. Such habits and routines can be anything from mannerisms of speech through to veiled prejudices, stereotyping, and inappropriate attitudes toward children, yielding teaching practices that cease to be dynamic as the teacher develops an individual rhythm of practice. Self-knowledge and its acquisition demands moral and intellectual honesty, a preparedness to reevaluate each aspect of one's individual practice, precisely when that rhythm has become static and repetitive.

A second area of inquiry will concern the reconciliation of roles. Janet (see chapter 3) was illustrative of the conflicting roles of (a) personal relations with children, (b) being a critic of their work, and (c) being an examiner on whose word careers hang. Students are "examined" through being given grades by a teacher on which there is little or no external check but which cumulatively have profound influences on a child's "career" as student. Yet simultaneously, the teacher must act as a critic of children's work, indeed help children through difficulties and problems of understanding that would seem to require a different kind of interpersonal relation from that of the examiner. In American schooling, the teacher has a multifaceted role, often with conflicts such as that of disciplinarian versus advocate. Self-knowledge requires understanding the demands of each sub-role and the consequent challenge of reconciling them.

Third, however, it would be a mistake to think that self-disclosure refers simply to professional practice and that self-enactment refers to me as a private individual, outside my role. Both personhood and role can be understood in both articulations. This takes us back to the moral demand for integrity-as-wholeness. In his essay "Morality and the Emotions" Bernard Williams (1973) reminds us that "a man who sincerely makes some moral utterance expresses his judgment of the situation, his beliefs about its merits, his moral outlook, his feelings on the matter—possibly his intentions. A man who makes an insincere moral utterance does not do these things, but hides his beliefs and his real feelings. But it is these that chiefly concern us: *the moral cast of the man lies below the level of the speech-act*" (p. 217; my italics). Both self-disclosure and self-enactment offer the opportunity for us to reflect not just on our personal or self-identity, but on who we really are, what our moral cast is. Because it must be the case that the "person" is ontologically prior to the "role," and our virtues are rooted in each of us as persons, though they are manifest in the different roles we have in life—teacher, parent, spouse—but the different actions in each role stem from my self qua person.

Yet we need to be aware not only of MacIntyre's point about self-understanding arising from our relationships, but that they are critically influenced by our cultural and intellectual traditions and the conversations in which they are articulated. Thus we may equally be influenced by individuals outside our own traditions, and these are often the most difficult to encounter in thinking about self-enactment. Personal knowledge is, in conclusion, a complex of elements of experience, commitment, and identity. But as I shall shortly argue, although we need to be aware of how our "moral cast" reveals where we stand, and how that is manifest in our dispositions and virtues, it is our dispositions that have primacy over mere knowledge and skill.

PART IV

The Virtues of the Teacher

Introduction

This final part of this book builds on the rationale articulated so far, and the focus therefore shifts from teaching and learning in general to the teacher and teacher education. In chapter 10, the teacher constructing an epistemological presence in the classroom will have a view of morality, be it Kantian, Aristotelian, religious, utilitarian, or other. Three specific approaches to moral agency are considered here and articulated through the notions of rules, relationships, and character. But, as this book adopts a broadly neo-Aristotelian stance, the view of morality implicit through this book—that is, the approach through character and virtues— has to be tested by (a) an examination of Fritz Oser's (1994) critique of it and (b) distinguishing virtues from personality traits and distinguishing dispositions from goals. In the final section of the chapter, the argument for the primacy of dispositions in the moral life, and thereby in teaching and in the education of teachers, is developed.

Chapter 11 outlines the significant possibilities for education coming from what is called positive psychology and how its direction connects to the arguments in this book. It then distinguishes three categories of virtues in teaching, namely those of character, intellect, and care. In the second section, four virtues of character discussed in parts II and III are elaborated: trustworthiness, sincerity, risk-taking and courage, and perseverance. Likewise, in section 3, the category of intellect is examined through the prism of critical thinking, specifically the work of Paul and Elder in the Critical Thinking Foundation, and it focuses on truthfulness, accuracy, open-mindedness, and impartiality. In section 4, a brief and selective critique of Nel Noddings's account of care ethics leads to an account of four virtues of care: tolerance, patience, compassion, and what she calls sympathetic attention. It should be stressed that the selection of these dispositions desirable in teaching is intended suggestively, not prescriptively, for teacher educators working with recruits to the profession.

The final chapter of the book turns to the avowedly practical. In section 1 the threads of the notion of the epistemological presence are gathered together almost as a manifesto, but that is incomplete without considering both teacher quality and a view of the problem of assessment of dispositions in teacher education. In section 2, a solution rooted in self-assessment by students is proposed, based in Oakeshott's distinction between self-disclosure and self-enactment. In section 3, it is argued that the challenge for teacher educators lies not in assessing would-be teachers, but in framing an assessment format in which self-assessment by students is seen as the central pillar of judging a person's virtues and competencies for teaching. A procedure for this is outlined containing faculty and student protocols. Within such a framework there then follows an example in section 4: open-mindedness. In the appendices to the book, four other protocols are drafted: truthfulness and trustworthiness, courage and the will, sympathetic attention, and integrity as wholeness. The final section of the chapter is a summary of the challenges for the development of teacher quality.

10

THE PRIMACY OF DISPOSITIONS AS VIRTUES

The region of the ethical, then, is a region of diverse, certainly incompatible and possibly practically conflicting ideal images or pictures of a human
life, or of human life: and it is a region in which many such incompatible
pictures may secure at least the imaginative, though doubtless not often the
practical, allegiance of a single person.... Any diminution in this variety
would impoverish the human scene.

(Strawson, 1961, p. 4.)

In section 1 of this chapter, three possible approaches to moral agency are discussed and developed through the notions of rules, relationships, and character. In
section 2, the view of morality implicit through this book—that is, the approach
through character and virtues—is tested by (a) an examination of Fritz Oser's
(1994) critique of it and (b) distinguishing virtues from personality traits. From
that examination, in section 3, the argument for the primacy of dispositions in the
moral life, and thereby in teaching and in the education of teachers, is developed.

I. Moral Agency: Rules, Relationships, and Character

The emphasis on the complex interrelations of knowledge and virtue needs an
account of a "moral agent," if it is to be coherent. Briefly, there is a common core
to most if not all moral points of view (Baier, 1965). The moral agent is, formally
speaking, someone who acts consciously in pursuit of valuable ends or according
to rules of conduct. Specific goals may be determined by someone else on whose
behalf the agent works, but the responsibility for the actions pursued by the agent
are his or hers. On this view, when a person is being blamed for an action, the statement "He ordered me to do it" is neither excuse nor justification, because agents
are assumed to be capable of choice—that is, they are autonomous (see chapter 8)
and they control their own behavior, even what they see (see chapter 7). The
central case of a person described as an agent demands that the person acts consciously and with intention.

The moral agent is therefore an individual who acts consciously and intention-
ally but often out of habit in *consideration of the interests of other people* as individuals

ɪcluding the interests of the agent as counting for one. Such
ʂts is a wide-ranging formal description of what the word
ʟerms of human behavior and action. It should be noted that,
many other considerations of moral thought, this is a contestable
ʌnt.

There has been a strong tendency in American culture to regard the word
moral with disapproval, so much so that it is sometimes seen as inflammatory.
Often the word "ethical" is used because of the bad press the word moral has encountered. One part of the problem is that "the moral" has been associated only
with sexual behavior; another is that "moral" is used to refer only to those behaviors that are profoundly controversial, so that being moral is regarded as entirely
subjective, often because people believe that nothing but a religious justification
for morality can be acceptable. The word "consideration" brings out the fact that
we *think* morally. Indeed we can describe morality as a form of thought, though of
course, it is thinking about what to do or thinking in action. It is practical. (Ethics might be thought of as moral theory.) This suggests that we can have moral
knowledge, for instance, as we might say to someone, "But you knew that was
not the right thing to do." Contemporary public life is littered with various types
of rogues confessing that they knew what they did was wrong. This suggests that
people do come to *know* what the difference is between right and wrong, between
what the moral thing to do is and what is not the moral thing to do. Being a moral
agent does not demand moral perfection, but it does demand a stance toward the
importance of the moral—that is, of considering other people's interests. Human
beings get things wrong in all kinds of areas, and moral action and thought is one
of them.

But considering the interests of others does not get us very far in articulating
what moral agency is. If we can and do think morally, and morality is a form
of thought, three matters surface: (1) What is distinctive about moral thought?
(2) How do we justify our actions morally speaking? (3) Why, if we know what is
the moral thing to do, do we not do it? This is not an exclusive account of the historically vast philosophical literature and thought on the nature of morality. But it
picks out, I think, some of the central issues of special significance for the teacher.
To get at some of the different stances toward this formal account, consider three
teacher educators on different occasions watching three different student teachers
conduct a lesson. All of the teacher educators notice that each student can be very
sarcastic at times with a particular child. The child is constantly put down and
subject to some intellectual bullying from the student. How each teacher educator approaches each student depends on how he or she sees his or her own moral
agency, but also what his or her moral position is. We can see this from the post-
lesson discussion. These are three characteristic moral responses to the student(s).

Consider first teacher educator Bill. Bill perhaps sits down facing his student
and asks, perhaps in a somewhat accusatory tone, "Manuel, why have you not
yet learned the rule that you must not single out students and bully them in this

way?" Bill's emphasis, morally speaking, is on *rules*. It is a classical liberal position, emerging from Hobbes, Kant, and Mill, widely articulated by John Rawls (1970, 1993), and by Lawrence Kohlberg (1981; 1984) in terms of the progress of moral development. For Bill, moral agency is about the rules that follow from our having obligations and duties to others.

Consider second teacher educator Eileen. She sits next to her student on a school bench and, putting her arm around her student's shoulders, says, "Anne, let us talk together about how we all seek to create caring relationships with children." Eileen's focus is on *relationships*. It is known widely as a feminist position variously articulated in our generation by Carol Gilligan (1982; Gilligan, Lyons, & Hanmer, 1990), Nel Noddings (2002), Mary Field Belenky and her coauthors (1986), and many others, with origins for some in the work of Martin Buber (1970). For Eileen, moral agency is about caring for others and, unlike Bill, who faces his student, Eileen wants to help Ann look out at the world the way Eileen does, with care for others, but asking especially what the child might have felt.

Consider third teacher educator David. He neither sits facing the student nor sits alongside, but invites the student to take a walk in the school yard, puffing metaphorically on his pipe as he talks. "Asia, I think I am rather surprised by you. It seems as though you are deliberately choosing to become the sort of person and teacher who hurts other people, but I can't believe you would choose that…maybe you were frightened?" This question emphasizes both the student as a person and as a student teacher in a role. The emphasis is on *character*, in terms of both who Asia is and who she is as a student. This moral emphasis is directly in the tradition of Aristotle, articulated in the present day by such scholars as Alasdair MacIntyre (1987) and David Norton (1995) and is being given much wider attention by contemporary philosophers, especially those advocating justification as reliabilist or responsibilist (see chapter 6).

Each of these responses might be used by teacher educators. Thus, in the spirit of entertaining alternatives, teacher educators might use one or the other of these questions, perhaps depending on the student, but their personal moral agency has to be construed within one or another of these frames. How each of these moral agents/teacher educators conducts his or her life and the moral underpinnings of their different responses can now be explored.

Rules

The primary mode of understanding morality in the classical liberal tradition is around the question "What is it right to do in this situation?" a question that represents a marked break with ethics of Aristotelian origins. For Immanuel Kant, for instance, the answers were built around categorical imperatives, such as "Act only as if you were a lawmaking member of the kingdom of ends,"—in other words, do what you would want to be followed by everyone. This formal idea needs substance. Obviously if the underlying principle is justice (as Kant, Rawls, and

Kohlberg argue), the rules turn out to be questions of obligation. If the principle, following Mill, was bringing about the greatest happiness for the greatest number of people, then all kinds of different calculations would have to be sought for. It is possible, I think, that if the underlying principle was "love your neighbor," then the outcomes of following Kant's rule would be different again. Therefore what is right to do, which rules to follow, have to be interpreted against such substantive views (e.g., justice, greatest happiness, love) of what the primary, or the group of primary principles, might be that form the criterion for the articulation and establishment of rules.

Integral to the idea of what it is right to do is the idea of moral duty, which implies legal duty. That is, the way in which the rules out there become connected to the individuals following them is through the idea that the moral agent is morally bound to follow the rules. But, when everyone has duties to everyone else in moral terms, reciprocity is created: one person's duty becomes another person's right. So rules get framed in a context of rights as well as duties, and these matter hugely in a democracy and a political framework, in which we speak of natural rights, human rights, and the rights of man. The Golden Rule, "do as you would be done by," characterizes the central feature of reciprocal rights and duties. Law consists of rules of one kind or another, so the rule of law demands that individuals know what a rule is, how to follow a rule, how to make judgments about the introduction of new rules, and the application of old ones.

An ethic of rules is thus focused on the individual following moral rules derived from principles of social organization (often thought of as implying a social contract). But when we take justice to be the primary principle of social organization, that will have to be interpreted across many spheres of human life—for example, issues of the fair distribution of resources (i.e., distributive justice and social justice), to matters of sanctions in which coercion is needed to punish malefactors (i.e., retributive justice), and more broadly in all rules of impartiality. However, this principle of justice (or any other) considered as primary in a democratic frame will often conflict in application with such principles as equality and liberty. An emphasis on freedom, for example, is often at the expense of equality and social justice, and these possibilities of conflict are inevitable between principles and rules. The upshot is that rules *do not determine their application.* Just as the rule "love thy neighbor" immediately evokes the question "who is my neighbor?" so every rule formally requires exactly that kind of thought in applying it, although we must note the role of habit mentioned above. Human beings have to constantly make judgments within this ethic of rules about *how* rules apply and what to decide when there is conflict and much else.

This matter of applying rules has led to one important feature of talk about the ethic of rules, as far as teachers are concerned. Richard Hare (1952) emphasized that each individual must build principles of action for him or herself, rooted in the Kantian principle that they should be universalizable. If, for example, I decide that at Christmas it is my duty to contribute more to charities than to my family, as a moral principle, then I would be constructing that principle for myself, although I would believe it is my duty in part because it could, indeed should, be of universal applicability. The ethic of rules demands that individuals construct, interpret, and weigh the rules as they act morally. One makes decisions of principle under this ethic, which then become our moral habits.

So we now have a picture of the person whose moral life is framed by an ethic of rules. He or she has a set of principles, derived from principles of social organization such as liberty or justice, which frame the moral life. Rules are followed and, in some case, created by individuals within a sense of duty and responsibility, as well as an awareness of their rights as human beings. Such rules must, of course, be followed autonomously: I must choose to obey the rules. When I obey the rules under the orders of others—that is, heteronomously rather than autonomously— I am not behaving as a full-fledged moral agent. Above all, I must constantly decide where they apply. The responsibility of the individual in respect of an ethic of rules is primarily cognitive.

Relationships

It was against the ethic of rules derived from central principles of classical liberalism that Carol Gilligan (1982) developed her important thesis that women thought about moral issues, especially dilemmas, not in terms of rules and principles, but in terms of relationships. Her target was Kohlberg's analysis of moral development. She has been followed by many different scholars, though not exclusively those whom we might want to label feminist, an adjective too often deployed as a substitute for thought. The distinction Gilligan was after is illustrated by this anecdote. The youth deserting from the army and coming back home will get from his father the stern and detached "Go back and take your punishment like a man," while from his mother he will hear the soft, welcoming "Come to me, my baby." The woman *naturally* feels differently about what is critical in a moral situation, so the argument would run. The most critical element in the moral notion of caring is contained in the word "we" in the example I posed: "Anne, let us talk together about how we all seek to create caring relationships with children." The focus is not on the individual teacher or parent caring for the child as if the child were a piece of antique furniture on which one lavished care and attention. Rather the focus is on the relationship between what Noddings calls "the one-caring" and the "one cared for," and her work will be discussed in more depth in chapter 11. The notion of justice is thought of from this perspective as detached, as paternal, without the receptivity, relatedness, and responsiveness characteristic of caring and typically thought of as maternal.

Centering the moral in relationships focuses on how "we meet the other morally" (Noddings, 1984, p. 5) and on the uniqueness of human encounters. It is empirically obvious, but worth indicating philosophically, that the experience we all have of the challenges of caring for and being cared for are complex and highly intricate. We have only to think of our relationships with our close family—our children, our parents, our siblings—to comprehend that complexity. From the inside, in Noddings's view, for the one caring there is a displacement of interest from my own reality to the reality of others. I feel your pain, so to speak. This goes well beyond a feeling of empathy, even beyond a sense of compassion: rather we see the other person's reality in the perspective of caring as a real possibility for *me*. "I must make a commitment to act. The commitment to act on behalf of the cared for, a continued interest in his reality through an appropriate time span, and the continuing renewal of that caring are the essential elements of caring" (Noddings, 1984, p. 16). For the one cared for, on the other hand, the reception of the authentic attitude of the one caring transforms the relationship.

Character

The fundamental idea behind an ethics of character is that knowledge, through education and self-knowledge, affords intrinsic rewards to the individual, issuing in the self-fulfilling conduct that Aristotle called *eudaemonia*. How we conceive ourselves and our lives is what matters. Being a human being demands taking responsibility for oneself and what kind of human being one is and who one becomes. Following ethical rules is subordinate to that self-discovery: insofar as rules instrumentally assist in a person's self-understanding, that is desirable but only instrumentally, not of itself. Who one becomes is one's own choice, a matter of one's own initiative; "the self is . . . a task, a piece of work, . . . the work of self-actualization" (Norton, 1995, p. 6).

Three things this ethics of character is not: First, it is not an elitist view of moral agency. Rather, framed democratically, there is, in Barber's phrase, "an aristocracy of everyone" (1994). Human beings are seen as invested innately with potential. Second, as Norton points out, this is not egoistic: rather by conducting this project of my self, that project will be of objective value to others. Most important, third, while it looks just individualistic, one's choices and one's development rest in interdependence with others.

But this is also a project appropriate for a democratic society. If the purpose of government is enhancing the life of human beings, and that can be done only by individuals themselves, then the major function of government is to provide the conditions for getting the best opportunities in position for individual self-discovery and self-development. As we have seen, the task of government then demands the removal of obstacles, such as poverty, that prevent such self-actualization (Norton, 1995, p. 80). Enhancing the life of human beings means enabling them to acquire moral virtues, understood as *dispositions of character*.

On Norton's neo-Aristotelian account of the ethics of character, the primary task is to engage the individual initiative through self-discovery—that is, in the old Greek phrase, to "know thyself." It is the creation of an identity (see chapter 6).

The foundation virtue, in Norton's account, is moral integrity, because it unifies the virtues, virtues once again being seen as dispositions of character—integrity as wholeness (see chapter 7), which brings together all aspects of the self (desires, interests, and roles) that we can think of as separable. In this tradition, connected to self-knowledge and integrity are Plato's cardinal virtues of wisdom, courage, temperance, and justice. Out of these cardinal virtues we fashion our character; we choose to become the people we are, and we do that on our own initiative. This applies to us as teacher educators. Our moral life is always a project in being—a task, in modern jargon, of continuous improvement. We need to ensure the connection of what Norton calls meaningful work and meaningful living. If virtues are dispositions of character, and dispositions are the contemporary currency of discussing the moral character of teachers, then on this account we can add self-knowledge and integrity to wisdom, courage, temperance, and justice. So, although the moral agent considers the interests of others, he or she may do so out of broadly different understandings of morality, but a clear understanding there must be if the morally requisite attention to the person of the student and the student in a role is to be supported and developed effectively.

These three examples illustrate how the moral identity of a teacher educator will yield different approaches to teaching. I am choosing to characterize teacher professionalism within this character perspective. The position influences how we judge ourselves as teachers, how we invite novices to see their own career development, and how opportunities are created for practitioners. It asks us to question the virtues in ourselves and the virtues in our own work. This overview provides a way to link the role, the men and women who occupy it, the moral demands it makes on us, and the practical arts of teaching to the institution of education. Distinctively different normative approaches to education will still exist, forcing the debate on educational ends and means, and the complexity of their interrelations, up into the culture of the profession. A profession can have unity of purpose with distinctiveness of perspective (see Sockett, 1993, pp. 90–92).

Yet the three examples also compel us to reflect on the continuum of teacher educator, student teacher, and the child in the classroom. While we are well aware that there are many social and cultural influences on a child's understanding of the world, the influence that a student teacher has will also be influenced by the quality of the teacher education he or she receives and which, in the short and long run, he or she represents in his or her work with children. The obligation on the teacher educator is to get the kind of depth of inquiry into seminars and professional work that profound work on self-revelation and self-understanding demands.

II. Virtues and Personality Traits

This neo-Aristotelian approach is not, of course, immune from criticism, and it is worth confronting one particular critique. Oser (1994) rejects any account of professional teaching based on virtues. He approaches questions of morality in teaching through the notion of professional responsibility, derived from an ethic of rules and obligation, which he equates with morality. Responsibility can, in his view, be empirically researched—that is, be testable—and be shown to be effective because its focus is on children's learning outcomes. Although he acknowledges the significance of placing morality within the act of teaching, he regards the notion of professionalism as completely lacking in research.

First it is sensible, though limited, to equate morality with responsibility. Responsibility is empty, of course, unless we know what for and to whom. Oser limits the teacher's responsibility as being for learning outcomes alone, and he does not discuss responsibility to whom, though we may assume the constituency of society, parents, and the child. This limited view of morality seems to be derived solely from its testability, so the responsibility turns out to be what connects teachers' acts and actions to children's learning only. One does not, however, have to be held to the paradigm of research as that conducted by the external observer on collections of teaching acts, because research may need to take the form of teacher-driven action-research because that approach puts teachers' moral autonomy at the center, out of which more thorough understandings of professionalism can emerge (Sockett et al., 2001). This alternative research model in fact focuses the teacher's attention exactly on the kinds of detailed features of teaching he elaborates (see p. 111) in respect of pre-service teachers (see Further Reading). But, models apart, there is nothing intrinsic to the concept of describing behavior in terms of virtue that makes it untestable through research.

Oser regards any statements of "virtues" as a kind of subjectively selected grab-bag, though as is apparent from the direction of this book, there are virtues constitutive of good teaching. However, he regards virtues as merely "personality features," which seems as though he needs to fit virtues into a preexisting psychological framework, a view rejected by those who call themselves positive psychologists (Csikszentmihalyi & Csikszentmihalyi, 2006). Quite how being honest or being fair are *just* features of personality is difficult to understand, not least because both seem necessary to being responsible as a teacher. Second, this seems to turn moral probity in the teacher into merely a measurable skill, the moral character of the teacher being immaterial to the learning outcomes, a view that seems excessively exclusive.

Oser distrusts the concept of virtue because his view of morality is exclusively Kantian, with the emphasis on rules, individual autonomy, and individual responsibility. Because he regards such a position as irreconcilable with the Aristotelian view, he is left with operationalizing a view of morality that, in this case, is determined by testability, rather than developing a moral argument for that position. For example, to recall the examples above, it can at least be argued that it would be a much more sophisticated teacher response to say to a child who stole, "Is a thief the kind of person you want to become and to be known as?" rather than Oser's teacher, who would presumably be unable to say to such a child much more than "you broke the non-stealing rule." Virtues to Oser are mere decorations, because his interest is in the tough empirical questions of cause and effect. We need not be ashamed of the concept of virtue. We need to find out how to research it, not to dismiss it as a priori untestable.

Oser (1994) rejects a virtues (dubbed a "personality") approach in general on four grounds: (1) it implies a teacher's character is superior to that of a child, is vague, and lacks justification, (2) there must be a "highest goal" to which a catalog of different virtues relate (e.g., responsibility), (3) the virtues describe an ideal when it is obvious teachers don't come close to these descriptions, and (4) such lofty requirements can't be met through teacher education (p. 79).

With regard to (1), Oser may well be unfamiliar with the vast philosophical literature on such virtues as honesty or fairness, but anyone familiar with the work of, say, Sisella Bok or John Rawls could hardly say that honesty and fairness were vague concepts, even understood as virtues, and, of course, part of that understanding is directly connected to matters of justification. The idea of a teacher's character as superior to that of a child is a misapprehension, derived presumably from the context in which, because a teacher is teaching something the child does not know (or there would be no point in teaching it), the teacher knows more than (and is in that sense superior to) the child. The term "superior" is misleading, because it seems to attribute to those who seek to understand teaching as a moral activity the idea that teachers must be morally superior, as if the institutional model were a seminary with novices.

It is difficult to understand (2). Those virtues elaborated in this book as central to teaching are not in service to some higher goal, nor are they hierarchically ranked. There is no reason for a higher goal—and it is difficult to say what that might be, except in Aristotelian terms the search for eudaemonia, or human flourishing. Education as human betterment might constitute a "higher goal," but this would be a "goal" in a very limited sense, because it is internal to what is done in teaching, not some kind of external outcome. But it is a typical fallacy of the empiricist mind to assume a need for ranking and hierarchies. The means can be constitutive of the ends, not just contingently connected (Sockett, 1973). No higher goal in personality terms is needed in teaching, because the goals are right there in the social practice (Hansen, 2001).

On the last two of his complaints about a virtues approach, Oser does not grasp that virtues are stable dispositions of character: they are not ideals—in Iris Murdoch's (2001) example, being Christ-like as an unattainable ideal that we constantly strive toward. Nowhere is the fundamental difference of approach between Oser's arguments and those in this book more apparent than in his claim that these self-selected virtues are just ideals and teachers don't come close to them. That misses the point badly. Finally, in (4) Oser describes virtues as lofty targets, impossible to meet through teacher education. That depends. It doesn't seem to me in principle difficult to have teachers thinking profoundly about themselves as moral professionals and addressing issues in their classroom contexts through a moral rather than technical prism or, for that matter, one constrained by "learning outcomes." Yet if we are to do empirical research as we must, and indeed Oser sees the empirical and the moral as necessary to each other in research, then we need to counter the claim that personality traits are the only way to handle virtues. Oser regards talk of virtues as of no value for empirical research as they can simply be reduced to personality traits (1994). This seems to me a mistaken reductionism. Taking virtues as personality traits limits exploration of the virtues and is too unsophisticated to encompass virtues and dispositions. To indicate why, distinctions need to be identified among personality traits, dispositions as a species of personality trait, and, in section 4, those dispositions called virtues.

Personality Traits

A personality trait can be any normative attribution made to stable kinds of human behavior, within the generally accepted classifications of the five-factor model: neuroticism, extraversion, openness to experience, agreeableness, and conscientiousness, with each factor set on a continuum to, respectively, emotional stability, introversion, closedness to experience, disagreeableness, and lack of conscientiousness (McCrae & Costa, 2005).

Dispositions are not synonymous with personality traits, because by no means all aspects of personality imply intention or actions in which intentions are embedded. For example, a disagreeable person—as understood in personality theory—does not have to set out to be disagreeable, and people who are not disagreeable personalities can indeed be very much so. Similarly, an extrovert does not have to say to him or herself, "How shall I be extroverted today?" Or "What would the extrovert do here?" Being an extrovert is not an intention but a way behavior is classified by others and then, perhaps, is accepted as a trait by the individual "owner." Equally, someone who is neurotic may manifest behavior that we would classify as such, but there need be no implied intention on his or her part. Indeed there would be something odd about a person describing himself as trying to be neurotic, though he could pretend to be neurotic. To intend to do something is to be aware that *this* is what one is doing (Searle, 1992, chapter 3). Indeed the neurotic person often, if not usually, does not see his or her behavior under this description and has to be shown by sympathetic psychotherapists when it is a matter of his or her personality. Intention thus implies, in its strong form, a conscious appreciation of what one is doing, which by no means all personality trait descriptors imply.

A disposition is a neutral, non-evaluative concept of a stable, long-lasting, maybe permanent, property that, unlike a personality trait, can be applied to physical objects. Sugar is soluble; glass is brittle. Solubility and brittleness are dispositions of sugar and glass, respectively. These facts about these dispositions enable us to predict how they will behave under the appropriate conditions (see Mumford, 2003, especially chapter 2). However, to say the glass broke because it is brittle is not an explanation of why it broke, only a confirmation of a property of glass.

The solubility of sugar did not cause it to dissolve, nor did the fragility of the glass cause it to break. Dispositions are not causal.

Equally, to say someone has a particular personality trait is not to explain that person's behavior, but to predict it. A person does not wash his or her hands continuously because he or she is obsessive-compulsive: the word "obsessive" functions here only as a way of describing what the person does, of classifying it as a type of behavior, not of explaining why the person does what he or she does, though from that description we can predict the person's behavior. It may be that all personality traits are predictions and empirically testable once criteria are established. The extrovert will do this and that, the conscientious person will be meticulous about this or that—given specific contexts. To say of someone that he or she has a disposition to X is likewise to predict his or her behavior or actions, but not to explain them, except insofar as we are putting an individual in a category of which we have numerous other examples. That a person is neurotic is informative but not explanatory.

Not only are human dispositions as character traits normative, they are distinguished from personality traits through always being acquired through learning. As we consider desirable dispositions for the teacher, we should stress that we are not trying to describe those elements of human behavior, types of personality traits, that are *not* open to learning, fostering, developing, and teaching. (This is of course not to say that individuals starting as students of teaching have a dispositional blank slate.) Once we start discussing human actions and behavior, therefore, we are necessarily using normative language away from the laws of nature. Our description of human actions in dispositional terms is therefore not mere description or prediction, but evaluation, too.

Finally, if the dispositions we think desirable in teaching are to be objects of intention, and if they are to be distinguished from temperament, then they will have what we may term a cognitive core. Dispositions are not nervous tics that just happen; rather we must understand reality (i.e., "use our cognition") as being like *this* for us to act or behave as our dispositions metaphorically prompt us. As we have seen in chapter 8, to be brave demands appraising this situation as fearful and being frightened by it, so we must note that it is not that our disposition to bravery prompts us, like some internal voice. Dispositions do not cause us to do anything. *Our actions stem from our cognitive appraisals of situations where our dispositions are embedded.*

The upshot of these claims is that dispositions are narrower in concept than personality traits. Like personality traits, they tend to be stable and long-lasting, and they can be predictive, but not explanatory. However, dispositions, unlike personality traits, are normative, requiring both description and evaluation. They are acquired through voluntary or involuntary learning, like many but not all personality traits, and they have a cognitive core. Dispositions as constructs resist the simplicity of personality theory. This is not to say that empirical research, suitably informed by moral thought and argument, on the development of those dispositions that are virtues is impossible.

III. Dispositions and Goals

Teacher education institutions in the contemporary political framework are faced with the demands of accreditation that require statements of desirable teacher dispositions as targets for the institutions, but there is too often a confusion between teacher dispositions and educational goals. No character strengths or virtues could be classified as goals, implying they could be completed, even though the difference of educational context may yield legitimately different emphases on precise educational goals. Teachers must be educated well enough to understand, and be prepared to espouse or to emphasize, different views of educational purposes. Many teacher educators and teachers, for example, regard social justice as a central educational purpose; this is historically new, being an outcrop of equality of educational opportunity. The emphasis on social justice began in the aftermath of desegregation and has continued as the demographic balance across the nation has shifted. Social justice, for some politicians, policy makers, academics, administrators, and teachers, is what the schools are for. The term functions as an institutional *goal* under some such rubric as "all children can learn," "treat every child equally," "no child left behind," or "equality of educational opportunity." Its reference point needs to be emphasized—namely, that today's teachers work in classrooms of diversity of race, gender, and income, in a multicultural society, and that the teacher's aim should be equality of treatment, and, in the case of children with special needs, there should be forms of compensation, with its manifold and controversial implications for curriculum.

An overarching description of educational purpose is given by Brighouse (2003):

> Education Policy should aim at ensuring that every child has a real opportunity to become an autonomous person, and should aim at rough equality of educational opportunity. Equal educational opportunity requires at least the following three things: the quality of the educational inputs in the school system should not reflect the level of wealth of the parents; they should not reflect the decision-making ability of the parents; and children with disabilities should get substantially greater educational resources than children without disabilities.
>
> *(p. 163)*

Yet social justice, which would be the catchphrase for Brighouse's last sentence, has been a locus of considerable confusion in discussion of teacher dispositions. Except in their role as citizens, or perhaps through unions, teachers have no input into the policy decision-making that Brighouse describes: *he is describing what the schools are for, not what teachers should be like.* The requirements he sets out are not in the same conceptual basket as, say, "open-mindedness" or "truthfulness" because social justice cannot be coherently described as the property of an individual. One may be disposed toward endorsing social justice as an educational purpose, in which case one would expect an individual's dispositions to be at least those of fairness and maybe compassion (but see section 4). Likewise freedom, as a broad educational purpose, could not be understood as a disposition because it does not describe the stable quality picked out by a disposition, it describes a social and political status to be enjoyed.

In 2002, the new accreditation guidelines from the National Council for the Accreditation of Teacher Education (NCATE) insisted that teacher dispositions should be considered alongside knowledge and skills and gave social justice as an example of a disposition. That irritated conservatives (e.g., Damon, 2002). Their complaint, roughly, was not that one should ignore children "left behind" or renounce principles of equality of opportunity, but that the notion of social justice is turned into an item of political faith and political priority, masquerading as a disposition necessary for a professional teacher. Insisting that teachers have this "disposition," in conservatives' view, is to make students toe an ideological, indeed a political, line. One way or another, of course, schools are vehicles of social engineering and political debate and perspective. Yet it is a political judgment that social justice should be a purpose or even the *primary* purpose for schools, not least because it implies the deployment of resources to accommodate the political preferences its advocates embrace. The problem is not merely one of toeing a line: conservative alarm focused on the idea that if "social justice" is a disposition that would then be assessed, an ideological/political test for would-be teachers would have been created. It would carry with it political baggage way beyond the primary significance of the underlying principles of equality of opportunity, quite apart from its incoherence as a disposition. It may well be, of course, that teacher education institutions, when they assert the need for a disposition called "social justice," are simply bundling together a package of desirable dispositions— for example, treating individuals equally and fairly or, say, having a special regard (i.e., compassion) for the underprivileged in society. But that still leaves open issues of educational purpose that cover a variety of views appropriate for examination in teacher education about which student teachers should be encouraged to be open-minded, if they are to be professionally autonomous.

For example, students might examine whether the commitment to social justice (a manifestation of the principle of equality) is more important than a commitment to children becoming free (a manifestation of the principle of liberty). After all, child-centered theorists (from Rousseau to A. S. Neill, including mavericks like Homer Lane) have consistently emphasized the centrality of the child's autonomy and the creation of a "free" learning environment. Indeed, there are critical educational issues about the development of "free persons," how that is done, and how freedom connects to freedom of choice (Peters, R. S., 1966; 1972): But perhaps most important is the problem of being free—intellectually and morally—in a social and cultural climate that, though it seems to espouse individualism, simultaneously creates huge pressures to conform. Engineering the schools for social justice need not produce the free, autonomous persons embraced in chapter 9. Engineering the schools for maximum freedom likewise need not produce social justice.

The purpose of these comments is not specifically to attack social justice as an educational purpose, but to put it in its place. It is one of various educational goals on which there will need to be political compromise. It draws attention to alternative educational values, such as freedom and scholarship. Social justice cannot be a virtue or a disposition, of itself, however desirable it may be as an educational goal. A line has to be drawn between distinguishing social goals for education and the dispositions required of the professional. This is an uncertain line over which there will be much debate and over which people of conscience may disagree—as is inevitable in a democracy. However, is it not a very odd paradox that American civil rhetoric is so permeated with talk of freedom, but in educational institutions, the word is hardly uttered these days? The tradition of educational thought about freedom since Thomas Paine and John Stuart Mill is ignored in much contemporary educational discussion. Moreover, the strong focus on social justice does seem to demand that teachers "get it": but this whiff of indoctrination suggests that teacher education is neglecting the education of teachers *as citizens,* within which discussion of democratic principles must take place (Gutmann, 1999) such that informed discussions about complex political principles can also take place. The three categories of teacher dispositions deployed in the next section could be held important by people of widely different political allegiances and ideas within a democracy. They do not describe educational goals, nor do they seek political identification with them.

IV. The Primacy of Dispositions

While dispositions are important to our moral lives in general, the focus here is on the professional teacher, a person engaged in teaching the young and in doing so necessarily engaged in the moral activity of assisting in the development of the young as persons. The language of virtue, in this argument, refines our talk about (a) which dispositions might be desirable, (b) what those dispositions are in descriptive reality and in evaluation, and (c) setting intention and self-awareness in the minds of practitioners and their teachers.

Why therefore are dispositions as virtues appropriate to teaching and teacher education? First, the application of the disposition as virtue, rather than the disposition as personality trait, to teaching is justified by the normative moral context of teaching. Techniques in teaching are always determined with regard to moral ends and described in the light of them. Similarly those dispositions to be fostered are determined by the professional contexts of teaching. Second, the normative context demands not just that the teacher have certain dispositions (e.g., truthfulness or open-mindedness) as virtues but that these qualities *also be taught to children*.

A moral or intellectual virtue shares three general characteristics of a disposition—it is stable, is learned, and has a cognitive core—but these characteristics are neither necessary nor sufficient for virtue. If we recall the six examples used in earlier chapters—truthfulness, open-mindedness, impartiality, courage, commitment, and self-knowledge—we can note the distinctive character of any disposition as virtue as threefold (with which personality theory need not be concerned):

1. To become virtuous (in any specific description) is the result of the individual's initiative; indeed it is an individual's achievement (Norton, 1995, especially chapters 4 and 5). We become virtuous by seeking to become generous, kind, and so forth through the specific contexts of our lives.
2. To call someone virtuous in a specific description implies that the individual has surmounted internal counter-inclinations (e.g., laziness or fear) or overcome external obstacles (e.g., lack of money) to be said to have such a virtue (Williams, 2002).
3. "Virtue is its own reward," or, more properly, being virtuous is always driven in its exercise by intrinsic motivation. To be truthful or generous for instrumental motives, for example, is not authentically to be truthful or generous.

A virtue is not therefore a dormant or passive disposition, like the brittleness of glass. Rather it is "a deep and enduring acquired excellence of a person, involving a characteristic motivation to produce a certain desired end and reliable success in bringing about that end" (Zagzebski, 1996, p. 137). To say of a person that he or she is compassionate is not merely to predict his or her behavior but to describe that person as motivated by compassion, seeking to bring about results issuing from his or her compassion.

Nor is a virtue a skill. While it is true that we may develop little habits—like counting to ten when we get impatient—to foster our virtues, the virtues themselves are not matters of skill. Ryle (1949) reminds us that we can forget a skill, but not a virtue (see chapter 9). Skills are also not inherently valuable, because they are always means to ends: skills can serve virtues "by allowing a person who is morally motivated to be effective in action" (1949, p. 113). Indeed virtues are psychically prior to skills: "the motivational component of a virtue defines it more than external effectiveness does, whereas it is the reverse in the case of skills" (1949, p. 115). There are also notable differences between intellectual skills (such as verbal, logical, or explanatory skills) and such intellectual virtues as open-mindedness, truthfulness, impartiality, and fairness (1949, p. 114).

Nor is a virtue a natural faculty; it is acquired. We may or may not have natural attitudes such as shyness or calmness; we may be strong or weak, beautiful or ugly; but for none of this can we be blamed or held to account as we can for our lack of virtue (1949, p. 105). Dispositions are open to moral appraisal—to praise and blame. Virtues are thus acquired by spending thought, time, and work on their development, because one's virtues address one's contrary inclinations. That may occur, for example, in how we control our primary emotions—love, hate, and anger—and such secondary emotions as jealousy and envy. The person who procrastinates needs to be persistent. The person who is lazy needs to develop all those virtues connected with effort and endeavor. Several philosophers (e.g., Zagzebski, 1996, p. 108; Peters, R. S., 1974, pp. 312–319) have addressed the detail of these internal obstacles to virtue. To say a person has this or that virtue, therefore, is to say that that person has (a) a desirable disposition with stability and predictability in his or her behavior, (b) a motivation to produce an end with certain desired features, and (c) success in his or her endeavor. "A person does not have a virtue unless she is reliable at bringing about the end that is the aim of the motivational component of the virtue" (Zagzebski, 1996, p. 136).

For Aristotle and his followers, therefore, moral evaluations of individuals focus on them as persons and their dispositions and virtues rather than on the acts. Roughly, they would be much more interested in evaluating a high school senior in terms of his or her dispositions as virtues than on his SAT scores or grades on the community service elective. To describe a good person is to describe the person's virtues. Zagzebski (1996, p. 15) maintains that a virtue is reducible neither to the performance of acts independently identified as right nor to dispositions to perform such acts. Rather than judging others (or indeed ourselves) just in terms of what we do (e.g., giving to charity), we judge in terms of the person's virtues or dispositions—for example, he is a compassionate man, she is a generous woman. In part, we do this because when we see a person acting, we actually may have no idea of his or her motive or whether this is a deliberate attempt to deceive or disguise the real motive, as the Hanssen example (see chapter 7) indicates.

Virtue theories thus insist that who the person is becomes more fundamental than what he or she does and how we describe it. The dispositions of the moral agent are therefore primary to moral acts. Educators are fond of a weak cliché that we can hate the act but love the person; the point of the remark, of course, is for us not to be blinded to who the person might become by some egregious act or indeed patterns of bad behavior. *Not exactly*—for virtue theorists. "Persons are ontologically more fundamental than acts; acts are defined in terms of persons," as Zagzebski puts it (1996, p. 79). And, she continues, "the moral properties of persons are ontologically more fundamental than the moral properties of acts, and the latter properties ought to be defined in terms of the former. Hence, virtues and vices are ontologically more fundamental than the rightness or wrongness of acts. The concept of right act ought to be defined in terms of the concept of virtue" (p. 80). Who the person is, in other words, is more fundamental than what he or she does and how we describe it, so we cannot disentangle coherently the act from the person, making the cliché empty.

Various philosophers in the past half-century have found Aristotelian arguments of this kind compelling. Virtue concepts such as courageous and truthful (descriptions of persons) are conceptually rich (Anscombe, 2000) compared to right and wrong (descriptions of acts), which lack content. "Thick" descriptions combine the normative and the descriptive elements of courage and gratitude (Williams, 1985). Virtue approaches may also provide "more convincing moral accounts of such personal goods as love and friendship" (Zagzebski, 1996, p. 18), as the stance of the individual can be taken into account. Moreover, we can address the moral qualities of an institution much more effectively through examining the virtues and qualities for which it stands than through examining its rule-book. Finally, we need an ethical perspective that embraces such central moral concepts as integrity (Norton, 1995), which is difficult for rules-based systems.

If we take our current practices in education, teachers operate with a default mode in which the act (the student's being able to perform, complete tests, do "good" work) is much more important than the student's character or person-hood. This is back to front. "Persons" (Zagzebski, 1996), to repeat, "are onto-logically more fundamental than acts; acts are defined in terms of persons." The default-mode teacher (formally) cares not a whit as to whether the student is diligent, persevering, or committed, because these are not outcomes put up for testing. In the classroom with an epistemological presence, therefore, the focus for the moral teacher must be on the moral and intellectual virtues being educated, not on the content performances demanded by the default curriculum.

Finally, Bernard Williams (2006), from whom the phrase "The Primacy of Dispositions" is borrowed, argues that individual dispositions must be replicated to sustain ethical life. "If ethical life is to be preserved, then these dispositions have to be preserved" (p. 75). Moreover, if we are to criticize or change the ethical life we have, this is not a cognitive matter, but a challenge to modify our dispositions. Only a dispositions account enables us to explain and understand the occurrences of ethical attitudes such as prejudice, confusion, and barbarism, to mention Williams's examples.

The cultivation of dispositions includes those intellectual virtues taught to children, but *they also become the prism through which a teacher understands teaching*. That is, any so-called methods a teacher uses in a classroom are governed not by judgments about effectiveness but by how they fit with the teacher's understanding of his or her own intellectual and moral virtues. In Darling-Hammond and colleagues (2005) something is made of the idea that teachers should have a vision, though teachers are not institutions. At one level, that is all right, but it cannot be a placeholder for a firm self-conscious inquiry of where the teacher stands, morally speaking: the moral cast, once again, of the teacher beneath the classroom persona. Teacher knowledge includes intellectual virtues, which include sensitivity to detail, open-mindedness in facing evidence, fairness in evaluating arguments, intellectual humility, perseverance, diligence, care and thoroughness, adaptability of intellect, insight into problems and theories, and the communications virtues of explanation, candor, listening, and, of course, practical wisdom and intellectual integrity. It is through a teacher's cultivating his or her own dispositions, at his or her own initiative, that the ethical framework of the classroom can be thoroughly rooted in the public and personal knowledge being exchanged there.

This argument for the primacy of dispositions, if correct, drastically changes the balance of virtuous dispositions of the teacher with regard to his or her knowledge and skill. It might imply, for example, selection methods that sought to find out what existing dispositions a candidate had, on the grounds that no institution could expect to install in any person "new" dispositions. It might imply much greater attention to the self-disclosure and self-enactment distinction indicated in chapter 9 as a framework for reflection. It might imply quite new forms of assessment. It would certainly yield a very different seminar discussion about children. Yet, it may be argued, this is impossible for teacher education in an abbreviated form of initial training, in which clinical training is the core. These issues will be discussed in chapter 12 after a more thorough account of the virtues of the teacher in chapter 11.

11

CHARACTER, INTELLECT, AND CARE

> After a detour through the hedonism of the 1960s, the narcissism of the
> 1970s, the materialism of the 1980s, and the apathy of the 1990s, most
> everyone today seems to believe that character is important after all and
> that the United States is facing a character crisis on many fronts, from the
> playground to the classroom to the sports arena to the Hollywood screen to
> business corporations to politics.
>
> *(Peterson & Seligman, 2004)*

From the playground to the classroom. The "character crisis" can be described
trivially—for example, too much sex, drugs, and rock 'n' roll—or it can, as this
book has implied, have a substantial meaning in that we are neglecting who children, students, and their teachers *are* in favor of assessable knowledge and skills,
with right answers being overriding. The crisis, in this view, centers on the intellectual and moral virtues or dispositions not being nurtured or taught in schooling at any level, except by default or accident. As far as our educational system is
concerned, when it comes to your development as a person, you're pretty much
on your own.

However, if we believe that schools should be held partly responsible for this
crisis, then its solution may also rest in understanding teachers of quality set against
a view of education and its purposes (see chapter 9). That quality must include
dispositions as virtues. In this chapter, section 1 outlines the significant possibilities
of positive psychology and how it connects to the arguments in this book, specifically in the distinction among three categories of virtues in teaching, namely
those of character, intellect, and care. Section 2 elaborates formally four virtues
of character discussed in parts II and III: trustworthiness, sincerity, risk-taking,
and courage and perseverance. Likewise, in section 3, the category of intellect is
examined through the prism of critical thinking, specifically the work of Paul
and Elder in the Critical Thinking Foundation, and it focuses on truthfulness,
accuracy, open-mindedness, and impartiality. In section 4, a brief and selective critique of Nel Noddings's account of care ethics leads to an account of four virtues
of care: tolerance, patience, compassion, and what she calls sympathetic attention.
It should be stressed that the selection of these specific dispositions desirable in
teaching is intended suggestively, not prescriptively, for teacher educators working
with recruits to the profession.

I. Classifying Dispositions as Virtues

In 2004, psychologists Christopher Peterson and Martin Seligman (2004) edited an 800-page volume, *Character Strengths and Virtues: A Handbook and Classification*. This important book arose from the development of positive psychology, which focuses on positive elements of human beings rather than on their varied disabilities which had, with the exception of developmental psychology, dominated the discipline. The informal subtitle to the book is a "Manual of the Sanities." The structure of the work is important (Peterson & Seligman, 2004, Introduction). The classification contains:

1. The six main *virtues:* wisdom and knowledge, courage, humanity, justice, temperance, and transcendence, gathered from historical and contemporary texts.
2. Twenty-four *character strengths,* grouped under each of the six virtues, drawn from broad-based discussions among psychologists:
    1. Wisdom and knowledge contain such strengths as creativity, curiosity, open-mindedness, love of learning, and perspective.
    2. Courage contains bravery, persistence, integrity, and vitality.
    3. Humanity contains love, kindness, and social intelligence.
    4. Justice contains citizenship, fairness, and leadership.
    5. Temperance contains forgiveness and mercy, humility and modesty, and prudence and self-regulation.
    6. Transcendence contains the appreciation of beauty and excellence, gratitude, hope, humor, and spirituality.

There are also *situational themes*—that is, specific habits that lead people to manifest given character strengths in given situations.

The 10 criteria for a "strength of character" include that it fulfills an individual's life (i.e., is based in an Aristotelian view of human flourishing), that it is morally valued in its own right, that it is manifest across situations and is stable across time, and that there are institutions capable of cultivating it in a society. Additionally, and of particular importance, individuals who display any such strengths are understood by a sense of ownership of a strength, an excitement in its display, in being invigorated by it, and in the creation of fundamental projects around it. This is especially true of the child as owner of the curriculum and the virtues implicit in it.

This approach through positive psychology is parallel to the philosophical argument in this book. First, its profound empirical approach on the basis of this avowedly abstract classification illustrates how character strengths (a) are educable, (b) are critical to human flourishing, and (c) can be exercised within all contexts—for example, in the study of subjects in school and in classrooms with an epistemological presence. Second, in paying attention to the circumstances of the development of character strengths, be it in family, work, or school, the book heralds a potential for understanding new ways of looking at schooling as the development of the individual's character strengths. Such work promises to contribute hugely to empirical bases on which education and teacher education can be structured, which, I will claim without argument, behavioral psychology and its intellectual descendants, including Thorndike, have drastically failed to do. Third, it demonstrates that a strong research partnership between philosophers and psychologists, between the moral and the empirical, is a necessary foundation for understanding character strength and virtue. Positive psychology, in this manifestation, embraces conceptual complexity and seeks to build out of historical and contemporary philosophical understandings an appropriate construct of character strengths to drive the empirical work, rather than simply operationalizing definitions of character strengths for purposes of measurement or assessment.

The abstract classification of character strengths and virtues necessarily has a somewhat arbitrary texture. The category of transcendence contains gratitude and playfulness that might as easily crop up as strengths within humanity. Some character strengths may well be regarded as virtues: open-mindedness, for example, has been so described in this book. Attention is paid to habit, but not so much to conceptualizing these character strengths or virtues as dispositions. However, Peterson and Seligman emphasize the significance of situation and context. It therefore *is* significant, psychologically and philosophically, to ask what are the character strengths, virtues, and dispositions of the teacher, as opposed to the priest, the lawyer, the soldier, the parent, or the politician. Positive psychology can thus be informed by analyses drawn from different professions and occupations to enrich the situational bases within which character strengths are researched, especially in terms of the facilitating conditions of their development. The common search is for a full enrichment of our understanding of human life, especially teaching.

In parts II and III of this book, six dispositions as virtues and their different connections to elements of public and personal knowledge have been articulated: truthfulness, open-mindedness, and impartiality in public knowledge and integrity as wholeness, courage, and self-knowledge in personal knowledge. These have arisen from epistemological considerations, but they need to be expanded to encompass dispositions as virtues in teaching and teacher education. Rather than using Peterson and Seligman's abstract classification, a set of three categories, determined by the professional task of teaching, is appropriate for teacher education. The teaching context demands constituent virtues of *character, intellect,* and *care* (Sockett, 2006). The categories frequently overlap, and the following list is intended as indicative, not definitive, and will, like much else, be a matter of argument, as Peterson and Seligman anticipate will be the case with their classification.

a. Virtues of *character* include trustworthiness, sincerity, and the virtues of the will, such as courage, persistence, endeavor, perseverance, and self-control (see Sockett, 1988).
b. Virtues of *intellect* include truthfulness, accuracy, clarity, consistency (e.g., in the application of rules), open-mindedness, and fairness and impartiality, especially in making judgments, all of which imply thoughtfulness.

c. Virtues of *care* include tolerance, tact, patience, discretion, civility, compassion, attention, sensitivity, and receptivity.

Integrity as wholeness is seen as an overarching virtue of *personhood*.

Why these? Such dispositions are immanent in both the practice and the content of teaching. *Character,* in this iteration, describes the kind of person the teacher is and his or her ability to get things done. Teachers must also pay attention to the development of character in their students. *Intellect* is the teacher's stock-in-trade, however the curriculum is construed, but students too must become seekers after truth. Teachers have children placed in their *care;* children also need to be guided to care about and for other people, to be constantly aware of the caring relation between themselves as individuals and other people. These three categories are, once again, profession-specific. Were we talking about priests or pastors, we might want to talk of spiritual virtues—humility, for instance. Were we discussing military officers, we would classify virtues of leadership, including physical courage. Were we discussing politicians, police, or doctors, the categories would differ again. This is not to ignore a host of prudential virtues needed in teaching from Peterson and Seligman's classification (e.g., leadership, vitality, and humor), but, for the moment, to focus on what seem to be nonnegotiable dispositions for the teacher.

However, while the context of teaching calls for these specific human qualities, those contexts can be immensely varied, as varied as the individual people who are teachers. The virtues as dispositions described above as virtues of character, intellect, and care do not function independently, given the complexity of human life and classrooms. The task in teacher education is not to impose a template of dispositions as virtues but to have teachers explore themselves and their professional work within the aspects of self-disclosure and self-enactment, to have them thereby be acutely and profoundly self-conscious, both as individuals and as individuals in a role. But differences are crucial, and teacher educators will need to be sensitive to difference rather than cast any shadows of ideological predetermination (see below). A kindergarten in rural New Hampshire is a different context from a high school in East Los Angeles, and Mr. Chips is a different person from Jaime Escalante. Differences of emphases too will mark differences between teachers. The scholar-professional mentioned in chapter 3 will stress the virtues of intellect, while the nurturer-professional will stress care, and the moral agent–professional will focus on character. The virtue as disposition, once again, has a cognitive core that is internal in the sense that the agent knows what he or she believes in and acts accordingly out of these virtues.

II. Virtues of Character for the Teacher

The clarification of the difference between educational goals or purposes and teacher dispositions does not imply that there is no connection. As has been argued, what the citizenry want from an education system will determine what they think the teachers ought to be like. Across each of these dispositions as virtues will also run the difference explained in chapter 9 between self-disclosure (when one examines one's actions in the light of episodes) and self-enactment (when one reflects on the dispositions themselves). But if both teacher educators and student teachers reflect on their work with either of these, they will need to work with an articulation of virtues of character as teacher dispositions of the following kind. Each will include understandings, commitments, perspectives, and choices.

Trustworthiness implies:

1. Realizing that trust has to be engendered and won, and that trustworthiness is a virtue to be developed in each child, in a class of children, and across schools;
2. Avoiding deceit, set within a sophisticated understanding of truthfulness (which does not imply never saying something false);
3. Continuing awareness that authority and the trust it implies may dissolve into power plays;
4. Continuing the open search for the truth with children cooperatively to provide the ground for understanding a shared world;
5. Valuing and articulating disagreement, and giving each argument due respect;
6. Acknowledging how trustworthiness can be undermined with children—for example, by prejudice, favoritism, or simple dislike;
7. Embedding in all work with children the value of trustworthiness, in relation to mutual responsibilities in classes or in groups or across a school;
8. Understanding that trustworthiness will be also manifest when other exercises of virtue are paramount—for example, in treating children fairly—as it is in truthfulness.

Trustworthiness is also one of the six "pillars of character" as defined by the Josephson Institute (http://josephsoninstitute.org/).

Sincerity implies:

1. Being motivated to say what one believes without dissembling and to be prepared to express views that may elicit disfavor,—for example in a faculty lounge;
2. Thinking clearly about one's beliefs, and judging the significance of their expression in a context;
3. Being sensitive to the problems of candor in the role of an "examiner" of children's work;
4. Being sensitive to the problems of candor in the role of "critic" of children's work;
5. Being sensitive to the problems of candor in handling children as individual persons, distinct from their work as learners;

6. Understanding the complexity of using irony (Roberts & Wood, 2007, p. 166) or the devil's advocate as a pedagogical practice.

The virtues of the will, discussed as courage in chapter 5, include a variety of virtues all of which describe getting things done. However, in teaching, the positive virtues of the will vis-à-vis teaching may be divided into three main categories: (1) acting in the face of a perceived danger or fear of a context (e.g., risk-taking and courage), (2) striving for a goal (e.g., persistence and perseverance), and (3) self-control (e.g., in concentrating, in listening to others, in the use of one's time, for example, in prudential virtues like punctuality and the problem of procrastination). "Desire, emotional response and choice...constitute the excellent formation of the will" (Roberts & Wood, 2007, p. 154). Each of these will be apparent in matters of will through these examples:

Risk-taking and courage imply for the teacher:

a. Clarifying what is the object of the risk and what the dangers are (e.g., for self-esteem in the event of failure);
b. Control of emotions appropriate to the task of encouragement;
c. Retaining a commitment to the goal embodying the risk, but continuously making course corrections;
d. Sustaining the commitment to the object of the risk over the long term if needed;
e. Consistently reappraising the appropriateness of the task that is the object of the risk;
f. Recognizing the ability to transfer the disposition of courage across different contexts.

The encouragement of children and students demands developing these qualities in children.

Perseverance includes persistence, and they share common threads; both dispositions do not imply any worthiness of goals being pursued. The larger frame is that of making an effort or striving. This disposition is distinct from courage or taking risks in that it is not premised on the presence of a situation to be regarded as dangerous. Following Peterson and Seligman (2004, pp. 229–247), perseverance implies:

1. Determination to achieve goals in the face of obstacles, difficulties, or discouragement (p. 229);
2. A "learned industriousness" in respect of goal achievement (p. 230);
3. Constant optimism and expectations of success;
4. Preparedness to tackle difficult tasks, with satisfaction coming both from goal achievement and from the exercise of will;
5. Self-control or self-regulation facilitating "overriding one's natural tendency to quit" (p. 234);
6. Persistence determined by value placed on the goal (p. 235).

For teachers, there is evidence that strong support by "observers" facilitates the development of persistence, probably because, for children, both pleasing the teacher as well as completing the task provides strong motivation (p. 233).

A Note on Weakness of Will: Procrastination

One of the most pervasive and characteristic issues of the will is procrastination (Surowiecki, 2010). "Procrastination needs no great pleasure to drive it and no activity to instantiate it. It is just the venerable sin of sloth" (Andreou & White, 2010, p. 11). There are two ways to look at weakness of will and procrastination in particular. First, you do something, as we say, against your better judgment. You know course A would be best, but you take course B. Alternatively, you turn a vague intention into a resolution (e.g., shift from "that closet needs cleaning" to "I will clean that closet tomorrow") that you then put off, thereby failing in your resolution (Stroud, 2008). Yet "the perplexing thing about procrastination ... is that, although it seems to involve avoiding unpleasant tasks, indulging in it generally doesn't make people happy" (Surowiecki, 2010, p. 110). Maybe needed efforts and tasks are postponed, not always simply from sloth, but due to a lust for perfectionism and a fear of not living up to standards. Or, of course, we could put something off because we have "better" things to do, things we choose over what we have put off. Procrastination therefore can manifest failures of persistence and perseverance and the lack of an ability to concentrate. Both teachers and students are schedule-driven, but within that, especially in higher education, there is plenty of room for delay.

Any teacher recognizes the widespread character of procrastination in themselves and in the children and students they teach. It is a classic instance of what needs to be in the moral classroom viewed as a problem to be shared and constantly discussed, not least because learning is difficult. Many freshmen students, in my experience, feel that procrastination takes them over, that they are helpless before it. One can speculate about means to help students combat these habits. Maybe they have no weapons to combat it, such as devising a schedule with care, not attempting to do the impossible ("today I will work in the library all day"), or not attending to study habits (e.g., sitting at a table to read, not lying on a bed). Procrastination, in this very brief account, is primarily a matter of poor self-control.

III. Virtues of Intellect: Critical Thinking

In his book *The Philosophy of Teaching,* Australian philosopher John Passmore (1985, chapter 9) articulates the significance of educating a person as a critical thinker, not a person with critical thinking skills. A critical thinker is seen here as having virtues of intellect. Being a critical thinker, however, contains a wide variety of dispositions and skills. The Foundation for Critical Thinking (Paul, 2000; Paul & Elder, 2009) describes a plethora of dispositions, skills, and attributes for critical and creative thinking. They distinguish three *levels of thinking* and *universal standards* that are, more or less, present in such levels: clarity, accuracy, precision, relevance, depth, logic, significance, and fairness. They also distinguish eight *intellectual traits or virtues* in critical thinking, namely intellectual integrity, intellectual humility, intellectual autonomy, intellectual empathy, intellectual courage, confidence in reason, intellectual perseverance, and fair-mindedness, pointing out the vices to which these qualities are virtues. (In chapter 5 their account of weaknesses in thinking was discussed.)

The important contribution made by this foundation is the production by 2010 of 17 short, accessible monographs aimed at students and faculty, and a further 6 aimed at faculty alone, providing an excellent intensive approach to critical and creative thinking (see Further Reading). This partnership between philosopher Richard Paul and psychologist Linda Elder also provides considerable depth both for the ideas and for the pedagogy it espouses. In an age in which public policy statements about education are full of the need for "critical thinking skills," it is surprising that the foundation's work is not widely used, especially in teacher education. As with Peterson and Seligman, the classifications deployed by Paul and Elder are different from those used in this book. For example, while accuracy is indeed a standard, it is also clearly an intellectual virtue and thus a habit of mind. Similarly with fairness, for example in making impartial judgments, this is not merely a standard but a disposition that is the property of the individual.

Of particular interest across the body of this work is that no central place is given to the concept of truth. Only in the discussion of being accurate do Paul and Elder question, "How can we find out whether that is true?" Critical thinking, we are told, is "self-directed, self-disciplined, self-monitored, and self-corrective thinking. It requires rigorous standards of excellence and mindful command of their use. It entails effective communication and problem solving abilities, and a commitment to overcoming our native egocentrism and socio-centrism" (Paul & Elder, 2009, p. 2). However, the universal standards described above only have point, not simply as flexing one's intellectual muscles, so to speak, but in getting that reasoning working in the light of truth. Critical thinking, in this iteration, must latch on to the world and its truths and falsities, as opposed to being a gymnastic exercise in human flourishing. While there is a strong emphasis on the critical thinker as a person examining the development and the critical modes as I have described them, the point of being a critical thinker, deploying all the standards and virtues expressed, must be to get at the truth. Those who use critical thinking in classrooms must be constantly sensitive to this lacuna in the work of the foundation.

That apart, the central emphasis of the work developed in Peterson and Seligman, and in the work of Paul and Elder, is to emphasize the overall importance of virtue in teaching. In the account given in parts II and III, in which virtues were connected to public and personal knowledge, truthfulness, accuracy, openmindedness, and impartiality, especially in making judgments, were stressed. Each of these implies thoughtfulness, clarity, and consistency (e.g., in the application of rules and such universal standards as described by Paul and Elder). These are of central importance in teaching.

Truthfulness implies:

1. Having an enthusiasm for the search for truth;
2. Becoming a person who is believed;
3. Being open to being corrected in matters of truth;
4. Taking the trouble to be accurate;
5. Understanding the connection with sincerity;
6. Understanding the relationship with trust and being trustworthy;
7. Valuing the distinctive types of conversation with distinctive criteria of truth;
8. Caring that children and students become seekers after truth;
9. Exercising considered judgment as to when not to be truthful.

Accuracy implies:

1. All the characteristics of truthfulness;
2. Rigorous and careful attention to detail;
3. Confronting counterevidence to one's beliefs;
4. Becoming reliable in describing memories or events;
5. Understanding how to get at truth, the methods, in different disciplines;
6. Being an efficient and effective investigator in terms of ways to acquire the truth;
7. Avoiding self-deception or sloppy recording or argument in all its forms;
8. Understanding how the connection between accuracy and the search for truth affects teaching.

Open-mindedness has these characteristics, drawn from the work of Bill Hare (2007; and see chapter 12 for further elaboration of Hare's work). It implies:

1. Intellectual humility in terms of one's own knowledge and abilities;
2. Understanding the need for ongoing inquiry as knowledge is not absolute;
3. Having students continue thinking about an idea, notwithstanding class consensus;
4. Attention to all possible sources of knowledge;
5. Accepting criticism from students and fostering a climate of open-mindedness;
6. Monitoring one's own ideas carefully to understand controversy;
7. Searching for counterevidence to my own views;
8. Welcoming diverse views without stacking the deck or having an agenda;
9. Commitment to research as an ongoing part of teaching;
10. Accurate and impartial presentation of subject matter and authentic questions;
11. Challenging students to produce evidence and argument.

Impartiality implies:

1. Profound respect for alternative or contradictory beliefs;
2. Withstanding the pressures of irrelevant interests to the context requiring impartiality;
3. Understanding the detail of contexts in which the exercise of impartiality is needed, especially in terms of what is seen as an observer;
4. Examining the reasonableness of the alternative or contradictory beliefs;
5. Developing the capacity to scrutinize the world;
6. Developing the capacity for judgment through thoughtfulness;
7. Understanding the objective, the subjective, and the inter-subjective;
8. Accepting but controlling the likelihood of prior commitments, emotions, and unconscious influences on our judgments.

These characteristics of intellectual virtues indicate that any intellectual activity or act demands that the person have several interlocking and overlapping dispositions. They demand other kinds of capabilities—for example, creativity or curiosity (Peterson & Seligman, 2004, chapters 4 and 5)—that are talents to be nurtured in different ways from the virtues. A disposition to be creative sounds odd, but not so curiosity or inquisitiveness, though they are value neutral. However, these are intellectual virtues specific to teaching, and they serve to fill out the picture of the desirable dispositions for the teacher to be developed in all students.

IV. Virtues of Care

In the last thirty years, Nel Noddings has developed a formidable account of care ethics. Three major concepts were originally at the core of this moral ideal of caring, in which the focus is on the relation, not the individual (see Noddings, 1984). Receptivity defines a relationship in which each is open to the other, building a context of trust and understanding. Relatedness suggests the ability of both to fashion the relationship, to contribute to it, to have it grow, and responsiveness implies the readiness to commit to a relationship, whatever it brings. These three dispositions connect deeply to moral sentiments. First is the centrality of interpersonal trust in receptivity. Second is the sense of building not merely one's self (as in Aristotle) but in building out of one's heritage as a child in a family those abilities to relate to other people, and those abilities that are psychologically profoundly connected to our parental relationships. Third, the idea of responsiveness implies the notion of commitment to the person, to the "other," as opposed to commitment to the "rule."

However, the relationship of care ethics to other ethical systems is uncertain: sometimes in Noddings's account care ethics seems to be able to stand alongside others, such as an ethic of justice as a principle, a utilitarian ethic, a religious ethic,

or a virtue ethic. Yet, she also makes the sharp contrast between an ethic of relation (i.e., care ethics) and an ethic of self-interest, which constitute the two paths to
morality identified in the title of her 2010 book, *The Maternal Factor: Two Paths to
Morality*. If by "self-interest" she means all ethical systems that start with the individual, then she is not just contrasting care ethics with moral egoism, because,
in many ethical systems, morality is marked by consideration of the interests of
others though it does not ignore the consideration of oneself (see, e.g., Baier, 1965,
especially page 93 ff. and chapter 10). Noddings summarizes care ethics as follows:

> In care ethics, we put little faith in broad, abstract principles. We may give
> them nominal assent, but we get little guidance from them. Nor do we
> substitute, as Confucians might, a myriad of specific rules to replace univer-
> sal principles. And we are wary of depending too heavily on our personal
> virtues as moral agents. We keep our attention on living others to whom
> we must respond in specific situations. In doing this, we draw on a fund of
> experience in caring and being cared for, but in every situation we must
> identify needs, analyze complex interactions, locate similarities and differ-
> ences between present and past situations, seek empathetic accuracy, main-
> tain an open channel between empathy and sympathy, consider the effects
> of our proposed current response on others in the web of care and evaluate
> the resources at our disposal. Contrary to the odd idea that *caring* can be de-
> scribed as a nice, fuzzy feeling, ethical caring requires a high degree of skill
> in critical thinking, but the required thinking is directed at the situations
> and practices of real life, not merely at the perfection of theory.
>
> *(2010, p. 243)*

Noddings sees the woman's experience as the "one primary candidate that has
been neglected" (2010, p. 6) in moral philosophy. There is not the space here to
describe in full the subtleties of Noddings's view of care ethics: indeed, following an all-too-brief examination of some of the issues her work raises, it will be
possible to incorporate specific virtues from her notion of "caring as a complex
virtue" (p. 137) into an account of the teacher's dispositions as virtues.

An overview of the theory's grounding now looks like this (Noddings, 2010).
Care ethics is located in natural caring, identified first as the instinctive care a
mother feels for her newborn, to which she *must* respond. Her caring becomes
natural to her such that the relationship of caring can then be seen as ethical. This
moves us, so to speak, not merely from nature to nurture, but from an account
of how the evolution of the human being provides the ground for our morality,
through the experience of motherhood. This caring relationship of human experience has its antithesis in male-developed theories in ethics (in which the female
perspective is ignored), especially those seeing morality as following rules and
principles. Worse still, the male of the species, unlike the caring female, is prone to
swagger his individualistic self and to be attracted by aggression and violence, not

merely sit in his study spinning out moral theory: "my interest," she writes, "lies in changing a male evolutionary trait—the tendency to aggression and violence" (p. 4). Relations are necessarily social, so, to Noddings, the paradigm underlying the moral must itself be social, not individual. "Care Theory...insists that relation is ontologically basic and the caring relation morally basic. We become individuals only within relations...the attributes we exhibit as individuals are products of the relations into which we are cast" (p. 101).

The richness of Noddings's full account is such that it raises numerous questions. First, the notion of evolutionary theory as primary may say too little because it says too much. That is, few would deny that our moral lives are in some sense rooted in the way human beings have evolved, and Noddings puts great faith in the development of genetics to further our understanding of this common knowledge about human beings. Few would further deny that individuals are, again in some sense, shaped by society, because we live in societies and always have. Noddings, as we have noted, argues that women's experience (e.g., in child-bearing and upbringing) has been ignored in the moral understanding of societies, but, however important, this is a narrow base (the experience of mothers) on which to build an ethic. "Narrow" may be thought too harsh (or typically male), but if we consider only "two paths to morality," the choice offered is too constricted in its perspective on human life. By that is meant that there are much broader features of the empirical world on which to construct an account of an evolutionary and social basis for morality, with answers to such questions as "What are the fundamental conditions for human society to exist at all?" and "How dependent are these conditions on the characteristics of human beings?"

An example of a much broader and comprehensive account of what is implied in social evolution is offered in Hart's (1961, ch. IX. 2) account of the minimum content of natural law. He articulates connections between natural facts and moral or legal rules in his claims for five features of life on the planet that, with the use of reason and given survival as an aim, human beings can address and out of which there would emerge moral and or legal norms, usually forbearances or prohibitions. (Noddings, differently, articulates connections between natural facts [mothers and their infants] to articulate the ethic of caring.) Human beings, Hart claims, are vulnerable to each other; out of that fact have arisen generalized rules of not harming others, which in turn generate rules of respect for other people. Again, while human beings differ in many ways, no individual is so much more powerful "that he is able, without cooperation, to dominate or subdue them for more than a short period of time" (pp. 190–191). There is therefore approximate equality that makes necessary a system of mutual forbearance and compromise as the base of legal and moral obligation. Human beings also have limited altruism, being neither "angels nor devils" (p. 191). This fact about us leads, once again, to conventions of mutual forbearance, which, in turn, lead to conventions of behavior. Fourth, the planet is such that resources are, in general, limited: this gives rise to rights of property (communal or individual) but also to a division of labor, which brings with it dynamic rules, as in contracts, hence the development of moral rules about promising and the creation of webs of trust. Finally, in Hart's account, human beings have limited understanding and strength of will. Controls are needed and sanctions must be used to limit the depredations of the villains. "Sanctions are therefore required not as the normal motive for obedience, but as a guarantee that those who would voluntarily obey shall not be sacrificed to those who would not" (p. 193). Required is "voluntary cooperation within a coercive system." This is a much more complex picture of social evolution undergirding morality than that rooted solely in the mother-child relation, and it is difficult to classify Hart's account as "male" in any significant sense.

Second, in this naturalistic story Noddings tells, she portrays the female needing to "read" both her infant and her man-protector she is with. Women have been a party to their own subordination, she claims, which has become an "obsessive tradition." Her account of the problems of male dominance is in some ways mild and in others ahistorical and apolitical, which is odd considering her strong emphasis on the "real world," which she accuses the likes of Kant and Rawls of ignoring. For instance, she is nothing like as caustic as John Stuart Mill in his 1869 essay on *The Subjection of Women*. Again, the paternal power she describes was not a given of man's nature. In his *Second Treatise on Civil Government,* Locke, for example, was adamant on the mistake of paternal power and the importance of partnership, not male dominance in a family (Second Treatise on Civil Government VI: 52, 58).

Finally, part of the weakness of Noddings's account of male behavior lies in what almost seems a contradiction. On the one hand, her attacks on individualism in its different forms in moral philosophy are focused on the lack of attention to the empirical self coupled with an emphasis on social conditions. Yet her remarks about male violence and aggression seem to float free from any historical account. Locke was writing in the context of a rural-agricultural society, one the Founding Fathers would have recognized and whose practical economy demanded man-woman partnership in the fields and in the home. For every paterfamilias, one could find the opposite—John and Abigail Adams, for instance. Mill was writing in the 1860s, just after laissez-faire capitalism was subjected to some controls in Britain in a society dominated by greed and, for the poor, the need to survive. Social reality had been drastically shaped by the emergence of capitalism and industrialization, with major effects on the human psyche. (Of course, Noddings could argue that capitalism and the market are "male inventions," which, though historically correct, is uninteresting.) She takes little account of the effects of competition, capitalism, the market, or Marx's analysis of their weaknesses. Women under laissez-faire capitalism were as likely to be employed in mines and factories as men, but later ceased to "work outside the home." So, while emphasizing the importance of the reality as opposed to theoretical constructs about human beings, her view of the reality of the political and economic character of society within which human beings actually live is curiously myopic.

Three features of her account of care ethics deserve additional comment. First, she writes, "We keep our attention on living others to whom we *must* respond in specific situations" (see above; my italics). What exactly is the force of the "must"? Is it natural or ethical? "Must" originates in the woman's (natural) care for the child, generalized to an account of ethical caring. The natural processes of empathy impel us to respond to needs, we are told, to which we "must" respond. Yet even at the natural level, if "must" means that we cannot help responding to the expressed needs of others in this way, that seems empirically false, as we can clearly do this on a particular occasion or as a matter of policy. But, she also argues, caring is educable, suggesting that the natural basis only tells an interesting story, because caring does not, like the goddess Athena, spring fully armed from the head of Zeus or, in more prosaic terms, from our nature. It needs to be nurtured. If that is the case, then "must" looks very close to, if not synonymous with, "ought." There is hard work to be done: "we have to develop children's capacity for caring" (Noddings, 2010, p. 79). If caring is educable, teachers and students can fail at it: its natural base looks overstated. Because how then are such failures of caring to be regarded? As blameworthy? As shameful? "Neither," I suspect, would be Noddings's response: rather constant reflection and self-analysis would lead us to see the situation differently as one in which we "must" respond, which emphasizes the nonnatural obligatory character of caring.

Second, it was noted above that Noddings insists that "relation" is ontologically prior to individuals and to individual acts. Care theory "insists that relation is ontologically basic and the caring relation morally basic. We become individuals only within relations . . . the attributes we exhibit as individuals are products of the relations into which we are cast" (2010, p. 101). (Contrast Zagzebski's claim that persons are ontologically more fundamental than acts; acts are defined in terms of persons. See chapter 10.) Is Noddings correct? If interpreted strongly, it implies no place for *individual* temperament, character, and wants. If interpreted weakly, it means no more than that we are social creatures. Two points may be made about her argument. First, it cannot be an empirical claim, or if it is, it could rapidly dissolve into a chicken-and-egg argument. To have "relation" you must have at least two individuals, logically and chronologically, even if the relation is between the woman and the child growing in her womb. If that is not an empirical claim, it is normative and an argument that can be resolved only by ethical reasoning. It is then difficult to see how that might be resolved, except by simply asserting the priority of one or the other. Noddings would claim that a great deal hangs on which is given priority, but given the fact that human beings are social creatures, does the question of priority matter? Will it not depend on the kinds of issues being raised?

Finally, her view of us as social creatures leads her to interpret (individual) autonomy as some kind of limitless free will (which she regards as incomprehensible, as there are constraints of culture, background, family and law, etc.) to be replaced by a limited autonomy that she describes as limited control. "Care ethics," she writes, "views autonomy as a state of limited, appropriate, and at least minimally satisfying control. It is anchored in a relational ontology, and the self it describes is a relational self" (Noddings, 2010, p. 115). This view of autonomy seems what most scholars of autonomy would aver, putting the relational ontology to one side. Many philosophers have made autonomy conceptually central to morality, but with the possible exception of Rousseau, not many have regarded it as practically unconstrained, not least because it is usually set within a theory of obligation. Yet, again, she detaches autonomy from its social and political origins. The historical significance of autonomy, specifically in regard to the Protestant Reformation, is that it provided a conceptual frame for describing the needs and rights of people to *escape* from moral or intellectual duress of one kind or another and attain freedom of choice (see also my remarks on autonomy in chapter 9). Equally in throwing off the shackles of feudalism and developing what Condren (2006) calls the "moral economy" of early modern England, the autonomous acts of those holding office were necessary to effective compliance with the oaths of office to which all office-holders swore: autonomy implied not some boundless free will, but individuals' commitments to uphold the common good as defined in their oaths. Autonomy was circumscribed but necessary to fulfill an oath of office. Autonomy thus has moral importance, not only in freeing individuals from Rousseau's chains, but in providing a structural basis on which individuals can escape intellectual or moral servitude and also be of service, implicit in Belenky and colleagues' (1986) account of women's lives.

Notwithstanding the critical direction of these all too brief and selective comments, Noddings's work is of immense significance as we address the virtues of care for the teacher. Caring is "a set of dispositions to respond positively in interpersonal relations" (2010, p. 28). We must help children develop a capacity for empathy, put it into practice, she states, and continually evaluate their success in building caring relations. This maxim should be applied to students training to be teachers. It has been suggested above that tolerance, tact, patience, discretion, civility, compassion, sympathetic attention, sensitivity, and receptivity (the latter three drawn from Noddings) comprise the virtues of care. Of these tolerance, patience, compassion, and sympathetic attention are taken here as salient.

Tolerance

In a diverse democratic society, especially one in which the level of public debate in the media is of low quality, it is of critical importance that teachers develop an understanding of the difficulty of tolerance (Scanlon, 2003), its range of application, and its limits. Phrases like "zero tolerance" abound in schools; the need for understanding is considerable. Religious toleration, probably initiated by Cyrus the Great after his conquest of Babylon in the sixth century BC, is enshrined positively in the free expression and establishment clauses of the First Amendment to the U.S. Constitution.

We tolerate another's (individual, group) beliefs or behaviors: that is, in tolerating beliefs or behaviors we accept them as expressions without having to agree with, support, endorse, or welcome them. Tolerance is active, not passive, even though we may in fact do nothing. The beliefs or behaviors of others with which we agree or of which we approve are, therefore, not candidates for our tolerance. We must distinguish between (a) those expressions with which we do not agree, support, endorse, or welcome and (b) those expressions with which we do not agree and which we believe should be prohibited or sanctioned in one way or another. So, one could support the practice of abortion or the death penalty, disapprove of it, or disapprove of it and want to see the practice prohibited (Forst, 2007). It is the last two options with which tolerance is concerned, and to tolerate something is always a matter of one's own volition.

Three further points indicate the significance of tolerance. First, it is required often in cases of beliefs or behaviors that are socially or politically controversial (controversial does not imply that everyone has to see it as such). Second, the challenges to our tolerance are primarily challenges to our conscience with regard to our beliefs (see chapter 5): we have to work out where we stand. Finally, to be tolerant is not to accept that anything goes. Rather we must wrestle with the boundaries between expressions (beliefs and behaviors) we accept without agreeing with them and those we think should be forbidden, either in the public domain of civil society or in private associations. Understanding what it is to be tolerant and addressing the difficulties of teaching tolerance are very profound in a diverse society in which racial and gender prejudice are not uncommon.

Tolerance therefore implies:

1. Examining whether one's own beliefs or behaviors demand tolerance from others;
2. Being active in critiquing the views of others with respect;
3. Developing "a spirit of accommodation, a desire to find a system of rights that others could also be asked to accept" (Scanlon, 2003, p. 198);
4. Being active in supporting those subject to intolerance;
5. Subjecting one's own views on controversial issues to rigorous scrutiny;
6. Developing judgment on handling opposing views to one's own that are intolerant;
7. Demanding tolerance from others as a civic right when one's own views are controversial (see Dagger, 1997, p. 197).

Patience

Patience may be considered more of a prudential than a moral virtue, but waiting at an airport is clearly different in moral terms from waiting for a stutterer to finish a sentence. Waiting at a checkout is morally speaking different from hearing a child reading, making mistakes, correcting herself, and struggling to the end of the sentence. We can lose our patience. Patience often involves bearing suffering or pain with equanimity. Indeed most cases of patience, like tolerance, involve *not* doing anything: a classic example is the czarist Russian general Kutuzov, who defeated Napoleon in 1812 by withdrawing from Moscow and waiting patiently for several months for French army discipline to fray and the cold weather to undermine them, which eventually led to their ignominious retreat and defeat, leaving 600,000 French soldiers dead. Jackson (1990) commented in his famous *Life in Classrooms* that many features of classroom life call for patience, and he dubs it the quintessential virtue of life in any institution (p. 18), because it includes self-control. Here patience is treated as a moral virtue, as it functions ethically in many occupations—teaching, nursing, medicine, family life. So while being patient may involve not doing anything, it remains of moral significance.

Patience implies:

1. Understanding that the test of being patient is entirely one's own;
2. Using self-control in the face of misfortune, suffering, or provocation;
3. Being even-tempered in the face of delay or setbacks;
4. Being able to discipline one's own thinking and handle the pace required to achieve a goal;
5. Accepting, but not succumbing to, the rhythms of institutional life;
6. Being steadfast in purposes that demand support for others;
7. Regulating the tendency to complain at setbacks.

Compassion

In 2009, author Karen Armstrong, a former Roman Catholic nun, launched the Charter for Compassion. Its first paragraph read:

> The principle of compassion lies at the heart of all religious, ethical and spiritual traditions, calling us always to treat all others as we wish to be treated ourselves. Compassion impels us to work tirelessly to alleviate the suffering of our fellow creatures, to dethrone ourselves from the centre of our world and put another there, and to honour the inviolable sanctity of every single human being, treating everybody, without exception, with absolute justice, equity and respect. (http://charterforcompassion.org/charterevent/)

This very broad account of compassion nevertheless leads us to criteria for compassion as a human virtue of care. It is extremely important not to confuse compassion with charity or love. In chapter 10, I asserted that teachers who place a loving relationship with the child above the child's intellectual and moral development simply misunderstand the purpose of teaching and the teacher's responsibility. So children should be helped to confront difficulty, rather than be hugged. Something similar is true of compassion. That is, it can be misplaced, even misdirected. It is a much more comprehensive matter than simply feeling sorry for someone: I may feel sorry for someone suffering under some description but, as

I might say, "He brought it on himself," in which case my being compassionate may be inappropriate. Whether the metaphor of "dethroning ourselves" quite describes compassion seems misleading in that no ethical requirement (*pace* Noddings) can hold that we reduce the importance of our individual self in relation to others, because our individual self must morally count for one, but no more than one. Such dethroning is a characteristic of saints and heroes (Urmson, 1958), people who go above and beyond what might be reasonable demands of any ethic and perform acts "which are good to do but not bad not to do" (Heyd, 2007).

Compassion implies:

1. Understanding that suffering can take many forms in varied contexts, social and individual;
2. Being able to imaginatively enter into situations in which suffering may not be perspicuous;
3. Clearly understanding the nature of the suffering the other is enduring;
4. Being or becoming competent in appropriate ways to relieve that suffering;
5. Taking steps to relieve that suffering;
6. Acting to restrain in appropriate ways those who are responsible for the conditions of suffering (see Noddings, 2010, chapter 3);
7. Judging the limits of compassion in terms of other desirable responses to a person's suffering.

Sympathetic Attention

Sympathetic attention stands at the heart of Noddings's view of those virtues composing care, and it is this conception of attention that will be used here. "Sympathetic attention is a complex virtue," she writes (2010, p. 174). It is interesting, however, that she is reluctant to use the word virtue because, she argues, a virtue is an individual possession and we need in care ethics a stance "towards the one who addresses us." This seems somewhat confused: there are obvious examples of virtues that are our possessions, but others whose meaning entails addressing others—for example, tolerance, patience, and compassion. But that apart, her account of sympathetic attention is paramount among the virtues of care, because it "involves skill, and that skill can be honed to a high level of competence." "As a virtue, sympathetic attention requires *commitment*. A person who regularly responds with sympathetic attention has committed herself to keeping open the channels from perception to feeling to motivational displacement. The carer...accepts the vulnerability that accompanies exercise of this virtue" (2010, p. 175). The focus is on the needs of the one being cared for, in Noddings's terms, not that individual's rights (2010, p. 177). Yet Noddings is also more concerned with attributes and habits such as "preservative love, holding, staying with, fostering growth," which are difficult to describe as virtues but nevertheless critical to caring.

The emphasis on the *needs* of the cared for rather than their *rights* is of immense importance in teaching. As teachers we may generally describe the child in the classroom as having rights to a safe and drug-free environment, quality teaching, bussing to school, help with college admission, and other things: our perception of the child in the classroom can easily become dominated by thinking of "the rights of the child," which can bypass the child as a person with specific, idiosyncratic needs. It becomes easy, therefore, not to give each child sympathetic attention because the child is a "third-grader," a bureaucratic description of a child with rights derived from that category, rather than a person with a developing social and personal identity. Yet if the argument throughout this book has any weight, the development of individual virtues (self- and other-regarding) must be intricately connected to who each individual child is and who they are becoming. We may not, as teachers, have the skills to do this, but Noddings helps us see the importance of it. The one being cared for is in relation with the carer, but both are individual persons with unique desires, wants, and ambitions.

Sympathetic attention implies:

1. Understanding that sympathetic attention demands the development of skills—listening, not hearing; seeing behind, not merely perceiving;
2. A strong unremitting focus on "reading" the needs of the specific individual;
3. Being prepared to surrender one's own priorities to another, as in motivational displacement;
4. A dynamic commitment to that individual, with children minimally in terms of their moral, intellectual growth;
5. Understanding the unique quality of the relationship with the individual and being open to its changing character;
6. Being mindful of the whole person and the context of that person's life—for example, family;
7. Being aware of one's vulnerability in these attitudes and commitment.

Finally, *integrity as wholeness* is a virtue of *personhood*. It provides a prism through which all these virtues of character, intellect, and care may be viewed by the individual. While a lack of it will be obviously manifest in interactions with other people, it is a matter of profound self-reflection and analysis. It implies:

1. Examining how my talents, capabilities, and virtues fit with the demands of the teaching role;
2. Examining how I address the conflicts and passions in my life and how they relate to each other;
3. Examining how I sustain my integrity through differing kinds of challenges—for example, marriage, a new school, or a new class.

Those separable aspects of the self—our faculties, desires, life-shaping choices—need to come together into a coherent whole, or as Noddings would put it, "concerned with moral life considered whole" (2010, p. 28). Conflicts have to be faced, not put to one side. Passions have to be measured, not allowed to become fanatic.

To some degree, the commitment to teaching as it meshes with internal values "must in some sense come to you," as Bernard Williams (1985, p. 169) put it. Another way of describing how a passionate commitment to teaching may be judged is the advice given to a person dithering about whether to become a teacher: "Don't, unless you feel you can't keep out of it." Norton's phrase "meaningful work and meaningful living" captures the achievement of integrity as wholeness, and the presentation to the students of an integrated personality provides a good model. However, "in the epistemically virtuous person the disposition of caring about the intellectual goods will derive in part from a disposition of caring about other goods, such as justice, human well-being, and friendship" (Roberts & Wood, 2007, p. 158). As we learn to care, such that it becomes a part of us, or who we are, so we will consistently encounter these other goods Roberts and Wood mention. This indicates, of course, that integrity as wholeness gives us our balance as individuals, and it leads to the care and love we develop for learning and knowledge.

12

THE EPISTEMOLOGICAL PRESENCE AND THE ASSESSMENT OF TEACHER QUALITY

> The challenge for our education system is to leverage the learning sciences and modern technology to create engaging, relevant and personalized learning experiences for all learners that mirror students' daily lives and the reality of their futures. In contrast to traditional classroom instruction, this requires that we put students at the center and empower them to take control of their own learning by providing flexibility of several dimensions.
>
> *(USDOE draft document, 2010,* Transforming American Education: Learning Powered by Technology, *p. 4)*

The familiar rhetoric around developing a twenty-first-century education system to meet the demands of the knowledge-based economy describes possibilities with which most of the population might feel some sympathy. Yet the most fundamental change in social patterns is that individuals in a modern economy are going to be free agents; with some exceptions, they can no longer expect to join a corporation or a smoke-stack industry and retire on full pension thirty years later. Career counselors tell undergraduates that they can expect to change careers five times in a working life. These changes demonstrate the importance of putting the individual child as a person at the heart of the educational engagement.

Yet this shift demands not merely different kinds of "personalized learning experiences" but the development of "twenty-first-century" moral and intellectual dispositions, virtues, and habits. Of what use to a company or to government is a closed-minded recruit? How useful is a human resource manager who can't be impartial? If we need entrepreneurs, let alone soldiers and sailors, we need people who are courageous and can take risks. How good at the job can an inaccurate bricklayer or electrician be? Our lawyers and doctors need to be sophisticated about their sincerity and how candid they are with their patients and clients. Do caregivers of all kinds manifest sympathetic attention, or are nurses more concerned with working the gadgets and filling in forms? If people work in teams on solving problems, they need to be trustworthy and familiar with creating or being a part of an environment of trust. All these intellectual and moral dispositions can be nurtured during schooling, and "learning powered with technology" will get no power at all if it ignores their importance, because people with competence and expertise without appropriate intellectual dispositions and habits of mind will have a barren life and cannot flourish as people or in roles (Peterson & Seligman, 2004, and see chapter 10). The teaching challenge becomes, in a proper use of the word, awesome.

For teacher educators, however, the quality of their work and the quality of their graduates is frequently under attack. As U.S. secretary of education Arne Duncan put it in an address at Teachers College in 2009, "by almost any standard, many if not most of the nation's 1,450 schools, colleges, and departments of education are doing a mediocre job of preparing teachers for the realities of the 21st century classroom," a widely held view among policy makers. Institutions of teacher education are responsible to the public, usually through mechanisms established by the states, for the quality of the teachers they graduate, and accreditation bodies vouch for their quality. It is unnecessary here to detail these mechanisms or accreditation systems, or to survey different institutional practices in formulating the judgments on individual candidates (see Further Reading). Institutions devise student assessment schemes, but needed is a scheme that connects strongly to dispositions, virtues, and intellectual habits.

This chapter articulates in section 1 what the epistemological presence in a classroom is, focusing on three questions constantly in the child's mind as he or she develops ownership of the curriculum. This gathers together the different pieces of the account that have constituted a central theme in this book. The articulation of the epistemological presence, however, can just be a feature of classrooms in schools: it must be pervasive in the education of teachers. This manifesto, if it can be called that, is therefore incomplete without an account of how teacher quality has to be assessed. The primary theme throughout this book—namely, the connection of knowledge to virtue, and the centrality of the person working out who he or she is, what he or she is becoming, what initiatives are needed for his or her own development, and how he or she sees him or herself—must stand at the center of the educational experience of the student teacher. Profound self-examination throughout that educational experience must be measured not against goals, but against the principles and virtues within which one's life is developing, being understood, and conducted.

Following the account of the epistemological presence, therefore, a view of the problem of assessment of dispositions in teacher education is outlined in section 2, followed in section 3 with a solution based in self-assessment by students. In section 4 a procedure is then outlined in which self-assessment is at the center, containing faculty and student protocols. Within such a framework there then follows an example in section 4, pertaining to open-mindedness. In the appendices to the book, four other examples are drafted: truthfulness and trustworthiness; courage and the will; sympathetic attention; and integrity as wholeness. Section 5 is a summary of the challenges for the development of teacher quality.

I. The Centers of the Epistemological Presence

There are four enemies of intellectual progress and the development of knowledge and self-knowledge in a child. The first is opinion, as in "Give your opinion on the Louisiana Purchase." Too often teachers believe that asking children to give their opinion is a way of valuing their thought or motivating them to think. But opinion is valuable only if it is rooted in analysis, examination of evidence and counterevidence, by people disposed to be impartial and made manifest in a judgment. The second is opinion's stablemate, simulation, equally inimical to coherent thought, as in "What would you have done if you were Thomas Jefferson?" Simulation develops the wrong sort of historical imagination, not least because it assumes that such a question is coherent. I am not Thomas Jefferson; I do not see the world as he saw it. How can I write anything intelligent in answering such a question? The third enemy is fun. Teachers manufacture all kinds of synthetic and shallow experiences so that child can have a "fun" classroom, the assumption being that things intellectual or serious are beyond enjoyment and have at best to be tolerated as part of the evil presence of school. The final enemy is love. Teachers who place a loving relationship with the child above the child's intellectual and moral development simply misunderstand the purpose of teaching and the teacher's responsibility. So children should be helped to confront difficulty, rather than be hugged. A classroom with an epistemological presence will not contain such enemies of the development of the person of intellectual and moral virtue.

In a classroom with an epistemological presence, the curriculum will become the child's own. By ownership is implied that the child sees the intellectual virtues as his or her strengths, is invigorated by them, is proud of them, and delights in paying attention to them in both curriculum and other contexts. That classroom or seminar room demands an atmosphere that has three primary categories of questions:

1. *Belief questions:* How do I know what I believe? What counts for me as evidence?
2. *Self-revelatory questions:* How do I see myself? Where do I stand?
3. *Search for truth questions:* What is truth? What is authority? To whom do I listen?

The child clambering on the bus after school should have a mind full of questions about the day's work—the symbol of ownership—not a mind filled with worry about what time he or she has tonight to memorize for tomorrow's test—the symbol of alienation from the curriculum. The principle applies to any learner, especially a teacher in training or a graduate student developing professionally. Thus the moral classroom in which that child/student lives will have an epistemological presence with those three centers—belief, self-revelation, and the search for truth. Through ownership, the student will come to love learning.

Belief Questions: How Do I Know What I Believe?
What Counts for Me as Evidence?

Knowledge begets ignorance, as Plato pointed out, thus at the heart of intellectual development lies the question, not the statement. Public knowledge has to be identified in terms of propositions (A knows p) that are formed within statements, which become the assertions a person makes (believing them to be true). Questions form a central part of our lives. That is, as with the child constantly asking why, getting an answer to a question lays bare a batch of new questions for the seeker after truth. Dewey's (1938) view of inquiry, crudely, sees the solution to a problem (arrived at through examining hypotheses and selecting one likely to work) as yielding equilibrium: but for the seeker after truth, any answer is necessarily provisional, given the new questions any answer (or solution) raises. Far from the solution bringing existential quiet, it may well do the exact opposite: create intellectual ferment.

A question is an invitation, whereas an answer is a terminus. The contemporary dominant place of the right answer, being both sought for and required in classrooms, spells doom for the active questioner. Teachers use all kinds of tactics to deflect difficult questions, but that is because they usually ask questions to which they know the answers, so questioning becomes a tool pressed into service for getting right answers. Such questions are not authentic questions for the teacher (since the teacher already knows the answer), and questions can be further undermined when posed with the teacher as devil's advocate (see chapter 4 on sincerity). Maybe teachers should always ask questions to which they do not know the answer.

Crucially, deflecting questions (e.g., "Ask me that later"; "Look it up on the web") cuts off dialogue, not least because such deflection smacks of insincerity. Yet if questions are authentic for the class—if they generate dialogue and the teacher does not know the answers—the opportunity for intellectual ferment occurs, governed by impartial consideration of possible answers. Yet not any old question will do. Dialogue is governed by a discourse that children are learning, in Oakeshottian language, to take part in a human conversation. Thus the subtlety of the way the teacher poses and encourages questions is within a framework of discourse and beliefs set out in chapter 5 (and see below). A balance is to be struck between the child's divergent question, which may or not be precise or relevant, and the "right-on" question that has clear relevance. But relevance to what? To the framework of discourse within which the inquiry is being conducted. For example, Columbus's voyages, to use W. Hare's example again, could spawn scientific, political, and historical inquiry, much of which (e.g., on navigation) could involve mathematical tools. "Off the wall" questions might, if pursued in a dialogue, produce real insights. For the teacher, the challenge is to so shape the child's questions that they remain the valued possession of their author without switching the questions into the teacher's agenda. Teachers set directions for the language and for the topics so that the developing child will learn, through being taught, how to understand what counts as relevant and thereby ask significant and searching (for truth) questions and develop ideas. The child comes to feel safe in taking intellectual risks with such ideas.

The interplay between the two questions noted in this section (How do I know what I believe? and What counts for me as evidence?) may well yield children who can appreciate alternative explanations but still not be able to commit to one or the other (see chapter 8). Evidence, of course, is not mere data, because, as virtue epistemologists urge us, it is the reliable or the responsible character of the agent that is the core of the justification. But that must include evidence as we commonly understand it, and it may be often contradictory: what seemed a long set of facts to be memorized about Columbus has suddenly become a charged inquiry in which students take different stands as they confront that evidence. The teacher may then, in such discussions, begin to play the role of the "neutral chairman" (see Stenhouse, 1983) to try to make sure the children are able to deliberate without feeling any need to come up against the (teacher's) right answer—in other words, to be open-minded. But that postponement of judgment is precisely what marks an epistemological presence that rejects the lust for the right answer in favor of thoughtful, careful weighing of alternatives and the making of thought-out judgments.

Self-Revelatory Questions: How Do I See Myself? Where Do I Stand?

A moral classroom with an epistemological presence is also one strongly monitored to facilitate the child's, as a historical individual, "world as I see it and as I articulate it." There are three areas of importance: (1) a child's educational conscience about his or herself, (2) a child's self-conscious view of his or herself as a learner, in both discovery and critical mode (see chapter 5), and (3) a child's belief in the validity of his or her experience and its place in his or her school learning.

An educational conscience can be most fruitfully pointed up through the question "Is this the best I can do?" This is, of course, the implicit demand of virtue epistemology: is the agent reliable or responsible in making a knowledge assertion? Doing your best can be, so to speak, an external challenge, asked by a teacher; but it needs to be internalized, a question that the learner constantly asks of him or herself and, if not satisfactorily achieved, creates a sense of disappointment in one's self, maybe shame or even guilt. Within this question is the pedagogical problem of getting children to respect themselves as learners, to regard themselves as trustworthy and truthful, but also persistent and persevering. Yet it can be of value to them only if they are interested. But interest here means "what they value" (see Further Reading). Children and students find interest in what they do, and that will come through their intensive participation—for example, by enjoying a question-driven curriculum. Doing one's best is a manifestation of self-respect, the initiatives the individual takes, and the will he or she reveals to do well by doing his or her best. If there is this intense interest in the content, and the determination to do one's best, there is less likelihood of slipping into the intellectual weaknesses (flaccidity or rigidity) in commitment to beliefs that were outlined in chapter 8.

Second, in some accounts of children at school (see Hersch, 1999), the school self is one whose self-conscious attentions lie in fellowship with friends, not in what is being taught. An epistemological presence in a classroom, however, emerges from a class being a certain kind of society, a society with a strong sense of communal purpose and strong social/intellectual identity. In his fascinating little book *Why Not Socialism?* philosopher G. A. Cohen (2009) describes a camping trip as an embodiment of socialist values—with common shared tasks, each contributing according to talent and skill, and a sense of common purpose. (He then asks what a camping trip would look like if it were market-driven by people making "rational"—self-interested—choices.) If we look at the social dynamics of a classroom, is it primarily an environment driven by self-interest, or by a common cause, like a camping trip? When my granddaughters were in fifth grade, they each took part in a musical production written by a teacher, for example, on the Lewis and Clark Expedition, which was a joyous community experience, with many but by no means all children contributing solo acts, but the whole grade involved in singing and dancing, some 150 children. This was extremely hard work for the children from which they got a profound enjoyment, but whatever else it was, it was not "fun." It was hard work—learning songs, dance routines, and so forth—and portrayed a marvelous sense of teachers' understanding how to create community. The epistemological presence demands that the self be committed to the community enterprise in the classroom and not solely to individual prowess or competitive attainments. Children can come to realize they can learn as much from their peers in a dialogic community as they can from the teacher.

The self-conscious view of oneself as a learner (in either discovery or critical mode) thus demands beginning to see oneself as a contributor, as a member of a community whose deep purposes are not just the fellowship of friends, important though that is, but fellowship in the enterprise of seeking after truth. Then, in a classroom with an epistemological presence, in the phrase Todd Endo often used, the whole is more than the sum of its parts, because all can learn and all can teach. The child is highly self-conscious about being a contributing learning self. The socialist versus market analogy is important here, because while there are privileged accesses to knowledge, my possession of knowledge does not imply that you cannot possess it. There can therefore be no sense of loss in making a contribution; indeed in making contributions, a child may expect reciprocal contributions to his or her understanding. Yet this self-consciousness is constantly mediated by opportunities to ask "Where am I going?" and "What do I want to achieve?"—not as grand, soul-searching questions, though they might turn out to be that, but as a constant reflective awareness about oneself.

The final segment of self-revelation lies in understanding one's own experience. Perry (1970) described a trajectory of positions—we might call them milestones—through which students give meaning to their educational experience. This study of Harvard students suggested four such positions: The initial position is basic dualism, when the student views the world as black/white, good/evil, and is dependent on authority. From that, given exposure to diversity of opinion, this dualism gives way to multiplicity, as the student starts to carve out intellectual autonomy, but as evidence and counterevidence drive the classroom experience, the student moves to a position of relativism subordinate, in which the student approaches knowledge questions analytically, and finally to a full relativism in which the student grasps the contextual character of knowledge and that knowledge is constructed. Putting on one side whether this constructivist view of knowledge is coherent, Perry is an observer. But we must believe that this account could make sense only if the achievement of these milestones was *how it appeared to the student*—that is, how the students revealed themselves epistemologically through understanding their experience and their progress to autonomy and in particular how their memories, perceptions, introspections, intuitions, understandings, reasons, and motives influenced what they represented in this trajectory.

One problem lies in the unity of person as student and person as self. As a student, I may well ignore my out-of-school life experience in the belief that my teachers know better or that my experience is irrelevant. That way lies the kind of disintegration shown by Hanssen (see chapter 7) or, at least, the failure to build the kind of integrity as wholeness needed for a meaningful life. Norton (1995) argues that the possession of virtues in a person is a result of a person's own initiative. But there are facilitating conditions: "the initiative to self-directed self-development remains latent in persons in the early stages of their lives, where it is overlaid by external demands." The problem of facilitation then becomes the "engagement of latent initiatives" (p. 82). Thus the individual's experience is primarily one of self-discovery through the kinds of mental capabilities (memory, etc.) described in chapter 9. The classroom with an epistemological presence becomes a "facilitating condition," one in which children are gradually released from the external demands of socialization in childhood into seeing themselves as taking the initiative in their learning, not being passive. But this is not simply initiative as students. Rather it goes deeply into their sense of themselves. If they begin to discover themselves in this sense, that will influence their vocational choices and how they approach all kinds of life-shaping choices—for example, whether or not to join a gang or whether or not to learn the guitar.

Truth-Seeking Questions: What Is Truth? What Is Authority? To Whom Do I Listen?

In part II, the basic elements of truth, belief, and evidence were expounded alongside the virtues of truthfulness, open-mindedness, and impartiality, which will be the core of personal dispositions contributing to a classroom with an epistemological presence. Truth, to repeat, is not to be seen as handed down but as something to be searched for. As we have seen, if a child does not continually examine alternatives and get the opportunity to reflect on his or her beliefs and their truth, he or she simply cannot progress to coherent self-understanding. The teacher's responsibility lies here, in having clarity about his or her authority and its moral and epistemological grounds (see chapter 3), but teachers must also, as seekers after truth, get themselves inside the knowledge and virtue set out in parts II and III.

The epistemological presence in a classroom is, of course, much more than an atmosphere. It implies processes and products. Teachers can articulate benchmarks and milestones that have no strongly sequential development but are normative characteristic dispositions, for example by paying detailed attention to, say, accuracy in one semester, then raising the student's awareness of obligations and purpose and focusing on open-mindedness in the next, building the habits of thought in a child that will become his or her dispositions. With regard to beliefs, without repeating the detail of chapter 5, three matters stand out: (1) helping children develop the capacity to understand beliefs without holding them themselves, (2) distinguishing between factual and opinion-based beliefs and their influence on judgment, and (3) given the complexity of beliefs, the capability to revise them in the face of new evidence. Lest this seem too formal, posit a class of non-Muslims getting to understand a Muslim's religious beliefs; seeing why they are what they are and what the stance of Muslims toward *their* religious beliefs is. That demands sorting out fact from fiction, in particular distinguishing the Koran's message from the bizarre fundamentalist versions of it seen in Saudi Arabia, contemporary Iran, and parts of Africa. Given contemporary American culture, it seems more as if the bizarre models are popular and likely to need revision. Yara Zidan, a young Muslim woman in my class, gives this account of herself:

> I don't feel as if it is my duty to go preach about how homosexuality is wrong according to Islam and Christianity. Other Muslims may read my remark and say I'm not a true practicing Muslim. However, I don't think I was put on the earth to tell others how they should live their lives or what they should believe in. I tend to use the Quran as a guideline as how I should live my own life. I do wear the *hijab* as a symbol of my identity as well for modesty. Hair attracts men and therefore to be respected by the opposite sex it is best that the man should see me in who I am and not my beauty. The stereotype of being "oppressed" because I chose to wear the *hijab* is ridiculous. I chose to wear it and my sisters chose not to. Those who were oppressed in wearing the *hijab*, I do feel sorry for them because it was done without the intention of being modest but being controlled.

A careful reading of this displays the intricacy a teacher faces in the sensitive handling of such matters in a multicultural classroom. Notice in particular the interweave of Muslim beliefs and the young woman's self-identity. Hence the need for teachers to be thorough in their understanding of public and personal knowledge and create the space for it in their classrooms and specifically in handling the three significant matters indicated about beliefs.

Thus, in the matter of searching for truth:

1. Knowledge will be provisional—not in the sense that nothing is true, but what is now ordinary truth may, at some point, change; hence the need for open-mindedness.
2. There will be constant attention to alternatives, which will counteract the inevitable egocentrism of belief.
3. Alternatives can delve deep into process, too, with alternative group identities being created within the classroom, quite apart from "understanding other cultures."
4. Children need to be helped to find validation and success in the development of all these dispositions and habits, through specific attention to such cognitive weaknesses as non-evidential belief, overconfidence, bias, or rushing to conclusions (Siegel, 2009).

The child, in such a classroom, is an epistemologist; the teacher is too, and the teacher needs to understand how his or her moral agency enables the establishment of that epistemological presence.

Love of learning and love of knowledge. Yet if the child owns the curriculum, and is proud of the strengths his or her dispositions provide, there must be a cogent relationship developing with content. Peterson and Seligman (2004) indicate that love of learning in children and students is seen as a desirable character strength by teachers, parents, and employers (chapter 7, p. 163 ff.). Love of learning is "a universal but individually varying predisposition to engage particular content or well-developed individual interest" (p. 163). It describes the way people engage with new information and skill or engage with new content if the strength is well developed. It engenders positive feelings in the process and as a consequence strengthens the motivation to persevere in the face of obstacles. It does not necessarily yield immediate achievement, and it is collegial, in the sense that deeper knowledge of content positions an individual "to make substantial and creative contributions to others' understanding of them" (p. 163). Motivation within love of learning is always intrinsic to the content, although in terms of competence, there can be different achievement orientations—for example, to mastery of the content itself or to ego-enhancement. Lovers of learning are optimists, placing great value on learning tasks. Their interest is characterized by "ongoing and ever deepening cognitive and affective relation with particular content" (p. 169). They don't need to be experts.

Love of learning, furthermore, needs to be nurtured if it is to be sustained; it needs challenges and "webs of relationships"—for example, between learners, between learners and teachers, between learners and parents, between teachers and parents, and so forth. The fact that it may decline in middle and high school is thought to be because the range of experience provided in a formal curriculum places limits on those things students are interested in. Culturally, failure to achieve is the source of guilt or shame in Western cultures, whereas in Chinese cultures, that shame or guilt arises from failing to *want* to learn (Peterson & Seligman, 2004, p. 172). For some students, the development of a love of learning may demand overcoming misperceptions, phobias, and present feelings.

The desirable interventions needed in teaching to develop love of learning are unsurprising. The classwork must be difficult but structured for learning. There must be meaningful and authentic connections to what is being learned. Students must know the teacher likes them and the teacher must indicate his or her consciousness of their efforts at learning. Strong connections to the teacher, and usually family support, enhance a love of learning. Group work also contributes, especially where groups are established with difficult challenges and given status, so that interpersonal goals become a feature of learning. The lover of learning has individual needs of "belongingness, competence, positive feelings and utility" (Peterson & Seligman, 2004, pp. 174–175). Complex tasks that involve shared perspectives, a caring teacher, and clear understanding of goals characterize interventions facilitating love of learning. Learning means, of course, the ongoing and unending process of coming to know or seeking for truth, which may be content-specific but which also implies the need for the right dispositions, such as those of character, intellect, and care described above.

Roberts and Wood (2007) give a philosophical account of love of knowledge. Love of knowledge, in the view of these philosophers, orients the will to knowledge. It therefore seems to describe the will of the seeker. They base their argument in Aristotle's account of there being a natural appetite for knowledge that "needs to be matured, formed, realized, completed" (Roberts & Wood, 2007, p. 154). They provide an interesting perspective on development of the love of knowledge in which the presumption, as in many child-centered theories of education, is that children want it, but the development is "often compromised or arrested short of its higher reaches" (p. 155).

> With further maturity... the child... wants true perceptions and beliefs, not false ones; she wants well-grounded beliefs, not vagrant, floating ones; she wants significant rather than trivial, relevant rather than irrelevant, knowledge; she wants deeper rather than shallow understanding; and she wants knowledge that ennobles human life and promotes human well-being rather than knowledge that degrades and destroys; she wants to know important truths.
>
> *(p. 155)*

The criteria for love of knowledge are that (a) a person wants the truth, (b) a person wants beliefs with range and depth leading to other beliefs, beliefs that in Roberts and Wood's terms are "load-bearing," and (c) worthiness, where the objects of knowledge to be loved "derive in part from caring about other goods, such as justice, human well-being and friendship" (p. 158). Finally there is a criterion of (d) relevance to the individual, with sufficient self-discipline to allow him or her to override less worthy motivations. However, there are two aspects to love of knowledge, those of acquisition and purveyance. With purveyance there is a concern for the well-being of others, and a motivation for a shared enterprise, through testimony or teaching or in shared enterprises (p. 165). Roberts and Wood, again, while not ignoring achievement, see love of knowledge as an ongoing process.

From these two accounts we get a much fuller picture of the seeker after truth, and, in so doing, we should stress the positive psychologists' claim that it leads to better physical and psychological health and well-being—that is, to human flourishing.

First, both accounts stress the significance of webs of relations, shared enterprises, to sustain, challenge, test the individual and to be enjoyed precisely because they often represent a struggle to overcome obstacles. This supports classrooms with dialogic space and an epistemological presence, in which tough problems are aired and explored.

Second, while there may be uncertainty over the natural or innate disposition to find things out, there is common understanding that such love of learning or of knowledge has to be nurtured and developed. The quality of the teacher thus comes into very sharp relief. Developing in children an intrinsic motivation and love of learning and knowledge is extraordinarily complex but arises primarily from the sort of person the teacher is, with the moral and intellectual dispositions he or she embodies.

Third, while achievement is important, the seeker after truth finds ongoing cognitive and affective relation with particular content (Peterson & Seligman, 2004) and the objects of knowledge to be loved derive in part from, to repeat, "caring about other goods, such as justice, human well-being and friendship" (Roberts & Wood, 2007, p. 158). This is a very strong claim, but it sets seekers after truth not in a frame of a myopic concern with some particular problem, but in the real world of actions and interactions, of moral principles and decisions about what life to lead.

In these psychological and philosophical accounts, it is not merely the teacher whose dispositions are to be understood in terms of character, intellect, and care, but also the seeker after truth: the children in the classrooms, Bruner's epistemologists (see chapter 5). In the love of learning or the love of knowledge, once again, dispositions have primacy.

II. Developing Teacher Quality: A View of Assessment

Self-examination—which we may call self-assessment—is a necessary part of teacher education, because it connects the role with the person and makes considerable demands on self-knowledge (see chapter 9). Indeed teachers badly need the habits of self-examination to balance the demands of assessment of their classroom quality made by their employers, lest their definition of who they are as a teacher be left simply to external decision-makers, much like the subjective knowers in *Women's Ways of Knowing* (Belenky et al., 1986). Students preparing to teach need to know how to conduct that inquiry. There is widespread use of reflective practice since the 1984 publication of Schön's (1995) book initiating the subject that goes some way to this self-examination. The bulk of such writing by students is reflection on classroom experience, often directed to observation of individual children, and the "journals" that emerge are usually graded. Yet here, we should recall Oakeshott's useful distinction (see chapter 9) between self-disclosure (in which I look at my actual practices, what I have done), and self-enactment (in which I examine the deliberation on and examination of those moral sentiments and virtues, principles and commitments to which I aspire, which I enact and which are the core of my personal identity). In principle, much of the writing student teachers do could be arranged under one or other of these heads, provided they interact. Reflective practice currently may be far too much weighted on self-disclosure without much inquiry into self-enactment. Reflective practice demands a balance between what I do *and* what I believe and what I am. That is not a navel-gazing exercise either, because it requires fellowship in its broadest sense: as MacIntyre (1999) noted, "genuine and extensive self-knowledge becomes possible only in consequence of those social relationships which on occasion provide badly needed correction for our own judgments" (p. 95; see chapter 9).

The overwhelming need to have pre-service teachers undertake such self-examination can present teacher-education institutions with a serious obstacle, namely the limitations of what continues to pass for assessment. The primary problem for the teacher educator as examiner is that he or she is used to grading student work against clearly defined goals, given the dominance of rational planning doctrines to which much educational practice, including teacher education, is in thrall. That doctrine holds that rationality demands the prior clarification of measurable goals after which the strategies and tactics for reaching these goals can be described. This ideal for school curricula became known in the 1960s as the Tyler Rationale, drawn from Ralph Tyler's work on the Seven Year Study begun in 1932 (see Tyler, 1969). Clarifying the goals thus describes the assessment and vice versa. Indeed, given the operational logic that a goal can be assessed is the main criterion in articulating it, so the story goes, goals and their assessment are logically linked. Rational planning on this doctrine also demands a sharp distinction between means and ends (which Auguste Comte and J. S. Mill also articulated as the logic of science) rather than the subtleties of means-ends interactions described by Dewey (see Dottin, 2010; Sockett, 1973). The model therefore simply does not fit with a deontological ethic of principles (such as Kant's articulation of what we know as the golden rule), with Aristotle's concept of human flourishing or eudaemonia, or with the care ethics described by Noddings (2010). In some ways, rational planning doctrines are the archenemy of teachers as moral professionals. In none of these views of morality does it make sense for a person to have measurable goals any more than it would in marriage. They have ideals or principles by which they live. To deploy that overused mechanical metaphor, the process is the product.

Reflection solely oriented to achievement of goals is far too narrow a perspective for a person teaching. Goals of reflective practice cannot be described, because a teacher as a reflective practitioner does not have goals as such; rather he or she proceeds reflectively. The procedures of self-disclosure and self-enactment are likewise not activities in which questions of whether teaching goals were achieved are paramount, because, in self-disclosure, the examination of teaching episodes and their outcomes does not need a primary focus on goal-achievement. Indeed whether goals have been achieved is likely to obscure the problematic character of most of the interactions. (For an excellent discussion of understanding life and professional life in terms of episodes, see Harré & Secord, 1972, chapters 8 & 9.)

Formally speaking, however, anyone with a degree (and sometimes without) can take part as a student in becoming a teacher, attending a course, and passing tests geared to such goals. Teacher educators are not allowed, we are told, to examine anything connected to character because it is inevitably subjective (and thereby "of course" ideological, prejudiced, or biased). In this highly litigious society, institutions and individuals dread being sued, from which the aura of objectivity around rational planning of goals and assessment provides some protection. A focus on goals diminishes the potential examination of "who the person is" who applies to become a teacher. In terms of assessing character, institutions thus feel bound to go for the *lowest common denominator* so that, provided the student does nothing criminal or egregious (e.g., molesting a child, or breaking the Honor Code) and shows aptitude in a set of goal-oriented formal dimensions, that student will pass and begin a career as a qualified teacher.

The case has been made throughout this book that the teacher's personhood and character is central to teaching as a moral activity, to which both examination through self-disclosure and self-enactment would contribute. Yet the very qualities articulated in the teacher's makeup, or so it has been suggested, cannot be assessed or judged in familiar ways, though there are often efforts to squeeze dispositions into behavioral categories. The context of teacher-education institutions manifests these tensions. First, if anyone can come, is it empirically possible to "re-educate" a candidate with a slew of undesirable weaknesses (if they have them) before graduating them to teach children? Are these kinds of dispositions too embedded by the age of 19? Worse still, could a candidate at exit feign the desirable qualities? Moreover, is it even possible to shift a weakness like closed-mindedness to open-mindedness in a student career, and, if so, what educational practices would support this? Second, how are institutions to handle those young people entering teaching with a sense of idealism and a sense that classrooms are where they want to be but have such character weaknesses as egocentrism or a basic inability to see the classroom as independent of themselves or simply fail in developing, say, sympathetic attention? Third, is it possible as a practical matter for universities and colleges, not to mention school systems, to recruit education students, often referred to as the cash cows of universities, using in-depth procedures, in a rigorous selection process that seeks to be much less arbitrary and capricious?

III. Toward an Assessment Solution

There is, however, a potential solution to these problems lying there in the framework of self-disclosure and self-enactment.

Recruitment. First, rather than accepting the *lowest common denominator*, institutions should seek out the *highest common factor* in recruitment and in teaching students. How might this work? First, institutions must take recruitment to teaching very seriously indeed. The admissions process must include the opportunity to make in-depth judgments about a candidate's character strengths and weaknesses primary; because recruitment processes are part of the education of the students and, like marriage, "not to be entered into unadvisedly or lightly but reverently, discreetly, advisedly, and soberly,"—reverently because the well-being of children is at stake, discreetly because the candidate is due all respect whatever his or her strengths and weaknesses, advisedly because significant judgments and commitments are being made to this and that person-candidate, and soberly because the institution's (and the nation's?) future is dependent on the quality of its students. If asked, positive psychologists can develop carefully constructed interviews to examine a candidate's trustworthiness, sincerity, perseverance, attention, truthfulness, open-mindedness, sense of fairness, impartiality, virtues of care, and, if his or her autobiography is explored, integrity as wholeness. Such tests would drastically inform the recruitment process. Institutions would admit, therefore, only those who could show through such tests that they are *predisposed* to the complexities of teaching, with those dispositions as virtues that have been indicated. Though in need of development, they will have both the intellectual and the moral qualities needed. (Note: I take the basis of this idea from Catherine Fallona and her colleagues at the University of Southern Maine.) The challenge then is to make recruitment the major responsibility of those responsible for teacher education, no doubt with faculty from psychology. If these predispositions as virtues are ones we want to see develop in the nation's children, we must want those qualities embedded in the candidates we select to become qualified teachers, if, we may hazard, the program cannot reform undesirable dispositions.

Self-disclosure and self-enactment. When the significance of the student's personhood is taken seriously, then how he or she views him or herself, and how he or she understands him or herself as a person and in a role, must be front and center in the process of the course and its assessment. A course might be framed from the outset as the enhancement of these predispositions such that all work (theoretical and practical) can be built around (1) self-disclosure, as reflection on classroom experience, and (2) self-enactment as examining the virtues, principles, and practices demanded by the role. Students then get an early grip on what personal qualities are needed in the role. Whatever is being studied, whether it be developmental psychology or classroom management, students will be consistently urged to see themselves within the conceptual or practical frameworks being articulated.

The patterns of self-disclosure and self-enactment are, from the outset, translated into "assessment tools" that are completely transparent to the students, framed within a learning community of students and teacher educators. The teacher-education curriculum, as well as the teacher educator's teaching itself, is always in play in the epistemological presence of the seminar room. Once students understand the qualities needed, reading about them and discussing them, they will begin the difficult process of self-examination, which, given a sophisticated recruitment process, will help students realize whether their interest in teaching is being enhanced or diminished. Counseling out is not then a process of weeding out undesirables but helping those individuals come to realize they have misjudged their attachment to the profession, their temperament, or their sense of themselves, and their need to seek other environments in which they can construct meaningful work and meaningful living, in Norton's terms (see chapter 7). This is to put such elements as taught courses or courses for the development of classroom skills within the emerging personhood of the student as a teacher, not just as topics that have to be covered under state regulations for would-be teachers. Such a framework of assessment becomes a framework of growth for the student. But, as Oser (1994) argues, the professional acts of teaching demand effectiveness *and moral* responsibility, and neither can be easily examined without the other; with that injunction in our minds, this framework for assessment of students learning to be teachers should both encompass all appropriate virtues and be the subject for tough-minded, rigorous inquiry such as the work of positive psychologists intimates.

Taking self-assessment seriously. This direction suggests a drastic shift in teacher education. Instead of viewing students as examinees, with the implicit assumption that "we will decide whether you are ready to teach" (in terms of all the grading systems used), the emphasis would shift to the student's making decisions about whether "I am ready to start a career as a professional teacher and to continue to learn to teach." Of course, teacher educators indicate that "we will help you come to that decision." But front and center in teacher education will be the articulation of those dispositions and virtues demanded by teaching. That is the logical and psychological base on which to build from the recruitment process to the learning experiences. There will still be cases in which the institution is not obliged to accept this self-assessment in terms of its public responsibilities. But the paramount weight of the assessment is done by the individual candidate, and the assessment process is presented as such. That immediately thrusts the motivational issue for teaching right into the psyche of the student; that will make students more focused on what they need to learn to do the job properly, efficiently, morally, and intellectually. This direction of thought resembles two other sorts of educational assessment. First, when a candidate presents a doctoral dissertation, he or she literally defends his or her thesis, by elaborating it and justifying its methods and conclusions. The onus is not on the supervisor to "get the student through." Second, the proposal may also be thought to resemble a candidate's seeking ordination as a priest, or a novice's being initiated into a religious order. That is, such candidates have not just to demonstrate their competence on paper, or that they can fulfill the practical requirements, but to show that their motivation is, so to speak, pure. That's not a false analogy: the rigorous self-examination is there because the life embraced is a life of service, not just a job (see especially Hansen, 2001). That is the *highest common factor* teacher educators must install.

IV. Procedures and Protocols for Self-Assessment

Such a framework for teacher education might be implemented through the following.

1. **An institutional description and explanation** of the dispositions as virtues (e.g., open-mindedness);
2. **A faculty protocol,** defined as assessment questions designed to explore what has been worked out in (1);
3. **A student protocol** in which each individual student, working with teachers and others, develops his or her own protocol, setting out the questions they need to wrestle with themselves in terms of either self-disclosure or self-enactment or both.

Description and Explanation

A teacher-education institution would develop a description and an explanation of the primary qualities required of the teacher. As indicated, the recruitment process becomes crucial, not least because of the perceived difficulties of failing students. This will require all relevant faculty to be well versed in the philosophical and psychological literature such that understanding of, say, open-mindedness is not reduced to a checklist. The purpose is to articulate those dispositions as virtues that define the institution's ethos and state the qualities of the teacher to be embraced. That will certainly demand seminar work among faculty themselves and also with area principals and participating teachers, such that the ethos being pursued and implemented is widely and coherently understood. That may mean a much sharper mission statement that is not platitudinous but quite specific. Moreover, this description and explanation will be dynamic, a possibility hugely enhanced by web-based technology in which discussion can be constant and continuous refinement and improvement of the description and explanation possible. Continuing faculty dialogue is essential, not just in the framework of committee meetings, but in the circulation of new readings, intensive evaluation, and identification of weakness. A learning community must be both moral and intellectual.

The Faculty Protocol

These discussions have a central task: to develop a faculty protocol for each of the qualities under consideration. (See next section for the protocol on open-mindedness.) This is a set of questions around a particular disposition that define that disposition for the student. The first challenge in articulating such a set of questions is that the protocol must have intellectual and moral depth and, when presented to students, each question may need to be backed by relevant reading of selected introductory extracts. The faculty protocol could be web-based with links to these readings. A second challenge is the scope and range of the protocol. For example, it will be noted in the protocol set out in the text and others in the appendix that there is some overlap. Crucially, this protocol should not be seen as different for students teaching different grades, because part of the emphasis of the protocol is to emphasize the professional community of teachers. Finally the protocol and its development should be shared with students, and students should be invited to critique and question the protocol's structure and content.

The Student Protocol

Each student then uses the questions in the faculty protocol to develop his or her own questions. Students should constantly be urged to take risks in developing these questions, because the student is asked to examine each question in each of the faculty protocols and to interpret that question as relevant to his or her own learning situation. Therefore no two student protocols will be the same. It would be expected that a student protocol would be a subject for faculty or student community advice, again, which a web-based environment can promote. The core feature of the student protocol, too, is its dynamism. Individual student protocols, like those of the faculty, will constantly change with theoretical and practical experience. It is in the iteration of changed protocols that faculty will discern what guidance is needed for student development.

The student will gradually learn the difference between questions of self-disclosure and self-enactment, and part of faculty advice will be to have students get what was referred to earlier as a balance between the two. Students may best be helped by describing self-disclosure topics within which they challenge their *pedagogical judgment.* So one would expect students to record problematic cases and for these judgments to be shared across faculty and the community of practice. Of special importance are the problems in judgment, to which the Abercrombie (1965) study (see chapter 6) provides some direction. In each item, too, the possibility of deepening and extending the sophistication of the teacher's understanding is present, suggesting not a reduction of, say, open-mindedness to a set of pedagogical habits but a constant development of improved judgments, especially if the twin discourses of self-disclosure and self-enactment are understood and explored.

Finally, it is critical that in a student protocol judgment be distinguished from decision-making. Focusing on a classroom decision merely provides the rationale for the action ("What did I do?"). Focusing on judgment ("Why did I do what I did?") widens the discourse by engaging with the factors that contributed to the judgment, because decisions in classrooms are the results of judgments, and judgment is logically prior to making a decision. Judgment is the quality of balancing competing kinds of claims (e.g., from different virtuous possibilities) and understanding their complexity. Judgments can be correct but implementation a disaster. However making good judgments is not something that can easily be taught, though wise and experienced individuals can prod students into examining and reexamining their judgments such that such self-reflection does become habitual. Good judgment arises from the constant self-examination being advocated—again, an achievement of one's own initiative. If judgments are educated, correct implementations will follow with experience.

To conclude on the procedure proposed: it is intended not as a blueprint but as a stimulus to thought. It has not been tested with students. Those engaged in teacher education will be able to use their contemporary experience to fashion the ideas implicit in this proposal for procedure. However, it does indicate the kind of direction that would follow from the arguments in this book, which, it is to be hoped, will provide that stimulus. It cannot be overemphasized that the description and explanation of each of these procedures will need to be discussed with students; appropriate reading or video examples can be shown, for example from http://gallery.carnegiefoundation.org/insideteaching/quest/collections.html. This website, Inside Teaching, provides numerous examples of these qualities manifest in classrooms (see also chapter 4). There is no substitute for depth: these procedures cannot be dealt with just by a bureaucratic committee dreaming up ideas, or trying to figure out how to get through accreditation, but only by dynamic, careful examinations of different philosophical and psychological material to ensure a sophisticated procedure (see Further Reading). Indeed, these details, it needs to be understood, are set within the overall shift to person-centered assessment advocated above, in which one might anticipate considerable variety of perspective.

The example given below is taken from W. Hare (2007, pp. 216–217) and from its elaboration (Sockett, 2009, pp. 301–303).

Table 12.1 Procedure and Protocol: An Example (for other examples, see appendices)

OPEN-MINDEDNESS: Description and Explanation (see ch. 11 & Hare, 2007, p. 216)

Intellectual humility in terms of one's own knowledge and abilities
Understanding the need for ongoing inquiry, as knowledge is not absolute
Having students continue thinking about an idea, notwithstanding class consensus
Attention to all possible sources of knowledge
Accepting criticism from students and fostering a climate of open-mindedness
Monitoring one's own ideas carefully to understand controversy
Searching for counterevidence to one's own views
Welcoming diverse views without stacking the deck or having an agenda
Commitment to research as an ongoing part of teaching
Accurate and impartial presentation of subject matter and authentic questions
Challenging students to produce evidence and argument

OPEN-MINDEDNESS: *The Faculty Protocol*	*OPEN-MINDEDNESS:* *The Student Protocol (example)*
1. Is the teacher someone, like Socrates, who seems to recognize the limits of his or her own knowledge and abilities, someone with a certain intellectual humility?	How often do I convey to students I am not a know-all and that as a class we need to approach knowledge with care and respect?
2. Does the teacher convey a sense that our grasp on knowledge is not absolute and final and that inquiry must be ongoing?	What ways do I have to convey that we are not just processing information but searchers on an adventurous quest for knowledge?
3. Does the teacher encourage the students to go on thinking about an idea even though consensus has emerged in discussion?	Do I respect divergence as much as consensus? Do I help students search for divergence even if we seem to agree?
4. Does the teacher remind the students not simply to take his or her word on matters under discussion but to consult other sources and to consider all the evidence?	How often do I present counterevidence? Do I ever use my personal authority to override students' questions?
5. Does the teacher draw attention to the way in which he or she has inevitably shaped the curriculum, and does he or she welcome critical comments from the students?	How often should I have the students discuss the curriculum, and what would help them critique their content learning?
6. Is the teacher someone who seems to monitor his or her own claims and ideas, signaling that an opinion, not a fact, is being expressed, calling attention to the controversial character of an idea or suggesting that he or she him or herself remains uncertain?	How do I have children work at the fact-opinion distinction? What pedagogies can I use to inform children what issues are controversial and why? How do I foster the notion that a "good" opinion is rooted in facts of the matter?

(Continued)

(Continued)

OPEN-MINDEDNESS: *The Faculty Protocol*	OPEN-MINDEDNESS: *The Student Protocol (example)*
7. Is the teacher someone who appears to have read widely, including authors who do not share his or her conclusions?	Am I always looking for books and articles on topics I am teaching? Am I excited by works that run counter to my own views?
8. Does the teacher give an idea an opportunity to be presented and heard, or is a signal given early on that it is not to be taken seriously?	How do I make sure everyone has a say and protect children trying to get a thought together in a classroom discussion?
9. Is the teacher someone who appears to include and welcome a wide range of diverse views without stacking the deck or having an agenda?	How do I get away from being committed to right answers in complex subjects, like history, as opposed to complex but axiomatic subjects like math?
10. In response to students' questions, does the teaching appear to have kept up with the subject?	How much do I coast from semester to semester, and how do I get children inside developments in all subject areas?
11. In terms of the knowledge the students already possess, does the teacher seem to present ideas accurately and impartially?	Should I be neutral? If not, how do I present different sides of a topic, or are there some areas (e.g., slavery) for which this does not work?
12. Is a question or a problem posed a genuine one inviting the students to think, or is it, as Dewey warns, an invitation merely to satisfy the teacher?	How do I develop in my students the sense that I don't want them to guess at what I think to get the "right answer"?
13. Does the teacher ask challenging questions that call on the students to support their beliefs with argument and evidence?	How do I challenge students for evidence without appearing threatening?
14. Does the teacher listen carefully and respectfully to questions and challenges from the students, showing in his or her responses that the points made have been given serious consideration?	How do I distinguish between a student giving a worked-out thought from a student just being voluble and thoughtless such that I can weigh how to treat each response with respect, but with judgment?
15. Does the teacher appear to have a ready-made answer to every query, especially an answer that employs a common, perhaps simplistic, theory or principle that explains everything?	How do I stop rushing to conclusions?

V. The Challenges to Teacher Quality

Whether teacher-education institutions are equipped to deal with the demands of this book is an open question. The central problem is the broad intellectual weakness of what is currently described as educational research. Of course, that is partly because there can be no discipline of education, because you can't define a discipline by its object of inquiry, but only by the methods used within that inquiry rooted in the empirical disciplines of sociology and psychology, or the discipline of philosophy, including moral philosophy, epistemology, and philosophy of mind. In this limbo, educational research seems not to be of much use, not least because it is too often cut off from its discipline-roots and also, let it be said, too often producing work of breathtaking triviality.

The central object of inquiry should be the practice of education from which arise questions of value and questions of fact. Value and fact cannot be separated. Philosophical analysis is thus critical to any educational inquiry, especially when the purpose of education is so muddied with the rhetoric floating around about the knowledge economy and the twenty-first century. Of immense damage is the excision of philosophy of education from initial training, let alone inservice education for teachers. Universities, devoted to the life of the mind, seem oblivious to the damage they are doing to the teaching profession. If the thoughts and aspirations of teachers are not rooted in the dispositions as virtues that have been the topic of this book, it is difficult to see how the profession can resist the second-rate political solutions currently being touted as educationally transformative.

Policy makers cannot grapple with the core problems of teacher quality that are implicit in this book. For instance, in the Chronicle for Higher Education of November 16, 2010, there is an article on the latest report on reform of teacher education.

> The report calls for a fundamental redesign of education schools that would integrate extensive hands-on preparation with the theory and content currently taught in education schools. That structure would bring in and reward experienced teachers to serve as mentors and clinical instructors for aspiring teachers. Coupled with that redesign would be more-rigorous accountability measures for education schools; better recruitment of potential teachers based on academic performance and the attributes that make good teachers; better placement based on school districts' needs; strengthened partnerships among teacher-training programs, local governments, and school districts; and the accumulation of better knowledge about which programs work.

There is a sense here not just of déjà vu, but of moving deck chairs around on the *Titanic,* of believing that bureaucratic or institutional changes of one kind or another will yield transformative change. It was so with the much-touted knowledge-base initiative of the late 1980s (see Shulman, 1987) that promised so much and yielded so little. This expert panel seems completely ignorant of the moral and epistemological questions embedded in teaching. This promulgation of a single model is itself a mistake, not least because it presupposes one type of teacher. Needed are initiatives that break the mold. For that to happen, a start needs to be made on "recruitment" and "attributes." That demands conceptualizing the quality of the teacher in terms of the primacy of moral and intellectual dispositions over knowledge and skills.

We return therefore to the significance of the questions with which this book opened: What is truth? What is authority? To whom do I listen? What counts for me as evidence? How do I know what I know? Teacher educators must embrace the radical character of these questions if they are to equip teachers effectively. Of course, teachers must have knowledge and skill, but, as we know quite well, most of the requisite skills are acquired on the job and from experience: schools retrain and socialize the graduates from teacher-education institutions. To develop teachers of quality, we need them to be developing a very profound view of themselves and of the world around them, because "our basic assumptions about the nature of truth and reality and the origins of knowledge shape the way we see the world and ourselves as participants in it. They affect our definitions of ourselves, the way we interact with others, our public and private personae, our sense of control over life events, our views of teaching and learning, and our conceptions of morality" (Belenky et al., 1986). These are the paramount questions for teaching and teacher education. A teacher of quality grapples with these life-enhancing questions right from the start, from a base of intellectual and moral virtues such that he or she builds a classroom with an epistemological presence.

APPENDICES

Procedures and Protocols

In using this procedure, faculty work conscientiously and thoroughly to describe and explain a disposition that they translate into a faculty protocol. That is shared with students and is seen as a dynamic document constantly inviting change and development.

On that basis each individual student develops a student protocol using the faculty protocol questions to delineate their own questions.

In both protocols, questions may invite self-disclosure and/or self-enactment, and the balance between both should be a matter of constant attention for faculty and students.

The procedure for development of protocols should include:

1. Creation of learning communities promoting extended faculty discussion on selected readings as prior to the development of a disposition description and explanation;
2. Generation of questions for the faculty protocol with provision for continuing faculty and student feedback to ensure the protocol remains dynamic;
3. Faculty explanations to students of the description and explanation and of the faculty protocol;
4. Continuing work with students in the development of individual protocols, including use of the protocol on evaluation by students of faculty teaching;
5. Creation of schedules for student protocol revisions and continued awareness of self-disclosure and self-enactment;
6. Arrangements for interchange through groups of student work on the protocols—for example, by continuously updated protocols being published on websites open only to group members.

The use of such protocols in assessment must be set against the philosophical background of the primacy of dispositions as has been outlined in this book. Students must come to understand its rationale.

These are examples:

1. Truthfulness and Trustworthiness

Description and Explanation

Making trustworthiness central to the relationship with individual students and the class
Avoiding deceit and understanding when to dissemble or avoid the truth
Understanding limits and opportunities of authority and avoiding power plays
Valuing and articulating disagreements, giving each voice its due
Avoiding all forms of stereotyping children and favoritism
Giving children contexts in which mutual trust can develop and be fostered
Being open to being corrected on matters of truth
Taking the trouble to be accurate
Exercising considered judgment as to when not to be truthful
Sophistication in matters of candor with children and with colleagues
Understanding one's own beliefs and searching for alternatives

---

Examples of Protocols

The Faculty Protocol	*The Student Protocol*
1. Do class interactions show a context of mutual trust and responsibility?	Why do some kids work well together in my class and others don't?
2. Does the teacher explore the truth of what he or she is saying and indicate the importance of truth through self-correction or justification for deceit?	How do I help the kids to understand the need to correct their mistakes to establish truth, not get the right answer?
3. Does the teacher understand the limits and opportunities of authority and the importance of avoiding power plays?	How can I resist overruling kids' thoughts and ideas because I need to "get on"?
4. Does the teacher indicate or acknowledge that other sources and authorities take a different view?	Do I really give every kid a chance to say what he or she thinks?
5. Does the teacher value and articulate disagreements, giving each voice its due?	Why do I find it difficult to explain ideas that I disagree with fairly?
6. What opportunities and context does the teacher provide for the development of mutual trust?	Why do some kids work well together in my class and others don't?
7. How does the teacher provide for and handle being open to being corrected on matters of truth?	Would it help me to try to ask many more questions to which I didn't know the answer?
8. Does the teacher always take the trouble to be accurate, avoiding having children make guesses?	I am not sure what's wrong with having kids guess. I need to work that out.

The Faculty Protocol	*The Student Protocol*
9. How does the teacher exercise considered judgment as to when not to be truthful?	What damage would it do to me in the class if the kids found out I had lied, even about work?
10. How sophisticated is the teacher in matters of candor with children?	How can I teach each kid that what I say about their work is always a considered judgment?
11. How sophisticated is the teacher in matters of candor with colleagues?	I'd like to say what I think to my supervisor and teacher, but I am not sure why I can't.

2. Courage and the Will

Description and Explanation

Clarifying what is the object of the risk and what the dangers are (e.g., for self-esteem) in the event of failure
Control of emotions appropriate to the task
Retaining the purpose while correcting the course
Sustaining the commitment to the object of the risk over the long term if needed
Judging the appropriateness of the task that is the object of the risk
Recognizing the ability to transfer the disposition of courage across different contexts
A "learned industriousness" in respect of goal achievement
Constant optimism and expectations of success
Preparedness to tackle difficult tasks, with satisfaction coming both from goal achievement and from the exercise of will
Self-control or self-regulation facilitating "overriding one's natural tendency to quit"
Persistence determined by value placed on the goal

Examples of Protocols

1. What is the teacher frightened of or nervous about in teaching, and what are the risks?	What exactly makes me nervous in teaching? Is it preparation? Unexpected behavior by children? What?
2. How does the teacher handle his or her emotions of fear in the classroom?	I must write about this classroom episode last week and examine how to control my anger from frustration.
3. How flexible or steadfast is the teacher in handling a risky pedagogical (or other) strategy?	Why have I given up having the kids doing some acting? Did I really lose control?
4. What is the quality of judgment in making decisions about taking risks?	Why is there a gap between what I think is possible and plan to do and my on-site decisions?
5. Does the teacher take risks in different contexts (e.g., in talking with the principal, other classroom teachers)?	Why do I find it difficult to ask for advice and help about the serious problems I have rather than the trivial?

(Continued)

(*Continued*)

6. Does the teacher understand the need for and acquire the habits of learned industriousness?	Why am I unable to organize myself for the demands of the program?
7. How optimistic is the teacher, and is the optimism justified?	I think I am always hopeful and confident about how things will work in my class, but when they don't work, am I substituting hope and enthusiasm for diligent work?
8. Does the teacher avoid difficult tasks or approach them minimally?	Why do I prefer to take the easy way out?
9. Is the teacher a quitter?	Why do I find it so hard to continue working hard with X, who needs so much? Am I expecting a reward or something?
10. Does the teacher appraise different difficult tasks according to their value or ease of achievement?	I need success at the straightforward, not failure at the difficult. Am I not brave enough? Or am I just not competent enough yet?

3. Sympathetic Attention

Description and Explanation

Understanding that sympathetic attention demands the development of skills—listening, not merely hearing; seeing behind, not merely perceiving
A strong, unremitting focus on the needs of the specific individual
Being prepared to surrender one's own priorities to another, as in motivational displacement
A dynamic commitment to that individual, with children minimally in terms of their moral, intellectual growth
Understanding the unique quality of the relationship with the individual and being open to its changing character
Being mindful of the whole person and the context of that person's life (e.g., family)
Being aware of one's vulnerability in these attitudes and commitment

Examples of Protocols

1. Does the student so handle him or herself in the classroom such that each child is listened to with attention; does the student have the peripheral vision in the classroom to spot children's needs?	Would sharing with the class the need to talk closely with each kid sharpen my attention to him or her?
2. When talking to a child, does the teacher engineer the space/time to shut out all other claims on his or her time, in and out of class?	I don't yet know how to do this; so I am making time in breaks, before school, and visiting children at home.
3. Does the teacher embrace the child's problems/needs as his or her own?	I can't do this. Why should I? I need to read the Noddings article.

4. Does the teacher provide a sense of dynamic commitment to each child and the class?	With 30 kids! This must be a joke. And anyway, some kids are unresponsive.
5. How does the teacher vary the quality of attention through a semester?	I do expect, as I get to know the class, to be able to ratchet up my attention to each child because I know them.
6. Does the teacher consider the significant others in the child's life?	I'd like to do this, but high school kids are really protective of life outside school. So I consider them and try to understand background.
7. Is the teacher aware of vulnerabilities in commitment and attention?	I dread the day when I am let down, yet I don't want my emotional commitment to the children to be less because of that. How can I cope?

4. Integrity as Wholeness

Description and Explanation

Examining how my talents, capabilities, and virtues fit with the demands of the teaching role
Examining how I address the conflicts and passions in my life and how they relate to each other
Examining how I sustain my integrity through differing kinds of challenges (e.g., marriage, a new school, or a new class)

Examples of Protocols

1. How does the student understand the fit between his or her talents and the demands of the classroom?	What can I do well? What do I need to work on? Is my love of acting a help or not?
2. How does the student understand the fit between his or her capabilities and the demands of the classroom?	What classroom requirements am I no good at? Why is my knowledge and love of music unusable in my class?
3. How does the student understand his or her dispositions as virtues and the demands of the classroom?	Who am I? Is this "I" a teacher?
4. How does the student address conflicts in his or her life?	Now that I am a student teacher, I have no time for anything else? How important is this? Is it to be expected in teaching?
5. How does the student understand the role of "student teacher" in contrast with "teacher"?	I was really confused when I heard a kid in my social studies class refer to me as "the student": I don't know what that tells me.
6. Are the passions in the student's life harnessed to teaching?	Some of my passions (hiking, swimming, for instance), seem useless in teaching. Do I need to be passionate about teaching?

(Continued)

(*Continued*)

7. How does the student address the challenges of teaching?	Why do I find it so much easier to teach girls than boys?
8. Who are the student's teaching models, and what qualities do they manifest?	I had a teacher in fifth grade I worshipped then, but what was she really like? What did my friends think of her?
9. How does the student relate to the demands of the search for truth?	I can see that truth is important, but I still can't work that as the priority in my teaching: we just use the texts—and I know some statements are false.
10. How does the student see the connection between meaningful work and meaningful living?	I began student teaching thinking I saw this connection. Now, I think I will take a break when I am qualified and maybe come back to teaching later. But why do I think that?

FURTHER READING

For a serious student of philosophy, *The Stanford Encyclopedia of Philosophy* (http://plato.stanford.edu/) is the best source on most philosophical topics. This comprehensive site is updated constantly.

For a serious student of philosophy of education, *The SAGE Handbook of Philosophy of Education* (Bailey et al., 2010) provides comprehensive papers on 34 topics, 20 being on the relationship between philosophy of education and educational practice.

For a more traditional and historical overview, Nel Noddings's *Philosophy of Education* (2006) provides an excellent base.

Refer to the References for full publication details.

Chapter 1

Mary Belenky, Blythe Clinch, Nancy Goldberger, and Jill Tarule (1986). *Women's Ways of Knowing: The Development of Self, Voice, and Mind.* The introduction (pp. 1–20) illustrates the intimacy of the connections between the public world and the self.

Charles Dickens. *Hard Times.* In particular, look at the plight of the women (Mrs. Gradgrind, Sissy, and Louisa) in the light of the previous reading. See also Nussbaum and Sen (1993) for further discussion of the novel.

Diane Ravitch (2010). *The Death and Life of the Great American School System: How Testing and Choice Are Undermining Education.* A sustained critique of the testing emphasis.

John Searle (1992). *The Rediscovery of the Mind.* A challenging book, but chapter 4 ("Consciousness and Its Place in Nature") is worth the struggle.

Chapter 2

Jerome Bruner (1996). *The Culture of Education*. An important book that locates the child in a culture.

Michael Williams (2001). *Problems of Knowledge: A Critical Introduction to Epistemology*. An excellent introduction to epistemology.

Gilbert Ryle (1949). *The Concept of Mind*. Contains articulation of "knowing that" and "knowing how."

Christine Kenneally (2007). *The First Word: The Search for the Origins of Language.*

Jonathan Dancy and Ernest Sosa (Eds.) (1992). *A Companion to Epistemology* (2nd ed.). There is a very clear entry (pp. 317–323) on "Other Minds"—our knowledge of the mental states of others.

Denis Charles Phillips (Ed.) (2000). *Constructivism in education* (Vol. 1). Ninety-Ninth Yearbook of the National Society for the Study of Education. A set of essays exposing contrary positions in the construction of knowledge. See especially Phillips's introduction to the issues.

Alasdair MacIntyre (1999). *Dependent Rational Animals: Why Human Beings Need the Virtues.* Very accessible. Chapters 1–4 focus on the animal-human distinctions. Chapter 3 is on the intelligence of dolphins.

Gareth Matthews (1996). *The Philosophy of Childhood*. A strong antidote for those inclined to "developmentally appropriate" education.

Max van Manen (1990). *Researching Lived Experience: Human Science for an Action Sensitive Pedagogy.* Van Manen's books are exceptionally sensitive to the concerns of children; this is one example.

Chapter 3

Joseph Raz (Ed.) (1990). *Authority*. Provides a good philosophical introduction to problems of power and authority.

Stanley Milgram (2009). *Obedience to Authority*. A social psychology work on problems of power/authority (Milgram does not make a distinction between them).

Lisa Delpit (2006). *Other People's Children: Cultural Conflict in the Classroom*. An important book for teachers, especially when viewed through the prism of the teacher's authority.

Philip Jackson, Robert Boostrom, and David Hansen (1998). *The Moral Life of Schools.* Now something of a classic in the observation of classrooms. The study of different teachers and how they use their authority is in part an extension of Philip Jackson's (1990) *Life in Classrooms,* a meticulous and well-wrought study.

Lawrence Stenhouse (1983). *Authority, Education and Emancipation*. An important book, not read much in the United States. His earlier *An Introduction to Curriculum Research and Development* (1975) is valuable for his particular insights into how the philosophical and the empirical cohere.

Mary Warnock (1989). "The Authority of the Teacher" (article). Deals with matters of professionalism and professionalization.

Chapter 4

Robert Jackall (2009). *Moral Mazes: The World of Corporate Managers.* Should be required reading for all university and school administrators, as it describes a picture of moral confusions between individuals and the roles they occupy.

Stephen Carter (1997). *Integrity.* A useful introduction to the varied problems of integrity in public life.

Karl Popper (1962). *The Open Society and Its Enemies.* One of the most scintillating books of the twentieth century. Its approach (and ferocious style) has been the object of much criticism, but it remains a splendid read. In particular, teachers and educators might find chapter 7, volume 1, on leadership, the most relevant, as it connects education to a democratic society.

Chapter 5

Paul Helm. *Varieties of Belief* (2004) and *Belief Policies* (2007) are important books for the philosophical study of belief.

Michael Oakeshott. *On Human Conduct* (1975) is an interesting example of Oakeshott's erudite style and somewhat idiosyncratic approach to life and politics. For educators and teachers, two of his essays in *Rationalism in Politics and Other Essays* (1962/2010), namely "The Activity of Being a Historian" and "The Voice of Poetry in the Conversation of Mankind," are important reading.

Ornstein and Hunkins (2008). *Curriculum: Foundations, Principles and Issues.* For those interested in philosophy of the curriculum, there is a collection of essays on various curriculum theorists edited by David Scott (2007) that forms a useful introduction.

Kurt Baier (1965). *The Moral Point of View: A Rational Basis of Ethics.*

Jeffrey Stout (1990). *Ethics after Babel: The Languages of Morals and Their Discontents.* Two of the most accessible books on morality.

William Hare (1971, 1979, 1985, 2007, 2009). "The Teaching of Judgment" (article), *Open-Mindedness and Education, In Defense of Open-Mindedness,* "Credibility and Credulity: Monitoring Teachers for Trustworthiness" (article), "Socratic Open-Mindedness" (article). Hare's work on open-mindedness is essential reading, as it is directed to teaching and teacher education as well as being philosophically robust.

Chapter 6

Guy Axtell (Ed.) (2000). *Knowledge, Belief and Character: Readings in Virtue Epistemology.* The book's introduction summarizes usefully the different approaches to virtue epistemology.

Robert Roberts and William Wood (2007). *Intellectual Virtues: An Essay in Regulative Epistemology.* An extremely important book, especially, but not only for, those interested in the moral-religion connections.

dum opinion in *Tammy Kitzmiller et al. v. Dover Area School District* District Court, Middle District of Pennsylvania (2005). A classic impartiality highly relevant to teaching is the judgment made in the ᴄ.. the Dover School Board, who sought to treat creationism as science. Using this text is an ideal way for student teachers to get inside the issues. Available at www.pamd.uscourts.gov/kitzmiller/kitzmiller_342.pdf.

Chapter 7

David Norton (1995). *Democracy and Moral Development: A Politics of Virtue.*

Mary Warnock (1987). *Memory.*

Richard Stanley Peters (1961). *The Concept of Motivation.*

Paul Hirst (1972/2010). *Knowledge and the Curriculum.* The connection between language and thought is central to our experience; for a provocative account see chapter 5.

Jesse Prinz (2007). *The Emotional Construction of Morals.* A clear but tough philosophical book on the emotions.

Richard Stanley Peters (1974). *Psychology and Ethical Development.* Chapter 7 on the education of the emotions is still the best introduction to the issues for educators.

Chapter 8

Samuel Freedman (1991). *Small Victories: The Real World of a Teacher, Her Students and Their High School.* A remarkable story of persistence and courage is told in this study of New York City high school teacher Jessica Siegel.

Paul Tillich (2007). *The Courage to Be.* A significant book that tackles the ontology of courage to make sense of it ethically.

Christopher Peterson and Martin Seligman (2004). *Character Strengths and Virtues: A Handbook and Classification.* Several chapters are valuable studies of the status of empirical enquiry in positive psychology, specifically the four chapters in the section on courage.

Chapter 9

David Hansen (1995). *The Call to Teach.* An important book on the self in teaching.

Kieran Egan (1998). *The Educated Mind: How Cognitive Skills Shape Our Understanding.* One of the most radical, provocative, and original books of the last two decades. Both theoretical and practical, Egan casts the mind as comprising five forms of understanding: mythic, romantic, philosophic, ironic, and somatic.

Dorothy Emmet (1975). *Rules, Roles and Relations.* An original setting out of the terrain in "person and roles."

Martin Hollis (1997). *Models of Man.* A much tougher assignment, but worth the effort.

Quassim Cassam (Ed.) (1994). *Self-Knowledge.* The classic philosophical articles on self-knowledge are collected in this book. But also see Conway and Pleydell-Pearce's (2000) article, "The Construction of Autobiographical Memories in the Self-Memory System."

Chapter 10

Jerome Bruner (1977). *The Process of Education.* Bruner's eighth/ninth-grade social studies curriculum "Man: A Course of Study" is an embodiment of the epistemological presence. See also the tenth-grade "Humanities Curriculum Project" by Lawrence Stenhouse (1983) in *Authority, Education and Emancipation.* "Man: A Course of Study" was attacked in Congress, and its funding was revoked, as it contained film of animals mating and Eskimos slaughtering seals, as well as detail on ancient Eskimo polygamy (see "Old School Values," *New Society,* May 22, 1975).

David Carr and Jan Steutel (Eds.) (1999). *Virtue Ethics and Moral Education.* A useful collection of essays connecting virtue ethics to moral education.

Pat Wilson (1974). *Interest and Discipline in Education.* An excellent, though neglected, Deweyan account of value in education.

"Committee on Obscenity and Film Censorship," Wikipedia, http://en.wiki pedia.org/wiki/Committee_on_Obscenity_and_Film_Censorship. The UK Committee on Obscenity and Film Censorship, which Bernard Williams chaired, published its report—one of the finest examples of the application of moral thought to social issues—in 1979. This has relevance, of course, to issues of censorship of novels in schools.

Marilyn Cochran-Smith and Susan L. Lytle (2009). *Inquiry as Stance: Practitioner Research in the Next Generation.*

Chapter 11

John Passmore (1980). *The Philosophy of Teaching.* An original account of critical thinking, but see also Stephen Brookfield (1991), *Developing Critical Thinkers,* and Peter Facione (2009), *Critical Thinking.*

Hugh Sockett (1997). "Chemistry or Character?" (chapter). Procrastination is a hugely important educational topic, as it connects to the very heart of autonomous disciplined work. It is not clear whether it is a symptom of attention deficit disorder of one kind or another. I have argued strongly that schools are using ADD and ADHD diagnoses because early upbringing has taught children to be promiscuous in their attention habits.

Julia Stratton (1982). *Pioneer Women: Voices from the Kansas Frontier.* A marvelous evocation of frontier life to illustrate the historical differences in women's roles. A more complex story is told in Drew Faust's (1997) book of women in the slave-holding South, *Mothers of Invention.*

Thomas Scanlon (2003). *The Difficulty of Tolerance: Essays in Political Philosophy.* Essential reading for those concerned with the topic.

Chapter 12

John Goodlad (1994). *Teachers for Our Nation's Schools.* As the speech by U.S. secretary of education Arne Duncan in 2009 illustrates, little has changed in universities and colleges of teacher education. Studying that has to start with Goodlad's book.

REFERENCES

Abercrombie, M. L. J. (1965). *The anatomy of judgment: An investigation into the process of perception and reasoning.* Harmondsworth, England: Pelican Books.

Adler, J. (2004). Reconciling open-mindedness and belief. *Theory and Research in Education, 2*(2), 127–142.

Andreou, C., & White, M. D. (2010). *The thief of time: Philosophical essays on procrastination.* New York: Oxford University Press.

Anscombe, G. E. M. (2000). *Intention.* Cambridge, MA: Harvard University Press.

Axtell, G. (2000). Preface. In G. Axtell (Ed.), *Knowledge, belief, and character: Readings in virtue epistemology.* Lanham, MD: Rowman and Littlefield.

Ayer, A. J. (1952). *Language, truth and logic.* London: Gollancz.

Ayer, A. J. (1957). *The problem of knowledge.* Harmondsworth, England: Penguin Books.

Baier, K. (1965). *The moral point of view: A rational basis of ethics.* New York: Random House.

Bailey, R., Barrow, R., Carr, D., and McCarthy, C. (2010). *The SAGE Handbook of Philosophy of Education.* London: Sage.

Barber, B. R. (1994). *An aristocracy of everyone: The politics of education and the future of America.* New York: Oxford University Press.

Barker, J. (1994). *The Brontës.* London: St. Martin's Press.

Barzun, J. (1959). *The house of intellect.* New York: Harper and Brothers.

Bayley, J. (1999). *Elegy for Iris.* New York: Picador.

Belenky, M., Clinchy, B., Goldberger, N., & Tarule, J. (1986). *Women's ways of knowing: The development of self, voice, and mind.* New York: Basic Books.

Bok, S. (1978). *Lying: Moral choice in public and private life.* New York: Vintage.

Bok, S. (1982). *Secrets: On the ethics of concealment and revelation.* New York: Pantheon Books.

Bowlby, J. (1988). *A secure base: Clinical applications of attachment theory.* London: Routledge.

Brighouse, H. (2003). *School choice and social justice.* New York: Oxford University Press.

Brookfield, S. D. (1991). *Developing critical thinkers: Challenging adults to explore alternative ways of thinking and acting.* San Francisco, CA: Jossey-Bass.

Bruner, J. (1968). *Towards a theory of instruction.* New York: W. W. Norton.

Bruner, J. (1977). *The process of education.* Cambridge, MA: Harvard University Press.

Bruner, J. (1996). *The culture of education.* Cambridge, MA: Harvard University Press.

Buber, M. (1970). *I and thou.* New York: Scribner.

Callahan, D. (2004). *The cheating culture: Why more Americans are doing wrong to get ahead.* Orlando, FL: Harcourt.

Campbell, E. (2003). *The ethical teacher.* Milton Keynes, England: Open University Press.

Carnegie Corporation of New York. (2006). *Teachers for a new era: Transforming teacher education.* New York: Carnegie.

Carr, D., & Steutel, J. (1999). *Virtue ethics and moral education.* London: Routledge.

Carter, Stephen L. (1997). *Integrity.* New York: Harper.

Cassam, Q. (1994). *Self-knowledge.* New York: Oxford University Press.

Chabris, C., & Simons, D. (2010). *The invisible gorilla: And other ways our intuitions deceive us.* New York: Crown Archetype.

Chignell, A. (2010). The ethics of belief. In *Stanford Encyclopedia of Philosophy.* Retrieved from http://plato.stanford.edu/entries/ethics-belief/

Clapham, A. (2007). *Human rights: A very short introduction.* Oxford, England: Oxford University Press.

Clifford, W. K. (1877/1999). The ethics of belief. In T. Madigan (Ed.), *The ethics of belief and other essays* (pp. 70–96). Amherst, MA: Prometheus.

Cochran-Smith, M., & Lytle, S. L. (2009). *Inquiry as stance: Practitioner research in the next generation.* New York: Teachers College Press.

Cohen, G. A. (2009). *Why not socialism?* Princeton, NJ: Princeton University Press.

Condren, C. (2006). *Argument and authority in early modern England: The presupposition of oaths and offices.* Cambridge, England: Cambridge University Press.

Conway, M., & Pleydell-Pearce, C. (2000). The construction of autobiographical memories in the self-memory system. *Psychological Review, 107*(2), 261–288.

Csikszentmihalyi, M., & Csikszentmihalyi, I. S. (Eds.). (2006). *A life worth living: Contributions to positive psychology.* New York: Oxford University Press.

Dagger, R. (1997). *Civic virtues: Rights, citizenship, and Republican liberalism.* New York: Oxford University Press.

Dalton, D., DiGiovanni, K., & Warner, T. (1996). *Morality's impact on discipline: An examination of an alternative learning environment.* Research study presented for a Masters Degree. Institute for Educational Transformation, George Mason University, Fairfax, VA.

Damon, W. (2002). *Bringing in a new era in character education.* Stanford, CA: Hoover Institution Press.

Dancy, J., & Sosa, E. (1992). *A companion to epistemology* (2nd ed.). Oxford, England: Blackwell.

Darling-Hammond, L., Bransford, J., LePage, P., Hammerness, K., & Duffy, H. (2005). *Preparing teachers for a changing world: What teachers should learn and be able to do.* San Francisco, CA: Jossey-Bass.

Degenhardt, M. (1998). The ethics of belief and the ethics of teaching. *Journal of Philosophy of Education, 32*(3), 333–344.

Delpit, L. (2006). *Other people's children: Cultural Conflict in the Classroom.* New York: New Press.

Dewey, J. (1938). *Logic—the theory of inquiry.* New York: Henry Holt.

Dewey, J. (1997). *Experience and education.* New York: Free Press.

Dickens, C. (2007). *Hard times.* New York: Penguin Classics.

Dottin, E. (2010). *Dispositions as habits of mind: Making professional conduct more intelligent.* Lanham, MD: University Press of America.

Downie, R. S. (1971). *Roles and values: An introduction to social ethics.* London: Methuen.

Downie, R. S., & Telfer, E. (1969). *Respect for persons.* London: George Allen and Unwin.

Dray, W. H. (1964). *Philosophy of history.* New York: Prentice Hall.

Egan, K. (1997). *The educated mind: How cognitive skills shape our understanding.* Chicago: University of Chicago Press.

Eisner, E. W. (1979). *The educational imagination.* New York: Macmillan.

Ellis, J. J. (2002). *Founding brothers: The revolutionary generation.* New York: Vintage.

Emmet, D. (1975). *Rules, roles and relations.* Boston, MA: Beacon Press.

Facione, P. (2009). Critical thinking: What it is and why it counts. *Insight Assessment Today* (pp. 1–23). Mibrae: California Academic Press. Retrieved from http://insightassessment.net/

Forrest, M. (2008). Sensitive controversy in teaching to be critical. *Paideusis, 18*(1), 80–93.

Forst, R. (2007). Toleration. In *Stanford Encyclopedia of Philosophy.* Retrieved from http://plato.stanford.edu/entries/toleration

Freedman, S. (1991). *Small victories: The real world of a teacher, her students, and their high school.* New York: Harper Perennial.

Gert, B. (1995). Moral impartiality. *Mid-West Studies in Philosophy, 20,* 102–107.

Gertler, B. (2008). Self-knowledge. In *Stanford Encyclopedia of Philosophy.* Retrieved from http://plato.stanford.edu/entries/self-knowledge/

Gettier, E. (1967). Is justified true belief knowledge? In A. P. Griffiths (Ed.), *Knowledge and belief* (pp. 144–147). Oxford, England: Oxford University Press.

Gilligan, C. (1982). *In a different voice: Psychological theory and women's development* (6th ed.). Cambridge, MA: Harvard University Press.

Gilligan, C., Lyons, N., & Hanmer, T. (1990). *Making connections: The relational worlds of adolescent girls at Emma Willard School.* Cambridge, MA: Harvard University Press.

Goffman, E. (1961). *Asylums: Essays on the social situation of mental patients and other inmates.* Harmondsworth, England: Penguin Books.

Goldschmidt, N. P., & Finkelstein, J. H. (2001, Oct.). Academics on board: University presidents as corporate directors. *Academe Online.* Retrieved from http://www.aaup.org/AAUP/pubsres/academe/2001/SO/Feat/gold.htm

Goodlad, J. I. (1994). *Teachers for our nation's schools.* San Francisco, CA: Jossey-Bass.

Gould, T. (1998). *Hearing things: Voice and method in the writing of Stanley Cavell.* Chicago, IL: University of Chicago Press.

Grant, G. (1990). *The world we created at Hamilton High.* Cambridge, MA: Harvard University Press.

Greco, J. (2010). *Achieving knowledge: A virtue-theoretic account of epistemic normativity.* New York: Cambridge University Press.

Griffiths, A. P. (1967). On belief. In A. P. Griffiths (Ed.), *Knowledge and belief* (pp. 127–144). Oxford, England: Oxford University Press.

Grossman, P. L., & Schoenfeld, A. (2005). Teaching subject matter. In L. Darling-Hammond, J. Bransford, P. LePage, K. Hammerness, & H. Duffy (Eds.). *Preparing teachers for a changing world: What teachers should learn and be able to do* (pp. 201–231). San Francisco, CA: Jossey-Bass.

Gutmann, A. (1999). *Democratic education.* Princeton, NJ: Princeton University Press.

Haley, A. (1976). *Roots.* New York: Doubleday.

Hansen, D. T. (1995). *The call to teach.* New York: Teachers College Press.

Hansen, D. T. (2001). *Exploring the moral heart of teaching: Toward a teacher's creed.* New York: Teachers College Press.

Hansen, D. T. (2007). *Ethical visions of education: Philosophy in practice.* New York: Teachers College Press.

Hansen, D. T., & Laverty, M. (2010). Teaching and pedagogy. In C. Bailey, R. C. Barrow, D. Carr, & C. McCarthy (Eds.), *The SAGE handbook of philosophy of education* (pp. 237–253). London: Sage.

Harding, S. (2003). *The feminist standpoint theory reader: Intellectual and political controversies.* New York: Routledge.

Hare, R. M. (1952). *The language of morals.* Oxford, England: Oxford University Press.

Hare, W. (1971). The teaching of judgment. *British Journal of Educational Studies, 19*(3), 243–249.

Hare, W. (1979). *Open-mindedness and education.* Montreal, Canada: McGill–Queen's University Press.

Hare, W. (1985). *In defense of open-mindedness.* Montreal, Canada: McGill–Queen's University Press.

Hare, W. (2007). Credibility and credulity: Monitoring teachers for trustworthiness. *Journal of Philosophy of Education, 41*(2), 207–221.

Hare, W. (2009). Socratic open-mindedness. *Paideusis, 18*(1), 5–16.

Harré, R. (1983). *Personal being: A theory for individual psychology.* Oxford, England: Blackwell.

Harré, R., & Secord, P. F. (1972). *The explanation of social behavior.* Oxford, England: Blackwell.

Hart, H. L. A. (1961). *The concept of law.* Oxford, England: Oxford University Press.

Helm, P. (2004). *Varieties of belief.* London: Routledge.

Helm, P. (2007). *Belief policies (Cambridge Studies in Philosophy).* Cambridge, England: Cambridge University Press.

Herodotus. (2003). *The histories.* New York: Penguin Classics.

Hersch, P. (1999). *A tribe apart: A journey into the heart of American adolescence.* New York: Ballantine Books.

Heyd, D. (2007). Supererogation. In *Stanford Encyclopedia of Philosophy.* Retrieved from http://plato.stanford.edu/entries/supererogation

Hirsch, E. D., Jr. (1988). *Cultural literacy: What every American needs to know.* New York: Vintage.

Hirsch, E. D., Jr. (1999). *The schools we need: And why we don't have them.* New York: Anchor.

Hirst, P. H. (1972/2010). *Knowledge and the curriculum.* London: Routledge.

Hirst, P. H., & Peters, R. S. (1979). *The logic of education.* London: Routledge and Kegan Paul.

Hollis, M. (1977). *Models of man: Philosophical thoughts on social action.* Cambridge, England: Cambridge University Press.

Hookaway, C. (2000). Regulating inquiry: Virtue, doubt, and sentiment. In G. Axtell (Ed.), *Knowledge, belief, and character: Readings in virtue epistemology* (pp. 149–163). Oxford, England: Rowman and Littlefield.

Jackall, R. (2009). *Moral mazes: The world of corporate managers.* New York: Oxford University Press.

Jackson, P. W. (1990). *Life in classrooms.* New York: Teachers College Press.

Jackson, P. W., Boostrom, R. E., & Hansen, D. T. (1998). *The moral life of schools.* San Francisco, CA: Jossey-Bass.

Jessop, C., & Palmer, L. (2008). *Escape* (Reprint). New York: Broadway.

Jollimore, T. (2006). Impartiality. In *Stanford Encyclopedia of Philosophy.* Retrieved from http://plato.stanford.edu/entries/impartiality/

Kazepides, T. (2010). *Education as dialogue: Its prerequisites and its enemies.* Montreal, Canada: McGill–Queen's University Press.

Kenneally, C. (2008). *The first word: The search for the origins of language.* New York: Penguin.

Kohlberg, L. (1981). *The philosophy of moral development: Moral stages and the idea of justice.* New York: Harper & Row.

Kohlberg, L. (1984). *The psychology of moral development: The nature and validity of moral stages.* New York: Harper Collins.

Kuhn, T. S. (1996). *The structure of scientific revolutions.* Chicago: University of Chicago Press.

Locke, J. (1690/1979). *An essay concerning human understanding*. Oxford, England: Oxford University Press.

MacIntyre, A. (1987). *After virtue: A study in moral theory*. London: Duckworth.

MacIntyre, A. (1999). *Dependent rational animals: Why human beings need the virtues*. London: Duckworth.

Mathews, J. (1989). *Escalante: The best teacher in America*. New York: Harper and Row.

Matthews, G. B. (1996). *The philosophy of childhood*. Cambridge, MA: Harvard University Press.

McCrae, R., & Costa, P. T. (2005). *Personality in adulthood: A five-factor theory perspective* (2nd ed.). New York: Guilford Press.

Merritt, M. (2000). Virtue ethics and situationist personality psychology. *Ethical Theory and Moral Practice, 3*(4), 365–383.

Milgram, S. (2009). *Obedience to authority*. New York: Harper Perennial.

Mitchell, M. T. (2006). *Michael Polanyi: The art of knowing*. Wilmington, DE: Intercollegiate Studies Institute.

Montmarquet, J. (2000). An "internalist" conception of epistemic virtue. In G. Axtell (Ed.), *Knowledge, belief, and character: Readings in virtue epistemology* (pp. 135–145). Lanham, MD: Rowman and Littlefield.

Moore, G. E. (1903). *Principia ethica*. Cambridge, England: Cambridge University Press.

Mumford, S. (2003). *Dispositions*. Oxford, England: Oxford University Press.

Murdoch, I. (2001). *The sovereignty of good* (2nd ed.). London: Routledge.

Nagel, T. (1989). *The view from nowhere*. Oxford, England: Oxford University Press.

Noddings, N. (1984). *Caring: A feminine approach to ethics and moral education* (2nd ed., with a new preface). Berkeley: University of California Press.

Noddings, N. (2002). *Educating moral people: A caring alternative to character education*. New York: Teachers College Press.

Noddings, N. (1996). *Philosophy of Education*. Boulder, CO: Westview Press.

Noddings, N. (2010). *The maternal factor: Two paths to morality*. Berkeley: University of California Press.

Noonan, H. W. (1999). *Routledge Philosophy Guidebook to Hume on Knowledge*. London: Routledge.

Norton, D. L. (1995). *Democracy and moral development: A politics of virtue*. Berkeley: University of California Press.

Novak, M. (1996). *Belief and unbelief: A philosophy of self-knowledge* (3rd ed.). London: Darton, Longman and Todd.

Nussbaum, M. (1997). *Cultivating humanity: A classical defense of liberal education*. Cambridge, MA: Harvard University Press.

Nussbaum, M., & Sen, A. (1993). *The quality of life*. Oxford, England: Oxford University Press.

Nyhan, B., & Reifler, J. (2010). When corrections fail: The persistence of political misperceptions. *Political Behaviour, 32,* 303–330.

Oakeshott, M. (1991). *On human conduct*. Oxford, England: Oxford University Press.

Oakeshott, M. (1962/2010). *Rationalism in politics and other essays*. London: Methuen.

O'Neill, O. (2002). *A question of trust: The BBC Reith Lectures 2002*. Cambridge, England: Cambridge University Press.

Ornstein, A., & Hunkins, F. (2008). *Curriculum: Foundations, principles, and issues* (5th ed.). Boston, MA: Allyn and Bacon.

Oser, F. K. (1994). Moral perspectives on teaching. *Review of Research in Education, 20,* 57–129.

Paley, V. G. (1986). *Boys and girls: Superheroes in the doll corner*. Chicago, IL: University of Chicago Press.

Passmore, J. (1980). *The philosophy of teaching*. Cambridge, MA: Harvard University Press.

Paul, R. (2000). Critical thinking, moral integrity, and citizenship: Teaching for the intellectual virtues. In G. Axtell (Ed.), *Knowledge, belief, and character: Readings in virtue epistemology* (pp. 163–177). Lanham, MD: Rowman and Littlefield.

Paul, R., & Elder, L. (2009). *The miniature guide to critical thinking: Concepts and tools.* Berkeley, CA: The Foundation for Critical Thinking.

Pears, D. (1963). *Freedom and the will.* London: St. Martin's Press.

Peirce, C. S. (1877, Nov.). The fixation of belief. *Popular Science Monthly, 12,* 1–15.

Perry, W. G. (1970). *Forms of intellectual and ethical development in the college years.* New York: Holt, Rinehart and Wilson.

Peters, M. (2008). Academic self-knowledge and self-deception. In L. J. Waks (Ed.), *Leaders in philosophy of education: Intellectual self-portraits* (pp. 145–159). Rotterdam, Netherlands: Sense Publishers.

Peters, R. S. (1959). *Authority, responsibility and education.* London: George Allen and Unwin.

Peters, R. S. (1961). *The concept of motivation.* London: Routledge and Kegan Paul.

Peters, R. S. (1966). *Ethics and education.* London: George Allen and Unwin.

Peters, R. S. (1972). Reason and passion. In R. F. Dearden, P. H. Hirst, and R. S. Peters (Eds.), *Education and the development of reason* (pp. 208–227). London: Routledge and Kegan Paul.

Peters, R. S. (1974). *Psychology and ethical development.* London: George Allen and Unwin.

Peterson, C., & Seligman, M. E. P. (2004). *Character strengths and virtues: A handbook and classification.* New York: Oxford University Press.

Phenix, P. H. (1964). *Realms of meaning: A philosophy of the curriculum for general education.* New York: McGraw-Hill.

Phillips, D. C. (1987). *Philosophy, science and social inquiry: Contemporary methodological controversies in social science and related applied fields of research.* London: Pergamon.

Phillips, D. C. (Ed.). (2000). *Constructivism in education* (Vol. 1). Ninety-Ninth Yearbook of the National Society for the Study of Education. Chicago, IL: National Society for the Study of Education.

Phillips, D., & Burbules, N. C. (2000). *Postpositivism and educational research.* Lanham, MD: Rowman and Littlefield.

Piaget, J. (1973). *To understand is to invent: The future of education.* New York: Grossman.

Polanyi, M. (1962/1974). *Personal knowledge: Towards a post-critical philosophy.* Chicago, IL: University of Chicago Press.

Popper, K. (1962). *The open society and its enemies: The spell of Plato* (Vol. 1). London: Routledge.

Posner, R. A. (2007). *The little book of plagiarism.* New York: Pantheon.

Postman, N. (1994). *The disappearance of childhood* (Reissue). New York: Vintage/Random House.

Preston, D. (2002). *Lusitania: An epic tragedy.* New York: Walker & Company.

Prinz, J. (2007). *The emotional construction of morals.* Oxford, England: Oxford University Press.

Putnam, R. D. (2007). E pluribus unum: Diversity and community in the twenty-first century. *Scandinavian Political Studies, 30*(2), 137–174.

Putnam, R. D., Leonardi, R., & Nanetti, R. Y. (1994). *Making democracy work: Civic traditions in modern Italy.* Princeton, NJ: Princeton University Press.

Quine, W., & Ullian, J. (1980). *The web of belief.* New York: McGraw-Hill.

Quinton, A. (1987). On the ethics of belief. In G. Hayden (Ed.), *Education and values* (pp. 37–56). London: Institute of Education, University of London.

Ravitch, D. (2010). *The death and life of the great American school system: How testing and choice are undermining education.* New York: Basic Books.

Rawls, J. (1970). *A theory of justice.* Cambridge, MA: Harvard University Press.

Rawls, J. (1993). *Political liberalism.* New York: Columbia University Press.

Raz, J. (1990). *Authority.* New York: New York University Press.

Rée, J. (1999). *I see a voice: Deafness, language and the senses-a philosophical history.* London: Harper Collins.

Riggs, W. (2010). Open-mindedness. *Metaphilosophy, 41*(1–2), 172–188.

Roberts, R. C., & Wood, W. J. (2007). *Intellectual virtues: An essay in regulative epistemology.* Oxford, England: Oxford University Press.

Rodriguez, R. (2004). *Hunger of memory: The education of Richard Rodriguez.* New York: Dial Press.

Ross, D. (1930). *The right and the good.* Oxford: Oxford University Press.

Ryan, A. (1997). *John Dewey and the high tide of American liberalism.* New York: W. W. Norton.

Ryle, G. (1949). *The concept of mind.* Harmondsworth, England: Penguin Books.

Ryle, G. (1958). On forgetting the difference between right and wrong. In A. I. Melden (Ed.), *Essays in moral philosophy* (pp. 147–159). Seattle: University of Washington Press.

Sacks, O. (1993, May 10). To see and not see: A neurologist's notebook. *New Yorker,* 59–73.

Saw, R. L. (1971). *Aesthetics: An introduction.* London: Anchor Books.

Scanlon, T. M. (2003). *The difficulty of tolerance: Essays in political philosophy.* Cambridge, England: Cambridge University Press.

Schön, D. A. (1992). The theory of inquiry: Dewey's legacy to education. *Curriculum Inquiry, 22*(2), 119–139.

Schön, D. A. (1995). *The reflective practitioner: How professionals think in action.* Farnham, England: Ashgate.

Schrag, F. (2010). Moral education in the "badlands." *Journal of Curriculum Studies, 42*(2), 149–164.

Scott, D. (2007). *Critical essays on major curriculum theorists* (New ed.). Abingdon, England: Routledge.

Searle, J. R. (1992). *The rediscovery of the mind.* Cambridge, MA: MIT Press.

Searle, J. R. (1999). *Mind, language and society: Philosophy in the real world.* London: Weidenfeld & Nicolson.

Sen, A. (2010). *The idea of justice.* Cambridge, MA: Belknap Press.

Sheldon, K. (2006). Getting older, getting better? Recent psychological evidence. In M. Csikszentmihalyi & I. S. Csikszentmihalyi (Eds.), *A life worth living: Contributions to positive psychology* (pp. 215–230). New York: Oxford University Press.

Shulman, L. S. (1987). Knowledge and teaching: Foundations of the new reform. *Harvard Educational Review, 57*(1), 1–22.

Shulman, L. S. (1999). Taking learning seriously. *Change, 31*(4), 10–17.

Siegel, H. (2009). Open-mindedness, critical thinking, and indoctrination: Homage to William Hare. *Paideusis, 18*(1), 26–34.

Smith, A. (1759/1976). *The theory of moral sentiments.* Oxford, England: Oxford University Press.

Sockett, H. (1973). Curriculum planning: Taking a means to an end. In R. S. Peters (Ed.), *The philosophy of education* (pp. 150–163). Oxford, England: Oxford University Press.

Sockett, H. (1988). Education and will: Aspects of personal capability. *American Journal of Education, 98*(2), 195–215.

Sockett, H. (1993). *The moral base for teacher professionalism.* New York: Teachers College Press.

Sockett, H. (1997). Chemistry or character? In B. Cross & A. Molnar (Eds.), *Constructing the character of children.* The Ninety-Sixth Handbook of the National Society for the Study of Education, Chicago (pp. 110–120). Chicago, IL: University of Chicago.

Sockett, H. (2006). Character, rules and relations. In H. Sockett (Ed.), *Teacher dispositions: Building a teacher education framework of moral standards* (pp. 1–17). Washington, DC: American Association of Colleges for Teacher Education.

Sockett, H. (2008). The moral and epistemic purposes of teacher education. In M. Cochran-Smith, S. Feiman-Nemser, D. J. McIntyre, & K. E. Demers (Eds.), *Handbook of research on teacher education: Enduring questions in changing contexts* (3rd ed., pp. 45–65). New York: Routledge.

Sockett, H. (2009). Dispositions as virtues. *Journal of Teacher Education, 60*(3), 291–303.

Sockett, H. T., DeMulder, E. K., LePage, P. C., & Wood, D. R. (2001). *Transforming teacher education: Lessons in professional development.* Westport, CT: Bergin & Garvey.

Sosa, E. (2009). *A virtue epistemology: Apt belief and reflective knowledge* (Vol. 1). Oxford, England: Oxford University Press.

Stenhouse, L. (1975). *An introduction to curriculum research and development.* London: Heinemann.

Stenhouse, L. (1983). *Authority, education and emancipation: A collection of papers.* London: Heinemann.

Stout, J. R. (1990). *Ethics after Babel: The languages of morals and Their discontents.* Boston, MA: Beacon Press.

Stratton, J. (1982). *Pioneer women: Voices from the Kansas frontier.* New York: Touchstone Press.

Strawson, P. F. (1961). Social morality and the individual. *Philosophy, 36*(136), 1–17.

Stroud, S. (2008). Weakness of will. In *Stanford Encyclopedia of Philosophy.* Retrieved from http://plato.stanford.edu/entries/weakness-will/

Sulloway, F. J. (1997). *Born to rebel: Birth order, family dynamics, and creative lives.* New York: Vintage.

Surowiecki, J. (2010, Oct. 11). Later. *New Yorker,* 110–113.

Sutton, J. (2010, Sept. 10). Memory. In *Stanford Encyclopedia of Philosophy.* Retrieved from http://plato.stanford.edu/entries/memory/

Taylor, C. (1989). *Sources of the self: The making of the modern identity.* Cambridge, MA: Harvard University Press.

Tillich, P. (2007). *The courage to be.* New Haven, CT: Yale University Press.

Tom, A. R. (1984). *Teaching as a moral craft.* New York: Longman.

Toulmin, S. (1972). *Human understanding: The collective use and evolution of concepts.* Princeton, NJ: Princeton University Press.

Tyler, R. W. (1969). *Basic principles of curriculum and instruction.* Chicago, IL: University of Chicago Press.

United States Department of Education. (2010). *Transforming American education: Learning powered by technology draft.* Washington, DC: USDOE.

Urmson, J. O. (1958). Saints and heroes. In A. I. Melden (Ed.), *Essays in moral philosophy.* Seattle: University of Washington Press.

Van Manen, M. (1990). *Researching lived experience: Human science for an action sensitive pedagogy* (2nd ed.). Albany: State University of New York Press.

Van Manen, M., & Levering, B. (1996). *Childhood's secrets: Intimacy, privacy, and the self reconsidered.* New York: Teachers College Press.

Waks, L. J. (Ed.). (2008). *Review of leaders in philosophy of education: Intellectual self-portraits.* Rotterdam, the Netherlands: Sense Publishers.

Warnock, M. (1987). *Memory.* London: Faber & Faber.

Warnock, M. (1989). The authority of the teacher. *Westminster Studies in Education, 12,* 73–81.

Waugh, A. (2010). *The house of Wittgenstein: A family at war.* London: Anchor.

Weiss, H. M. (2002). Deconstructing job satisfaction: Separating evaluations, beliefs and affective experiences. *Human Resource Management Review, 12*(2), 173–194.

West, C. (1989). *The American evasion of philosophy: A genealogy of pragmatism*. Madison: University of Wisconsin Press.

White, J. (2007). *What schools are for and why*. Impact Series, No. 14. London: Philosophy of Education Society of Great Britain.

White, P. (1996). *Civic virtues and public schooling: Educating citizens for a democratic society*. New York: Teachers College Press.

Williams, B. (1973). *Problems of the self*. Cambridge, England: Cambridge University Press.

Williams, B. (1985). *Ethics and the limits of philosophy*. Cambridge, MA: Harvard University Press.

Williams, B. (2002). *Truth and truthfulness: An essay in genealogy*. Princeton, NJ: Princeton University Press.

Williams, B. (2005). *In the beginning was the deed: Realism and moralism in political argument*. Princeton, NJ: Princeton University Press.

Williams, B. (2006). The primacy of dispositions. In B. Williams (Ed.), *Philosophy as a humanistic discipline* (pp. 67–76). Princeton, NJ: Princeton University Press.

Williams, B. (2006a). *Philosophy as a humanistic discipline*. Princeton, NJ: Princeton University Press.

Williams, M. (2001). *Problems of knowledge: A critical introduction to epistemology*. Oxford, England: Oxford University Press.

Wilson, P. (1974). *Interest and discipline in education*. London: Routledge and Kegan Paul.

Wittgenstein, L. (1922). *Tractatus logico-philosophicus (TLP)*. C. K. Ogden (trans.). Originally published in 1921 as "Logisch-Philosophische Abhandlung." *Annalen der Naturphilosophische, 14*(3/4).

Wittgenstein, L. (1971). *Philosophical investigations* (3rd ed.). London: Macmillan.

Wittgenstein, L. (2010). *Tractatus logico-philosophicus*. Retrieved from http://www.gutenberg.org/ebooks/5740

Woozley, A. D. (1966). *Theory of knowledge: An introduction*. London: Hutchinson.

Young, I. M. (1990). *Justice and the politics of difference*. Princeton, NJ: Princeton University Press.

Zagzebski, L. T. (1996). *Virtues of the mind: An inquiry into the nature of virtue and the ethical foundations of knowledge*. Cambridge, England: Cambridge University Press.

INDEX